"Thoughts For Each Step
...Every Day!"

"Acknowledgement"

I am truly grateful to my patient partner in life, Elaine. She has been very helpful to me in the editing of the manuscript. Her expertise in spelling and sentence structure has been a blessing to me. It seems I am always in a hurry to write as thoughts would come so vividly to me and I found myself failing to use the correct spelling, sentence structure and even selecting the correct tense or word for the thought being conveyed.

I appreciate my children (Tammy, Wade and Melissa); my son-in-law Clayton and daughter-in-law Dawn; and grandchildren (Johnathon, Brandon Kyle, Savannah, Brandon Wade and Dawson) who are personal character and experiences prompted thoughts and ideas for certain devotions.

I do appreciate the hard work of many scholars who spearheaded translations and paraphrases of the Holy Scriptures and particularly to those whose works are utilized in these devotions: Amplified Bible, New Century Version, King James Version, New King James Version, New International Version, Revised Standard Version, J.B. Phillips in Modern English and the Message.

I acknowledge appreciation to readers of my first four books, which shared encouragement in my desire to write a daily devotional and expressed their eagerness to receive a copy.

"Thoughts for Every Step

...Every Day!"

--Contents--

Introduction   Page 003

Step 1-January   "Beginning A New"   Page 004

Step 2-February   "Bountiful Love"   Page 036

Step 3-March   "Blowing In the Wind"   Page 066

Step 4-April   "Buried, Yet Alive"   Page 098

Step 5-May   "Basic Leadership"   Page 130

Step 6-June   "Begotten Of God"   Page 162

Step 7-July   "Battle Scars & Victory"   Page 193

Step 8-August   "Back-To-School"   Page 225

Step 9-September   "Back-To-Basics"   Page 257

Step 10-October   "Bearing Fruit"   Page 288

Step 11-November   "Blessings & Gratitude"   Page 320

Step 12-December   "Bountiful Gifts Of Life"   Page 351

Step 13   "Building A Future"   Page 383

"Thoughts For Each Step
...Every Day!"

"Introduction"

Just a note to inform you regarding the method and material that we wish to present in this book. The title tells the story. It is a book of thoughts that have been prepared with you in mind. We trust that each thought will bring inspiration and instruct for living daily with Jesus throughout the year.

We have used the words 'step" and "day" in our title. The twelve month span of a year has been divided into chapters or as we labeled them "steps." As you take steps throughout this year, we desire for you to grow and glow with God's peace, power, promises and presences.

We have labeled each devotion as a daily thought. Walking through life day by day, we want you refreshed and restored.

May you have a wonderful experience as you walk with Jesus in the way of life.

Step 1 – January

"Beginning Anew"

Well, the past year has come to an end and we are privileged to enter and enjoy a new beginning. Every step we take will be a step we have never taken before and every day will be a day we have never participated in. Yes, we may go in the same direction at times and perform the same duties; yet the future is now moved into the present.

January is a month of new beginnings. It is a time to re-evaluate the past year. A time to consider where we failed and why we made the mistakes we did. It is also a time to learn from our fragility and our flaws. Oh, yes, we are filled with humanity's ability to fail and falter. We so often fail to read the instructions or follow our instinct resulting in a conflict, confrontation or collapse. As we review, we come to the conclusion that sometimes we just went with the flow or got caught up with the fancy of the moment. But we can live and learn and that will enrich our lives for a new beginning.

Therefore, let us dedicate our abilities and devote our acknowledgment of God in living a life which will honor God and built a harmonious relationship with those we come into contact with. Let us determine that our attitude and our actions will portray a concern and a commitment to our faithfulness every step and every day. Let our words, our walk and our worship be a blessing to our Heavenly Father, our family, our friends, and the fruitfulness of our country.

As you read each thought throughout this month, may you be enriched and encouraged to "be strong and be of good courage." The Hebrew nation had lost their leader Moses, yet was about to venture into a new era with God in the much awaited Promised Land. Therefore, God spoke unto Joshua, and reminded him that he would guide him every step, every day. Be assured that God will do the same for you as you listen to His Words and lean on Him for guidance

January – Day 1

Text: Exodus 14: 13-15 NIV

(In response to the people's cries and concerns) Moses said, "Do not be afraid. Stand firm and you will see the deliverance the Lord will bring you today. (The Lord has said) move out."

Thought: "Get ready, get set, and go"

At the start of most races, there are signals such as get ready, get set, go! The gun fires or the flag is waved and they are off – building speed and heading into the turns and toward the straight away.

In the text, the Hebrew nation had come to the Red Sea in their fleeing from Egypt bondage. The mountain ranges extended skyward to their left and to their right. Behind them they could see the advancing Egyptian armies. In the path before them lay a monster body of water—the Red Sea.

Fear griped their hearts. Frantic cries of desperation bellowed forth. "Did God care about their situation or was this His plan all along?"

God not only opened the Red Sea for crossing, but destroyed Pharaoh and the Egyptian army as they attempted to cross.

Friends, God does care about your every situation. And when it seems hopeless, He becomes our Help! He will make a way. He will eradicate hopelessness and establish a fresh touch of hope within our life.

He will do what is necessary to provide for us. He can open doors and close doors. He is in control of every day as we must allow Him to guide our every step.

We must remember something that is very important. Listen, then line up and follow Him in the path that He leads us.

Talk With God:

Heavenly Father, we are thankful that you are aware of our every situation. I am renewed and refreshed in knowing you are prepared to stand with us, speak to us and allow us to move forward step by step through this day. I know you will lead in the way most beneficial for me. I love you and thank you for loving me. Amen.

January – Day 2

Text: II Corinthians 4:16 Amplified Bible

"Therefore we do not become discouraged – utterly spiritless, exhausted, and wearied out . . . our inner self is being (progressively) renewed day after day."

Thought: "Making the Routine Exciting"

Have you been guilty of saying, "every day, the same old routine?" I feel like I am in a rut. I sometimes feel like a robot simply obeying commands to perform. The joy and justification of doing what I am doing doesn't exist. When I wake in the morning sometimes I dread facing the day and the duty that is ahead.

Well, if you have—and most of us have—listen up! I'll tell you a secret of how to make a routine become a fresh new experience every day.

It's really very simple. Just begin your first step with Jesus. As we begin to walk with Him from step one to the final step of the day, each day will be brighter and better.

The Apostle Paul in his letter to the church at Corinth, simply reminded them that there was no reason to faint but to forge ahead in a renewed relationship with God

He knows our anxieties and our aspirations. He knows our normal routine and how we feel about our daily environment and encounters. He loves us and lives to lift us up to enjoy the day that He has made. He understands and is able to undergird our lives with His love, His light and His liberty. In these attributes, we are able to view life in a renewed perspective and in a positive note.

As we walk with a Godly attitude, we will develop His quality of character and demonstrate a refreshed quality of life.

Talk With God:

Lord, I am thankful that today is the first day of the rest of my life. It is not going to be a routine of normal daily activities but a renewed excitement of living and being able to do something for the glory of God. Amen.

January – Day 3

Text: James 1:25 NIV

"the man who looks intently into the perfect law (God's Word) that gives freedom, and continues to do this, not forgetting what he has heard, but doing it – he will be blessed in what he does."

Thought: "Hear & Hearken"

An athlete was never made by mere instruction. He had to practice and participate. A soldier was not trained by the mere study of his manual; but by drills that developed his skills. A farmer does not produce a successful crop by scattering seeds across a dry rocky soil but by learning and laboring the art of cultivation of soil and seed.

If we profess to be a child of God, we need to prove it by daily practicing it.

It is not the faint of heart that wrestles and win. It is the one who stands still, sincerely listening and searching every thought to learn from the inspiration and instruction of God as He speaks through His Word and His Spirit. It is the one who then acts upon that advice. It is the one who breathes in faith and breathes out fear. It is the one who is renewed by God.

For you see, the perfect law of God is a law that regulates the love and the liberty that flows from our heart and mind. It determines our attitude and action toward our Heavenly Father and all humanity. It governs our life and guides our steps each day.

Remember: the more you practice what you know, the more you shall know what to practice. Therefore, let us be challenged to listen, learn and live the Word of God. It is life.

Talk To God:

Jesus, it is a delight to know that we can have a great day by simply putting into practice what you share with us in Your Word. Enable me to embrace Your Word with confidence. Help me to believe it and be a beacon of
of it. Amen.

January – Day 4

Text: I Corinthians 2:2 Amplified Bible

"For I resolved to know nothing – to be acquainted with [nothing], to make a display of the knowledge of [nothing] and to be conscious of [nothing] – among you except Jesus Christ, the Messiah, and Him crucified."

Thought: "Be Your Best, But Be God's Best"

Today is our (Elaine and I) only son's birthday. He is now married and they have two wonderful children. He has a good job and is doing well. During his childhood and into adolescent, he was "all boy." Since I loved baseball, I wanted him to be a baseball player. However, he had different plans. He wanted to play football and that he did very well. He was all-conference for two different schools during his high school days. He was very athletic. I attended every game during his Junior High and High School days. I enjoyed watching him succeed in football, even if it was not baseball. It still made me proud.

Friends, God enjoys every physical, financial, and business success story you write about your life. He delights in what you achieve. However, He is very concerned about your spiritual success. You see, what a parent may want a child to be in the arena of sports; is a total (and minor) thing compared to what our Heavenly Father desires of us in this life. The Apostle Paul had an education, an elite position and earthly power; yet he allowed his relationship with Jesus to be his priority. So must we.

God desires our total devotion. He desires to develop in us the unique and undergirding quality of character that will write a story of success that our individual heart, all humanity and our Heavenly Father will view and voice approval. God has given us the right to choose and to commit our self to the task. Let us choose not only to be a success story but a spiritual giant for God.

Talk With God:

"Heavenly Father, I wish to thank you for life and the liberty to choose our personal interest and our personal involvements during this journey of life. I wish to seek your guidance and grace in making the right choices and being committed to do what will put you first in my life, provide for my family and
and promote your Kingdom. Amen"

January – Day 5

Text: 1 Samuel 15:17 Amplified Bible

"Samuel said, "When you (Saul) were small in your own sight, were you not made the head of the tribes of Israel and the Lord anointed you?"

Thought: "Little Is Big"

Size is not always an indication of importance. We all stop to look at a big man walking in a crowd. But he is not always superior to his less noticeable companions.

There are small things which wield a mightily influence. A rudder is a small thing compared to the ship which it steers. Springs are little things, but they are sources of large streams. Nails and pegs are little things, but they hold the parts of a large building together.

In our text, King Saul was head and shoulders above everyone else, yet he fails God because he fails to be little in his attitude toward God. He was unwilling to surrender His total being to God and yield in submission to God's plan and purpose in life.

God wants us to enjoy life. He is in control and desires that we experience blessings. Yet, to take hold of His promises, we must be willing to walk His path.

A little time with the Master, Jesus Christ, at the start of each day will enable us to handle the bundle of daily activities that await us. It will provide a fresh and fortifying strength to face each situation.

A brief moment each day sharing the love of God may aid someone who may be headed into something bigger than themselves.

God gave you His all; now give God back a little.

Talk With God:

Sweet, Holy Spirit, we humble before you this day. Help us to yield our total being to you each step of the day. Teach us to walk in honor and humble obedience to your divine plan for us this day. Amen.

January – Day 6

Text: Philippians 3:14 NIV

"I press on toward the goal to win the prize for which God has called me heavenward in Christ Jesus."

Thought: "What Is Our Focus?"

Three men, all engaged at the same employment were asked what they were doing. One man said he was making ten dollars an hour. Another replied that he was cutting stone. The third man said he was building a cathedral. The difference was not in what they were actually doing, although the spirit of the third might quite possibly have made him the more expert at his task. They were earning the same wage; they were all cutting stone; but only one held it in his mind that he was helping build a great edifice. Life meant more to him that to his co-workers, because he saw further and more clearly.

Life is important and our focus should have meaning, regarding of what we are doing in life.

How clearly and openly do you walk and work at your life's task? I know it is not always easy to see benefits in what you are doing; but it is important. It will make a difference in the health and the happiness of your heart and your head.

With the help of our Creator and Caretaker, Jesus Christ, we are able to realize the value of life and the validity of living a contented and committed lifestyle. It keeps our eternal focus in perspective as we progress each step every day.

Talk With God:

Dear Lord, it's me again. I come before you requesting your assistance in staying focused on my reason for living I want to enrich my life and one day enter heaven. I want to enable others to focus on you and your eternal reward. Please use me and O Lord don't refuse me, for surely there is a work that I can do. Amen.

January – Day 7

Text: Psalms 118:24 NIV

"This is the day that the Lord hath made, let us rejoice and be glad in it."

Thought: "A New Day"

We live but once. The years of infancy, childhood, adolescent, teens, young adult, middle age and old age once past is gone forever. It matters not how ardently we may wish to live them over; it avails us nothing.

The past is no longer ours. It has gone beyond our reach and what we have made it shall remain. There is no power in heaven or on earth that can or will change it. The record of our past stands forth in bold characters, open to the all-seeing eye of God.

Some things we may regret, others we hope to remember forever.

However, the present moment alone is ours. It is a gift of God to experience and enjoy. It may be an opportunity for repentance or it may be an occasion to celebrate. It may be an eventful day to note in our journal. It could be a day of battle. But do not forget, it is the day God hath made and we have a responsibility to be content and celebrate in our Spirit.

Today is a day which we've never had before and which we shall never have again once it is past. But what are we going to do with it. Are we going to let this precious span of time slip by or make good use of it? The best thing to do is perform each task with pride, praising God for the opportunity to serve Him and humanity.

Talk With God:

O precious God, hear me when I praise you and when I petition you. I desire to please you and perform my daily task with pleasure. It is my hope that I have your help in being what I need to be this day. Strengthen me to shine for you. Amen.

January – Day 8

Text: Matthew 6:33 NIV

"But seek first his kingdom and his righteousness, and all these things will be given to you"

Thought: "Christ Makes the Picture of Life Complete"

Did you know that your life is like a giant jigsaw puzzle? And in order to complete it every piece must be located and locked into its place.

I thought of this recently as I read about a husband and wife who had purchased a large jigsaw at a garage sale. Because the scene on the box was so beautiful, they decided to glue each piece in place on a sheet of paneling and then hang the completed picture on a wall for display. They worked on their project for several evenings, but to their dismay they discovered that one small piece was missing. And the empty spot detracted from the beauty of the picture.

Friend, our life is a puzzle and a piece of that puzzle is Christ. If He is missing, the whole picture is marred. It is incomplete and the picture loses its inspiration.

How beautiful is the picture of your life? Is a piece missing?

Don't allow the visible beauty of your conduct and conversation be marred by leaving the touch of the grace of God from it. Include Him in each step of your day.

Let the refreshing Spirit of God renew you in such a way that you will never subtract from the portray of life but always stand out being the complete picture of His holiness.

Talk With God:

Thank you Lord for being a part of my life. In fact, thank you for giving me life. I want to always include you in order that my life may portray a magnificent and majestic scene of your compassion and care Amen.

January – Day 9

Text: Psalms 118:27 NIV

"The Lord is God and he has made his light shine upon us."

Thought: "In His Spotlight"

You may have never thought about being in the spotlight. However, as a believer, every day you are in the spotlight of God. He is focused on you.

He is aware when you awake feeling all washed out. He sees you when you hop from bed singing a song (oh, you mean you have never done that—try it sometimes). He knows when you hurt or when you just want to hide. His light shines on you revealing every aspect of your being. God is acquainted with all our emotions and our experiences. And you know what—He cares.

You may have to take a step of faith to get going, but every step you take He is with you and will strength you all the way. He is willing for you to talk to Him about "whatever." He is waiting for you to express your feeling and your faith (or lack of it) with Him.

This is why He blesses us with today. It is time to shine in His spotlight. It is a time to be renewed, refreshed, revived, and restored. It is a time to commit our all to Him in order that we may be our all for Him.

Talk With God:

Sometimes Lord, physical hurts and pressures of mind does not permit me to truly express myself; however, I desire to lean on you today. I long to feel your embrace and experience your energy renewing me for this day. Shine on me showing me where I stand and what steps I need to take. This I ask in your Name. Amen.

January – Day 10

Text: Philippians 4:8 Amplified Bible

"whatever is true, whatever is worthy of reverence and is, honorable and seemly, whatever is just, whatever is pure, whatever is lovely and lovable, whatever is kind and winsome and gracious, if there is any virtue and excellence, if there is anything worthy of praise, think on and weigh and take account of these things—fix your mind on them."

Thought: "Mind Set"

An old Chinese proverbs says, "You can't keep the birds from flying over your head but you can keep them from making a nest in your hair." In other words, you can't thoughts from be said and heard, but you can keep them from being meditated upon.

Solomon in his proverbs penned, "As (a man) thinks in his heart, so is he." Therefore, what we fill our minds with as we prepare for the day will establish our mind set for that day.

If we take the advice of the Apostle Paul in his letter to the Philippians, we will begin our day focusing on the things of heavenly nature – truth, honesty, justice, purity, loveliness, and kindness. For these things portray a life that is anticipating goodness, graciousness and Godly to accompany them throughout the day.

Such virtues will prepare a mind to combat negative thoughts and control any negative response. Such virtue will strengthen our mind and spirit to response in a positive way to those confrontations and conditions that prevail in our path of daily living.

Set your mind to celebrate your heavenly nature and your mind will control your earthly nature.

Talk With God:

Thank you God for equipping our mind with the quality of character that will enhance our life and enable us to live each step of this day for the honor of you and the happiness of our being. This is my soul cry and my sincere commitment. Amen.

January – Day 11

Text: Isaiah 42:9-10 KJV

"Behold, the former things are come to pass, and new things do I declare. . .sing unto the Lord a new song."

Thought: "A New Song"

We are told that a lark will never sing while perched on its nest. But when it leaves and begins to wing its way toward the sky, you'll hear its lovely song. The higher the bird ascends, the louder and sweeter its music becomes.

This is true with humanity. Most people do not have a happy song as long as they pause and ponder the troubles and trials of this present life. They may sing songs of gloom, agony and despair, but they need a new song. A new song offering lyrics of praise and perpetual thanksgiving.

Therefore, let our thoughts rise above to the things of heavenly nature – the perfect love of God and the promise of His presences. For in His presences, our life is lifted by His abiding and amazing love giving us a new song. It makes possible our ability to forget the past and feast in the present.

The prophet Isaiah reminded the Hebrew people that God was able to release them from captivity and restore them. It was time for a new song of deliverance and delight.

It is time today for a new song of victory. Soar above your situations and sing a song of celebration.

Talk With God:

Lord, I am neither a songwriter nor a singer; but I desire to sing a song of victory as I travel throughout this day. Let my every step vibrate with chords of peace, praise and power. I will turn my attention from yesterday to this day given me. I will walk in newness of life. Amen.

January – Day 12

Text: Psalms 23:4 Amplified Bible

"Yes, though I walk through the [deep, sunless] valley of the shadow of death, I will fear or dread no evil; for You are with me; Your rod [to protect] and Your staff [to guide], they comfort me."

Thought: "Shadow of Death"

What a scary thought! No one likes to talk, must less, taste of death. Yet, it is an event everyone must experience.

But did you know that we are living in the shadow of death every day. The shadow of death may refer to any distressful time of our life. Even today you may be experiencing sickness, sorrow, suffering or separation that causes a deep shadow of feeling sapped of life.

Therefore, be reassured, you do not have to fret or fear the hardships of daily living nor the harsh reality of dying. The Good Shepherd stands ready to rescue, restore and render guidance to you.

The psalmist David reaffirms the comfort of God in walking the valley. He promises the power of His rod (the Holy Spirit) and His staff (the Holy Word) will ever be available to uphold us in time of darkness and dread; disappointment and discouragement; distractions and defeats.

Life is rough and grows ridged at times, but permit the Lord to call you to cheer, comfort and courage. He is the Good Shepherd and does care for His sheep.

Talk With God:

I am so glad to know that in the midst of hardships and harsh realities, we have a caring and compassionate Shepherd and Savior to uphold us. I am grateful that I can call upon Him and know He will lift me up above the shadows. For this is my praise and my prayer. Amen.

January – Day 13

Text: Proverbs 3:5 Amplified Bible

"Lean on, trust and be confident in the Lord with all your heart and mind, and do not rely on your own insight or understanding. In all your ways know, recognize and acknowledge Him and He will direct and make straight and plain your paths."

Thought: "Don't Be Fooled, Trust God"

Has this ever happened to you? You see a glowing report of a new miracle product advertised in the pages of the newspaper or magazine, or promoted on the radio or television; and you determine that you have got to try it. You declare it is just the thing that you been waiting for. Therefore, you push aside everything and purchase it; only to find it fails to live up to its billing.

Friend, Satan has been in the business of overselling his "product" in every possible avenue available for thousand of years. He first encountered humanity in the Garden of Eden. What happened? Adam and Eve rebelled against God and reached for the product. It led to disappointment and disbarment.

Just because it feels good, looks good and may taste good; does not make it right. Just because everyone else is trying it, doesn't mean it is okay.

God is our Creator, trust Him and He will provide what you have need of. Solomon's Proverbs again provide a wonderful insight for us to hold on to. When we trust God, He will direct our paths. We must learn to lean on Him for wisdom and understanding. We must build confidence in His ability to led us even if it is through the flood or through the fire of disappointments and distress. He will lead us each step every day.

Talk With God:

Lord, it is so easy to be swayed to go one direction then another; however, let me know your will for my life and lead me in the way everlasting. I need you and I want you to be my guide throughout this life. I want to enjoy your refreshing and renewing touch of life. This I pray in your Name. Amen.

January – Day 14

Text: Psalms 119:11 NKJV
"Your Word have I hid in my heart that I might not sin against you"

Thought: "Hidden Word for Open Living"

Probably the best piece of advice ever offered parents is the one found on most medicine bottles: "Keep out of reach of children."

Little children don't always know what's best for them. If you don't believe that, just turn a child loose in an unfenced yard near a busy intersection or leave your medicine cabinet unlocked. DANGER in capital letters comes to mind. Children do not have the wisdom or knowledge of adults.

Neither do adults have the wisdom of God. We sometimes do not know what is best for us.

Just as God gives grown-ups to help children survive; He gives us His Word and His Spirit to help adults survive. In His Word we find instruction, inspiration and interesting stories that reveal great truth for living, loving and leading.

We are challenged to "Study the Word of God" and "Search the Scriptures." We become blessed of God when we read the Word, remember it, and reflect it in our steps of life.

The Word will strengthen us each step of the way, sustain us in reinforcing the truth to our children and separate us from any evil that rises against us.

Talk With God:

Jesus, you are a friend indeed. And I am so glad that I can hear your instruction and experience your inspiration when I meditate on the truths of your Word. I find it to be a spring of living water, a letter of loving instructions and a basket containing loaves of divine Bread. As I drink and digest your spiritual food, I will grow into spiritual maturity. Thank you for that promise. Amen.

January – Day 15

Text: Psalms 46:10 KJV
"Be still and know that I am God"

Thought: ""Stop & Say"

Have you ever had a morning like this? You bounce out of bed, confident that today will be a great day; only to run into a brick wall (not literally). There are no clean towels available in the bathroom as you step from the shower. The top you had planned on wearing was in the dirty clothes basket. On the way to kitchen, you almost trip over a misplaced toy left by the kids or grandkids. The toast burns as you apply your makeup or the daily newspaper has not arrived yet. Then you encounter a traffic jam that makes you a little late.

What a day and it has just begun! You wish you could just do a back stroke and rewind—getting a fresh start.

I often say on days like this –mama said there would be days like this.

And when they happen, just remember. God is still God. He hasn't changed and He does not encounter things that cause Him to become confused and lose control.

Therefore, pause and ponder the reality that God is still God and He cares about you. You never see the rainbow until after the rain. You never know His healing power until after the pain. You never see the sunrise until after the night. And you will never know the victory until after the faith. He allows good days and bad days to come into our path; yet His presence remains sweet and steadfast. It is up to us to stay true in the midst of despairing and difficult days by focusing on Him.

We must seek to know Him in His fullness and begin to partake of His fruit. It will give us nourishment and necessary perspective for pressing forward.

Talk With God:

Today Lord, I stand still and speak words that are pure, positive and progressive regardless of little things that attempt to derail me. I acknowledge your omnipresence, omnipotence, and omniscience. I will trust you as I wade through the marsh of minor conflict. I will rejoice in your constant companionship. Blessed be your Name. Amen.

January – Day 16

Text: Luke 18:27 KJV
"The things which are impossible with men are possible with God."

Thought: "No way without God"

Just suppose I were to sit down to the piano and announce I was about to play Beethoven's Fifth Symphony. Then suppose I were to say, "I am totally unfamiliar with Beethoven's music plus the fact, I have never played the piano in my life." Of course those who heard me would either take me as an idiot or a joker.

Yet many who would not presume to play the piano without knowledge of music or the instrument will presumptuously enter upon the higher art of living this life without the inspiration, instruction and interpersonal relationship with the Creator of life. As I, due to ignorance, would make a mess of playing Beethoven's music; so those untutored and undisciplined in the art of successful living without God, would make a mess of their life. Many have attempted and many have failed in living a wholesome and wonderful life.

However, the great Counselor of life stands ready to assist you. Jesus is able to transform your life into a true instrument that makes a melody of praise each step of the way. Tell Him your desire and trust Him to make a way for you.

In our Scripture text today the writer Luke shares the words of the Savior Jesus Christ. Jesus is answering a question regarding salvation. He states it is impossible to borrow, buy or barter for spiritual redemption. It is a gift of God.

Therefore, you and I must look to God for our salvation and spiritual success.

Talk With God:

Heavenly Father, I am well aware that life is hard and the load is sometimes heavy; that is why I need you. I need you to stabilize me on a strong foundation (your Word) and strengthen me each day (by your Holy Spirit) and help me to shine and share in the joy of life. I thank you for your love for me, for lifting me up, for lighting my path and for helping me learn how to walk in appreciation and anticipation. Amen.

January – Day 17

Text: Psalms 23:5 NIV

"You prepare a table before me in the presence of my enemies. You anoint my head with oil; my cup overflows."

Thought: "A Very Special Day"

Today is a very special day. It is my sweetheart's birthday. I have had the opportunity to share her birthday with her for over forty years. It has been a joyful occasion each time. This birthday has been a special treat to her for she was taken out for a delicious meal the day before (by our son and his family) the day of (by our oldest daughter and her family and the day afterward (by our youngest daughter and her son). I tagged along for the side treats of being part of her life (ha).

A celebration in such a matter brings a real and rich reminder to my heart. A reminder that I have the unique pleasure of tagging along with God each step every day. Each day provides the opportunity of walking with God in the direction that He leads. The psalmist declared, "Where He leads me I will follow." He will always lead me in the path of success and in the end celebration.

He will always prepare a table of blessings before me regardless of the situations I find myself in. Our text declares uses the word "enemies." Age is the only enemy of birthday celebrations; however, problems, pressures and people sometimes become enemies in our path. We must rely on the fact that He is leading and we are following – stay close – and He will led us through to victory and celebration.

He will touch me and fill my life with His abiding and anointing presences, power and purity.

Talk With God:

Thanks Lord, for our promise of life and leadership. Thanks for your courage and comfort as I look to you, love you and learn to enjoy the companionship and celebration together. Guide me this day, govern my steps and give me reason to celebrate. Amen!

January – Day 18

Text: I Peter 5:8 Amplified Bible

"Be well-balanced—temperate, sober-minded; be vigilant and cautious at all times, for that enemy of yours, the devil, roams around like a lion roaring [in fierce hunger], seeking someone to seize upon and devour."

Thought: "Beware"

In the Australian bush country grows a little plant called the "sundew." It has a slender stem and tiny round leaves fringed with hairs that glisten with bright drops of liquid as delicate as fine dew. Woe to the insect, however, that dares to dance around it in the sunny air. For while its attractive clusters of red, white and pink blossoms are harmless, the leaves are deadly. The shiny moisture on each leaf is sticky, and will hold any bug prisoner that touches it.

The Disciple Peter challenges us to be renewed and reinforced in Godly character and caution knowing the enemy lures and is ready to launch on us.

As we go down the path of life, we must beware of Satan's sundew enticements of evil. The flowers of temptation may at first appear inviting and harmless; but everywhere we go we find people that have been trapped by these deceptive blooms.

We must stand fast in our belief that God will inform us regarding the tricks of Satan, instruct us to avoid becoming enticed, and inspire us to walk in worship of our Redeemer and Reinforcer of life. As we consider the day before us, let us prepare ourselves through a daily renewal of our commitment to Him.

Talk With God:

Blessed Redeemer, I love you and appreciate you. You are my constant companion as I launch out into the day. You will prepare me with a song and prompt me with a sweet spirit throughout the day. I desire to please you and put the enemy in His place by resisting His temptations and by reassurance of where I have placed by trust. On you O Lord do I lean and learn the way of life. Amen.

January – Day 19

Text: Psalms 119:116 NIV

"Sustain me according to your promise: and I will live; do not let my hopes be dashed."

Thought: "Lest we forget"

A story is told of a man having stopped for gas, then drove quite a distance before he noticed he had left his wife behind. (I can't imagine such happening) So, he contacted the police to assist in notifying the station that he was enroute for her. When he arrived, he admitted with great embarrassment that he just hadn't noticed her absence.

You say, how could he have forgotten his wife? But wait! It is not much different in the lives of many in their relationship with God. Individuals fail to remember the One who created them and in His compassion died for their redemption. How is this possible? I don't know but it happens.

We must develop a daily routine of keeping our relationship glowing and growing. It is done through our conversation with God (in Bible Study and prayer) and our commitment to worship and walking with God daily. If we stay in constant contact with Jesus, we will never lose sight of Him.

The Psalmist declares that God will sustain us according to His promise. His promise is dependant on our desire to keep His commandments and our dedication to serve Him.

Where is our help and our hope in this life? It is neither in our possessions, positions nor our pleasures; these will dissolve away in a moment of time (by destructive powers, downsizing and disabilities). It is in our relationship with God.

Talk With God:

What a privilege to talk with you O Lord. Let it be like a fresh breathe of air and a refreshing drink of water. For if it becomes this, we will long for it daily and never forget to utilize the opportunity to obtain either. I love you, need you and want you. Amen.

January – Day 20

Text: II Corinthians 3:2 KJV

"Ye are our epistle written in our hearts, known and read of all men."

Thought: "A Letter Of life"

I read a simple poem one day that related a beautiful and bold message.

Friend, you are writing a book, a chapter each day;

By the deeds that you do and by the words that you say.

Men read what you write, whether faithless or true;

Please live what the Gospel is to you.

You and I are writing each step we take and every day of our lives a story – notes on our life. It may be good news or bad news. It all depends on the way you look at it. It may please humanity but does it please God.

If we live according to the Word of God, it will be no problem to be content in our relationship with God and with God's creation—man.

As you arise in the morning, begin your salutation by greeting God with a smile and saying "good morning Lord" not a sour frown and a slanderous "good lord, it's morning." Then continue throughout the day noticing things that God has placed along your path to provide you a wonderful ideal to express in your letter of life.

Therefore, from the rising of the sun to the going down of the same; let us write the good news living in tribute to His Name.

Talk With God:

It is my desire Lord to live in a way that will honor your Name and give hope to others I come in contact with. Please enrich me with Your Word and enable me by Your Spirit to make a holy presentation of your Person, your Plan and your Purpose for all humanity. For this I believe is your will for me. Amen.

January – Day 21

Text: John 10:10 KJV

"I am come that you may have life and it more abundantly"

Thought: "I Want More Than to be Alive"

It has been said, the real purpose of humanity's existence on planet Earth is not to make a living, but to make a life – a worthy, well-rounded, wonderful instrument of life.

And I agree.

Life is more than material gain, a meal fit for a king, mental accomplishments, a magnificent job or a marriage made in heaven. Many enjoy such benefits but still lack satisfaction and happiness.

Anyone can make a living, but not everyone has experienced real life. That is evident by the escalating crime rate, the economic collapse, the ever-increasing construction of mental facilities and prisons, the corruption of society and the contamination of the environment. Not everyone seems to have a life filled with contentment.

Jesus Christ came that whosoever might be forgiven, granted freedom, given fortitude and have a fantastic life. It is available to all.

As you start a new day, step into the light of life found in the presences of God (His abiding Word). Light up your life with the character of Jesus expressed in the hope and the happiness of this life and the life to come.

His life is filled with the love, liberty, laughter, longsuffering and living contentment.

Talk With God:

I thank you Lord for vacating the splendor of heaven to give this world value and a valid life. I am indebted to you and desire to enjoy the life given by you. I want to express the blessings of possessing abundant life. In your precious Name I pray. Amen.

January – Day 22

Text: Psalms 23:2-3 NIV

"He makes me to lie down in green pastures: he leads me beside quiet waters. He restores my soul; He guides me in paths of righteousness for his name's sake."

Thought: "God leads and I'll follow"

Every time I read the 23rd Psalm I am reminded of the game "follow the leader." If I follow the game's leader, I have an opportunity to win the game. I may have to circle a tree, jump a stump, hop like a rabbit, shoot a basketball through the hoop, or stand on one foot. However, if I follow I will succeed.

God is My Shepherd and He leads me in places that will bless me and build me up. It is up to me to follow. And keep in mind, He will never lead me where He will not go Himself.

Each new day is an opportunity to start all over again…to cleanse our minds and hearts and grant us clarity to our vision. Let the past burdens and bags of garbage be cremated and buried.

This day offers us the opportunity to move ahead free of the clutter and confusion of the past. And there is no better companion to take each step with than Jesus Christ who is our supernatural and spiritual guide.

He leads into the restful, refreshing, and restoring moments of each day and enables us to reflect Him as our leader.

Talk With God:

Today, I will arise and with allegiances follow you Lord. Where you lead me, I'll go. I know you never lead me into harm's way but always in the heavenly path that reflects your image and inspiration. Thank for your willingness to direct my life. I love you, Amen.

January – Day 23

Text: II Timothy 1:12 KJV

"For I know whom I have believed, and am persuaded that he is able to keep that which I have committed unto him against that day."

Thought: "Confidence is Keeping Your Chin Up"

It has been said there is only a slight difference between keeping your chin up and sticking your neck out; but it's worth knowing.

As far as the posture of the head, there is very little difference; however in the conditions of life not knowing the difference could cost you your head.

A person sticks out his neck when he attempts something without the facts of life or foundation of living. And many people are doing that in regard to daily living. They attempt to crawl in the valley, climb the mountains and claim the mountain top without the power and presences of Jesus Christ.

Friend, humanity does not know the ropes of life and in his attempt to succeed will fail if he tries it alone.

A person who keeps his chin up is expressing an inner courage and confidence. He believes he will not drown when crossing the river of trials. He has blessed assurance that Jesus will be true to His Word and our commitment to Him.

So, don't stick your neck out; but keep your chin up.

The Apostle Paul reminds Timothy that God will keep what you commit to Him. As we commit our total being (mind, body and spirit) to the Lord, we can move forward with confidence and courage each step of this day.

Talk With God:

Lord, I definitely do not want to loose my head, but I do want to possess courage and confidence. Teach me to be submissive and serve you with my whole heart. Help me to be dedicated to your will and to demonstrate my willing to be lead by you. Amen.

January – Day 24

Text: Hebrew 12:1-2 Amplified Bible

"let us strip off and throw aside every encumbrances—unnecessary weight—and that sin which so readily (deftly and cleverly) clings to and entangles us, and let us run with patient endurance and steady and active persistence the appointed course of the race that is set before us."

Thought: "Traveling Light"

I have found that the art of packing for a trip is learned the hard way. Suitcases crammed with what one thought were basic necessities soon become unbearable burdens to be dragged from one stop to another. They weigh one down with their mostly unnecessary contents.

Along life's journey, we often convince ourselves that we need things that are actually unessential for the trip. We carry burdens that would be better let go or left behind. We overburden ourselves with failures and fears, weaknesses and wrong attitudes, plus hurts habits and hang-ups.

The Word of God says, "Lay aside anything or anybody that would hinder our progress and hurt our chances of making heaven our eternal home." It may be an attitude, an addiction (habit or hang-up), or associates (unhealthy relationships).

We must begin each day taking inventory of our baggage, isolating ourselves from the non-essentials and being inspired by our God to hold a steadfast course.

In traveling light we are able to fight off the enemy's attacks, able to move quickly in performing the task at hand and able to help carry the burdens of others.

Talk With God:

How true it is – we humans are so gullible in thinking we have to have this or do that to make our journey safer and more successful. Yet, how foolish we really are. Lord, help to keep our basic needs small, our focus straight and our desire strong. For this we ask in your Name, Amen.

January – Day 25

Text: Malachi 3:6 KJV

"I am the Lord, I change not"

Thought: "A Changeless Christ in a Changing World"

It is evident that we live in an age of change, civil disorder, crime and conflict. Human bonds are broken. Hearts, homes and holdings are shattered. Disillusion, doubt and distress grip our hearts.

Yet God desires for us to know that amidst the floods of change, chaos and carnage; there is a Heavenly Father that never changes. He is always the same loving, lifting and liberating God from start to finish. He extends His hands to take hold of each of us and to never release us again.

Have you considered looking up in the hour of today's uncertainties and behold the hand of the Savior? He is ever ready to save, satisfy, secure and safely lead you to higher ground.

No matter neither the condition of humanity nor the calamity of the world, Christ is the anchor and answer to the times of which we live.

In His presences, there is power, peace and provisions for daily living. He is able to enrich and equip you in the morning for the day ahead. He is able to grant you a steadfastness that will make you surefooted regardless of any change of direction that may occur this day. He is the One who will direct you when detours confront you in the course of life.

What a foundation to build each day and what a focus to take each step.

Talk With God:

Although our times are unsettled, there is no greater day to live in than the present. It could be the day that you return for your people and rapture us into your eternal presences. At that moment, one of the greatest changes ever will occur—we will be changed into an eternal being where never again will we be affected with changes brought about by earthly conditions. Thank you for that consolation and courage. Amen.

January – Day 26

Text: Hebrews 3:14-15 KJV

"For we are made partakers of Christ, if we hold the beginning of our confidence steadfast unto the end. Today if ye will hear his voice."

Thought: "Begin With an End In View"

Each day has a commencement and it should end in celebration.

God did not intend for us to make a start and not finish the task. It may take endurances and effort on our part, but God will see us through.

The writer of the book of Hebrews challenges believers to have confidence regarding our relationship with Christ now and our residence with Christ in the near future. The key is to a firm commitment to the work of Christ on Calvary and the change He has made in our heart.

I am afraid this is where our great nation has failed. We had a strong beginning – total surrender and submission to the will, way, worship, and work of God; however, we have grown restless and rebellious. We have compromised our confidence in our beginning.

As you walk this day, renew your commitment to your spiritual beginning – your conversion and commitment to Christ. You will find that each step will be filled with power, peace and the promise that al is well..

Remember: you are on a journey and moving toward a destination. One day you will safely reach that heavenly shore as you move ahead with the unmovable grace and gift God has bestowed upon you.

Talk With God:

Lord, what a promise, if we will stay tuned to your will and stay true to your way; then we are assured that all things will work together for good. We have begun the journey of this day with you and at its close, we will celebrate in thanksgiving. Amen.

January – Day 27

Text: Genesis 1:1 Amplified Bible
"In the beginning God (prepared, formed, fashioned), and created"

Thought: "How Quick We Forget"

A the beginning of the class, the teacher asked George to go to the map and locate North America. George did it without any problem.

The teacher told George that he was correct and she was proud of him. Then she asked the class, "Now, Who discovered America?"

The class responded in rousing unison, "George!"

The story of God's relationship with humanity begins with the simple revelation and realization that it is He who creates. And all the things that He forms and fashions are good. This thought is repeated throughout the pages of recorded history.

It is God that created rest for your last night. It is God that has created today for you. And it is God who desires for you to be filled with His presences in order that you may have a blessed, bountiful and beautiful day.

Yet, how often we forget this simple spiritual truth!

Regardless of what happens, happiness comes from Godly contentment prepared within us by His Spirit and His Word. We are to enjoy life and experience liberty. God loves us and will not leave you alone when conflicts and crises arise.

Trust Him today and allow Him to fashion your attitudes and actions in accord to His will. It is His good pleasure to bless us and bestow His grace and goodness upon us. Receive it and rejoice in it.

Talk With God:

I truly am thankful for every good gift that you have made possible. I acknowledge your love and receive the fullness of it this day. You are not the author of confusion or conflict; therefore I will receive your grace and guidance to endure the trials, escape the traps and enjoy the trip through this day. Amen.

January – Day 28

Text: Proverb 14:12-13 NIV

"There is a way that seems right to a man, but in the end...the heart may ache, and the joy may end in grief."

Thought: "Nothing Can Go Wrong!"

The world's first fully computerized airliner was ready for its maiden flight without pilots or crew. The plane taxied to the loading area automatically, its doors opened automatically, the steps came out automatically. The passengers boarded the plane and took their seats.

The steps retracted automatically, the doors closed automatically, and the airplane taxied toward the runway. Everything happened without a hitch.

As the passengers leaned back in their comfortable seats, a voice came over the intercom. "Good afternoon, ladies and gentlemen. Welcome to the debut of the world's first fully computerized airliner. Everything on this aircraft is run electronically. We're cruising at 35,000 feet. Just sit back and relax. Nothing can go wrong...Nothing can go wrong...Nothing can go wrong..."

God created man in a perfect state of being; however, he gave man a will to decide as to whether he would dedicate himself to following His divine will and remain perfect or disrespect God and lose his perfected state of being. We know the story. Man failed.

However, humanity still lives today thinking that nothing can go wrong doing it his way. It seems we fail to learn from the past. Because of that, failure will occur over and over again in the history of mankind.

We must come to our senses and trust an all-knowing and all-powerful God to dwell in us and direct us in our ways of life.

Begin today by looking into His Word, learning from His Word and leaning on the truths of His Word to sustain you and supply you with the knowledge and the grace to live.

Talk With God:

Lord, today, I am aware that things can go wrong when I attempt to proceed on my own merits and mental capabilities. Govern my self-imitative and guide me in your Word. Amen!.

January – Day 29

Text: Psalms 119:159-160 Amplified Bible

"Consider how I love your precepts; revive me and give life to me, O Lord, according to Your loving-kindness! The sum of Your Word is truth. And every one of your righteous decrees endures for ever."

Thought: "Revive Me and Give me Life"

The entire 119th chapter of Psalms is an expression of the importance of God's Word. The chapter describes in detail and with delightful terminology the beauty, boldness and blessings of the Word of God. It talks of the Word in terms of endurance and having no end. It acknowledges that the Word builds and breaks apart. It makes clear the power and potential of God's Holy Word.

Today, let us examine a portion of its power and promise. The Word (precepts) of God is truth and is able to triumph in life. The Word is refreshing, reviving and restoring.

This day, as we meditate on the Word of God, will make for a day of allegiance to His will, anticipation of His wonders, accomplishment of our work and assurance of success. It will be an anchor of the soul, an answer to our confrontations, an anointing for the crises, and an advertisement of His glory and grace.

Allow Him to revive you and give you life simply by acknowledging His Word and accepting its truths.

Talk With God:

Well, God again, I will have to admit that abundant life is found only in You. Your Word makes it very clear and the walk of life verifies it. Accomplishments and achievements that are enjoyable, enriching and eternal are made possible through a daily renewal of our relationship with you. Revive me, I pray, O Lord and let real life reign within my being. This I pray, Amen.

January – Day 30

Text: Isaiah 45:2-3 NIV

"I will go before you and level the mountains; I will break down gates of bronze and cut through bars of iron. I will give you the treasures of darkness, riches stored in secret places."

Thought: "My, What God Has In Store!"

A young fellow asked a rich, old businessman how he made his money. The man nodded sagely and said, "It was 1932, the depth of the Great Depression, and I was down to my last nickel. "I invested that nickel in an apple that I polished all day. At the end of the day, I sold that shiny apple for 10 cents. "The next morning, I invested those 10 cents in 2 apples. I spent the entire day polishing them and sold them for 20 cents. I continued this for a month and accumulated a fortune of $1.37. "That's amazing," the young man said. "Then my wife's father died and left us 2 million dollars."

We will never earn the earthly nor eternal blessings of God; we must inherit them through Jesus Christ.

Friends, we have no idea what God can do for those who will allow Him to guide them each and every step of the way. The pleasure of His grace, the power of His glory, and the promises of His Good News will enrich, enable, and exalt our lives. It will allow us to endure, escape and eradicate our tempter. He will provide a renewing of our commitment daily, refreshing of our spirit daily and a rewarding of our faithfulness daily. His delight is to deliver us, develop us and direct us every step of the way.

The prophet Isaiah declares in chapter 45, a promise of restoration to the nation of Israel and proof of God's eternal supreme power and sovereignty. It is a word of encouragement. He declares that God will do what is necessary to bring about restoration.

God doesn't change. He will lead you and level the obstacles. He will build up anything that will help or break down anything that will hinder your liberty in Him. God will open doors of blessings. It is up to you and I to accept the facts – God loves us and desires to lead us. He delights in His people.

Talk With God:

My heart is humbled as I think of what you have already done for me. Yet, I rejoice knowing that I have only tasted and touched the surface of your abundant life for me. I anticipate your daily renewing and daily revelation that will come my way as I trust you. Amen

January – Day 31

Text: Psalms 16:8 KJV
"He is at my right hand I shall not be moved"

Thought: "Concreteness comes when God's in My Corner"

What a promise! When I acknowledge and accept the fact that Jesus is standing by my side each day, I have the blessed assurance that I will not be shaken.

I may feel the winds of adversity and experience the waves of attacks; but in Him I have an anchor that will grant me a sure foundation and focus for living.

Today may be the last day of the first month of a new year; but I will begin it with a reminder that it is the first day of a lasting experience with God who is with me each new step I take throughout the year.

I will shout hallelujah, speak with honor, stride in holiness and stand humbly before my Heavenly Father and all humanity.

I am convinced that when there is righteousness in the heart, there will real beauty in the character, rich harmony in the home, right order in the nation and reign of peace in the world. I cannot afford to be a part of the guilty party that is destroying our world. "I must be steadfast, unmovable, abounding in the work (and Word) of the Lord."

I must live my life in my world (my home, my job, my city) walking in the presences of the Righteous Justifier and Judge, Jesus Christ.

Talk With God:

Thank you Lord for being in my corner, walking by my side. It is my delight and my desire to be lead by You. I count it my pleasure to experience your dialogue, your discipline and your direction. I ask that you never leave me nor forsake me but love me and fortify me. This I pray in Your Name. Amen.

Step 2 – February
"Bountiful Love"

February is the month of love based on the celebration of Valentine's Day on the 14th day of the month. During this month's devotion, I would like for us to consider the depth of God's love and the demonstration of that love to one another.

Let take a brief look at the legend of St. Valentine. The story begins in the third century with an oppressive Roman emperor, Claudius II, and a humble Christian martyr, Valentinus. The emperor had ordered all to worship twelve gods and made it a crime to worship any other god with a sentence of death. Valentinus refused to cease serving God. He was imprisoned and awaiting impending death.

However, during the last few weeks of his life; his blind daughter, Julia, was brought to the cell for instruction and inspiration to live without his aid. During this time, a remarkable restoration occurred. While praying one day, a light shone into the cell and his daughter received her sight.

On the eve of his death, Valentinus wrote a last note to Julia, urging her to stay close to God, and he signed it "From Your Valentine."

His sentence was carried out the next day, February 14, 270 A.D. He was buried at the Church of Praxedes in Rome. It is said that Julia planted a pink-blossomed almond tree near his grace. Today, the almond tree remains a symbol of abiding love and friendship.

On each February 14, St. Valentine's Day, messages of affection, love and devotion are exchanged around the world.

Let us be willing to share the love of God because he has enabled us to see His glory and experience His grace. Let us be willing to share a love for God and a love from God every day and every step of the way throughout the entire year not just this month.

You may share your love on Valentine's Day with another by gifts of candy, cards, calls, colorful bouquet of flowers, a complimentary meal, a compassionate kiss and hug, or a cozy sat by the fireside. However, let us be personally concerned for one another and offer daily a prayer of guidance and a purposeful word of gratitude and growth.

February – Day 1

Text: John 3:16 Amplified Bible

"For God so greatly loved and dearly prized the world that he [eve] gave up His only-begotten (unique) Son, so that whoever believes in (trusts, clings to, relies on) Him shall not perish – come to destruction, be lost – but have eternal (everlasting) life."

Thought: "Love Is Initiated By God"

Love is of God! Because God is love! Therefore, love is initiated by God and is an imitation of God.. We are able to know His love because He first loved us. We are able to show His love because He first showed us.

"Love is a gift, take it, and let it grow. Love is a sign we should wear, let it show. Love is an act, do, and let it go." This is what love is all about -- A deed, devotion, a dedication.

As we trust God with our heart, cling to Him with our head and rely on Him with our being; we are able to be filled with a fuel that can set the world aflame.

Therefore, as you trod the path of life today, shake off the complacency, stir up some compassion and spread some cheer. It will be well worth the effort.

Share a smile; it will make others wonder what you have been up to.

It should always be the desire of everyone to avoid destruction and possess a delight for life. Therefore, we must fall in love with Jesus, who in turn will help us to love ourselves and love one another.

Talk With God:

It thrills my heart O Lord to sing the chorus, "O How I Love Jesus." For I do love you with all my heart, mind, soul and strength. I do thank you for loving me and leading me to such a revelation and realization. Govern and guide me in your love; and teach me how to give in love. In your Name I pray. Amen.

February – Day 2

Text: 2 Peter 1:19 NKJV

"And we have the prophetic word confirmed, which you do well to heed."

Thought: "Hear the Truth!"

Punxsutawney Phil is a groundhog that is taken out of his cage in Gobbler's Knob, Pennsylvania, each February 2 to predict the weather. According to legend, if Phil sees his shadow, there will be 6 more weeks of cold weather. If he doesn't see his shadow, spring will come early.

Of course, this is all in good humor and bears no honest revelation of the weather conditions. No one to my knowledge takes Phil's predictions seriously. Furthermore, I've read that he's unreliable—more often wrong than right.

There is One, however, who is always right and whom we must take seriously. The Disciple Peter in his second epistle echoes a warning and a welcomed revelation. He reminds us that God is truth and the truth must be acknowledged and accepted.

When writing this letter, Peter must have been thinking of that day on the Mount of Transfiguration with James and John as recorded in the Gospels (Luke 9). In the company of the great prophet Elijah, the patriarch Moses and the Person of Christ; God the Father spoke of the Christ as His Beloved Son and challenged all to hear Him!"

Jesus is the One who is never wrong and who will never lead us astray. We must consider His revelation to us (coming from His Scriptures, His Spirit and His spectacular creation) each day of our life in order to know the climate and conditions of our relationship with God.

Talk With God:

"Lord, I am thankful that we have a true report and a true revelation of the present and promised (not predicted) conditions that can prevail in our heart through a right relationship with you. I love you and delight in knowing you will always be with us and never hide your presences from us regardless of the existing conditions of life. Amen!"

February – Day 3

Text: Romans 8:28 NIV

"And we know that in all things God works for the good of those who love Him, who have been called according to His purpose."

Thought: "It Will Work Out if we Walk In love"

The Apostle Paul declares to the Roman believers that if we love God and accept His call to follow and fully obey Him, then we can be assured that all things will work out for the good.

Think with me for a moment!

If you find yourself today stuck in traffic due to road construction, rude drivers, rough weather or whatever reason, don't despair. There are people in this world for which driving is an unheard of privilege.

Should you have a bad day at work; think of the man who has been out of work for months.

Should you despair over a relationship gone badly; think of the person who has never known what it's like to love and be loved in return.

Should you grieve the passing of another weekend of rest, recreation and relaxation; think of the person who in dire straits, working twelve hours a day, seven days a week to supply the needs of her children.

God has been good to us; therefore, let us prove our love to Him by loving Him, living for Him (in appreciation) and lifting Him up in praise and thanksgiving.

Talk With God:

O Lord, I do love you and I do believe you will work out all things for the good of those who love you and live according to your plan and purpose. Therefore, Lord, help me to be gracious when things don't go according to the way I think; but express gratitude knowing it will go according to your plan for my life. For I wish to please you, praise you and purposefully demonstrate to others your great love for humanity. In your name I pray. Amen.

February – Day 4

Text: Matthew 6: 25, 33 NIV

"Therefore I tell you, do not worry about your life, what you will eat or drink; or about your body, what you will wear. Is not life more important than food, and the body more important than clothes? – But seek first his kingdom and his righteousness, and all these things will be given to you as well."

Thought: "Love God and Live Good"

Some people look into a mirror in the morning and upon seeing a gray hair, they go ballistic or make a quick call to the beauty salon for an appointment to correct the problem by coloring their hair.

I don't have to worry about that. My hair has been gray (really, it's white) for over 25 years (and I am only 62).

But in situation like this, do we ever stop and think about the cancer patient in chemo who wishes she had hair to examine.

Do you ever find yourself at a loss pondering what is life all about, asking what is my purpose? Friend, be thankful. There are those who didn't live long enough to get the opportunity.

So, when we look in the mirror; let us consider what is important in life? Do we consider the way we look, what we wear, where we go or who we are as the important things of life? I pray that we do care about our appearance and the appropriateness of where we go; but I pray most of all that we are glad for God's redeeming grace.

In our text, Jesus is encourages us to seek His kingdom (filled with life, love and liberty); knowing that other benefits necessary will be granted – even if some of them are only for a short while.

Talk With God:

Lord, I don't understand all your ways of life. I will never know completely regarding sickness, sorrow and suffering; but I can be grateful for every blessing I am given. Help me to love you and love others in this life. Amen.

February – Day 5

Text: John 15:12 KJV

"This is my commandment, that ye love one another, as I have loved you."

Thought: "Love Is Fulfilling"

If you look back over your days, you find that the precious moments of life which stand out are those experiences that have been done in a spirit of love.

An old country love song written by Bobby Daren in the early 1960's expresses this so well – "Every night I sit here by my window,

staring at the lonely avenue;

watching lovers holding hand and laughing;

thinking about the things we use to do;

Things like a walk in the park;

things like a kiss in the dark;

things like a sailboat ride;

what about the night we cried."

Our past lives are lived in memories of love.

This is God's will for our lives. He designed us to love and be loved. He desires that we love one another and enjoy the love of others. He is determined to bring this commandment to a lively reality in your life by giving you His love.

His love is real, righteous and will reign forever.

In His love we are able to recall memories of love, render moments of love, receive meaningfulness in being loved and rest majestically in His love.

Talk With God:

Lord, I have received from you real and righteous love, which exceeds any degree of love in this world. Therefore, I desire and determine to love my self, love my spiritual sister and brother, and love the sinner and my Savior. Amen.

February – Day 6

Text: I Samuel 16:7 NKJV

"For the Lord does not see as man sees; for man looks at the outward appearance, but the Lord, looks at the heart."

Thought: "God Looks for a Heart of Love"

Two individuals didn't check the thickness of the ice on a lake prior to venturing out on it. The lake appeared to be solid. But shortly after they began walking on it, both received an unwanted dousing in the chilly water. That mistaken judgment could have resulted in tragedy.

When Samuel went to anoint the new King of Israel, God reminded him to not look at the natural abilities or the physical appearance of Jesse's sons in making a decision. He was cautioned and challenged by the Lord Jehovah, commanding him to look for a heart of love. God would reveal to him the one to be chosen the new king – for only God could see the heart of man.

Be careful in your daily walk and don't make the wrong mistake by judging a situation by the outward appearance only. We do not know what path a person has to walk, the pain one may be enduring or the problem confronting someone.

How hasty and harsh sometimes we response without even knowing the situation. How unholy and unthinking we react to situations of life.

Let the amazing and anointing love of the King of Kings direct our thoughts, our talk and our timing in response or relationship with someone this day.

Talk With God:

Today, Lord, create within me a clean heart and an upright spirit that I may use caution and comfort in my reactions and responses throughout this day. Don't let me be quick to judge or quick to justify. Help me to not question nor quarrel, but with quality of character and quietness of spirit provide healing and hope. This I plea. Amen.

February – Day 7

Text: Romans 8:28 Amplified Bible

"For good to those who love God and are called according to [His] design and purpose."

Thought: "Love Gives Purpose"

I recently read a brief statement in the book, "Apples of Gold." This is what it said,

"I am only one, but I am one.

I cannot do everything, but I can do something,

And what I should do and can do,

By the grace of God I will do."

Friends, every one of us can do something. The lifting grace and loving grace of our Lord will enrich us and enable us to accomplish the task for His glory.

His design and purpose for humanity is to be saved by grace, stabilized in faith, strengthen by love, and set aside for a purpose.

I can not tell you what your specific task is in life, but I can tell you that God has included all in His plan. He needs you and wants you to allow Him to fill your life with His favor, His faith and His fellowship.

Walk this day believing that you are an instrument of the living God and you will bring inspiration to all whom you will encounter.

Talk With God:

"Jesus, I love you and long to walk with you this day. I will surrender my life and serve you in whatever capacity you wish. I am your ambassador and I am to fulfill my purpose because I am loved by you. Amen"

February – Day 8

Text: Ephesians 3:19 Amplified Bible

[That you may really come] to know – practically, through experience for yourselves –the love of Christ, which far surpasses mere knowledge)without experience; that you may be filled (through all your being) unto all the fullness of God – [that is[may have the richest measure of the divine Presence, and become a body wholly filled and flooded with God Himself!"

Thought: "Love Is the Spice of Life"

Does your life grow sweeter as the days go by?

If not, maybe you need to add a little spice to your life. And if you do, what is the best spice for life?

Recreation! It is good and good for us, but it is not fulfilling.

Rest and relaxation! It will boost and benefit your life; however, too much will make you lazy.

Resources! Yes, I agree we need food, finances, and fixtures. Yet, these things will only be a temporal blessing.

What about the real and reliable love of God? What a spice for life!

Did you know that the life that is inhabited by the love of God has been proven to have an increase in personal happiness, in peace of mind, and in performance of life's duty than any other medicine, material and mind set?

So, add a little spice in life by inviting the presences and power of Jesus Christ daily. Trotting the trail of life and talking with the Master step by step will increase your value of life and the validity of life.

Talk With God:

"Lord, we are truly thankful for every blessing you have given to us in this life. However, we desire to become sweeter, stronger and spiritually mature; and we believe we can through your love. Therefore, fill us to overflowing with your love that we may become sweeter as the days go by. We desire this in your name! Amen.

February – Day 9

Text: I Corinthians 13:13   NIV

"And now these three remain: faith, hope and love. But the greatest of these is love"

Thought: "Love Is the Greatest"

One of the greatest boxers of all time was Cassius Clay (aka Muhammad Ali). He would shout loudly prior to and after each match, "I am the greatest." His record proved him to be one of the greatest, if not the greatest of all boxers. However, today he suffers from Parkinson Disease caused by the blows to the head during his boxing career.

I would rather have love, the greatest virtue of life, inspiring my life and granting me the promise that in the end I will be better off than when I started.

I do believe we should put forth our best effort in whatever we endeavor in life, but let us be assured that the end will be greater than the beginning. And with love as our foundation and focus of life; we will be enriched, enabled and endure. For love is the medicine and master over all moral evil and provides the cure and the control of its infectious nature.

Be rooted in the love of God this day and watch your life produce fruit unto Godliness. Apply His love to all circumstances and conditions.

Talk With God:

"Today, O Lord, I will declare that the greatest virtue of life – YOUR LOVE – will uphold me and utilize me in making my day a day of victory. I will lean on you as you love through me. For you are the greatest – you are love. Amen!"

February – Day 10

Text: I Corinthians 13:1 KJV

"Though I speak with the tongues of men and of angels, and have not charity, I am become as sounding brass, or a tinkling cymbal."

Thought: "Charity is God Clarity"

A small town newspaper carried as a regular feature the sermon of a local minister. In preparing the sermon of the weekly edition, the typesetter mistakenly inserted an "l" for the letter "h" in the "charity." The text of that week's article said, "Thought I…speak with tongues of men and of angels, and have not CLARITY, I am become as sounding brass, or a tinkling cymbal."

This error suggested to my mind a deeper truth: without charity (love) there is no clarity in the message we seek to convey to a needy world.

Our walk, our work, nor our words will present the truth humanity needs unless we have a clear understanding of our relationship with God. Confusion reigns in our world and we must possess and present a clear revelation of God to a wandering world. That revelation is that God loves each of us.

Is our lifestyle clearly the message of God? It is if our words are pure and positive. It is if our walk is progressively promoting the will and way of God. It is if our works are demonstrating a love for the Heavenly Father and all humanity.

Talk With God:

Thank you Lord for allowing me to comprehend that you love me and laid down your life for me. Thank you for accepting me and appointing me to share your great love to others. Keep me unspotted and unblemished by daily cleansing me and challenging me to walk in purity of your love. Amen.

February – Day 11

Text: II Corinthians 5:14 Amplified (*personal emphasis*)
"For the love of God controls and urges and impels us, because we are of the opinion and conviction that (*Christ died for all*)."

Thought: "Love Is Essential"

During the 1800's, as Springfield, Illinois, neighbor was drawn to the door of Abraham Lincoln's log cabin one day by the lusty crying of the two sons. Lincoln said, "Their trouble is just what is the matter with the whole world. I have three walnuts, and each boy wants two."

Yes, when someone desires more than their share of that which is available; personal greed, pride and pure jealousy erupt. Such action breed's discontentment, division and direct conflict.

We must attempt each day to seek that which is essential and that is love. To have a sharing concern and satisfying love is evidences of a life that is filled with the love, the law and the life of God.

Are you doing your part in maintaining a right relationship with our Heavenly Father and all humanity? If not, today is a good beginning.

The writer of our text is declaring that if we believe Christ died to provide love to a lost and living world; then we must die to this world's philosophy of "what's in it for me" in order to prove our love for the world.

Love is essential to life itself.

Talk With God:

O Lord, I am glad that you put humanity before your own desire. I am glad that you yielded to the Heavenly Father's will and died on Calvary. Thank you for making me aware that love is most essential to this life and the life after death. Amen.

February – Day 12

Text: II Corinthians 8:8 NIV

"I am not commanding you, but I want to test the sincerity of your love by comparing it with the earnestness of others."

Thought: "Love is Faithfulness"

A story was told of a young man who courted two girls at the same time without either of them knowing about the other. One day he wrote one of the girls this note: "Dear Jane, I love you with all of my heart. You are my only love." Then he wrote the same thing to his other girlfriend except he changed the name to Sue. Only after dropping the notes into a public mailbox did he realize, too late, that he had put the letters into the wrong envelopes. Soon, instead of having two girlfriends, he had none at all.

The great sin today is unfaithfulness. But, friend you can't love God and love the glory of this world at the same time. You must devote your love sincerely and singular to God only if we intend to buddy with Jesus, be a blessing to others and build His Kingdom.

In Paul's letter to the church at Corinth, he is telling them that God doesn't measure our love by how much to give or do but by what we have left when we give. It is easy to give a lot if we have a lot left; but difficult to give much and have little left.

The more we give, the more God will assure us we will have.

God gave His all for humanity and He expects no less from humanity. We must be willing to love Him and to love one another as He loved us. We must develop faithfulness.

Talk With God:

Thank you for Lord for being faithful to the plan of salvation that you founded and fulfilled by your great and gracious love. Enrich me step by step and enable me day by day to prove my faithfulness by being a person of love. Amen.

February – Day 13

Text:	Psalms 3:5 NIV
"I lie down and sleep; I wake again, because the Lord sustains me."

Thought:	"A New Environment of Love"

Today is day of acknowledgement. I hereby acknowledge that it is the birthday of our only daughter-in-law, Dawn. She is married to our son, Wade. I am glad she is a part of our family. She is special even if she was born and brought up in California (just kidding). She has adjusted well to our every changing climate, easy going social conditions and enjoying new challenges (hunting) in the Natural State of Arkansas. Her love for her family has enabled her to endure and to enjoy her new environment.

Her setting up new residence in another state totally different from that which she was accustomed reminds me of a grand spiritual revelation. When God calls us out of the environment of the bondage of sin and blindness of selfishness into a new environment of love, liberty and genuine love; we find it a time of caution as well as celebration.

Dawn was hesitant to try new food dishes, navigate in slow and uncongested traffic and not fear when storms or snow and ice were in the forecast. The new believer learns that God's peace, power and purpose will sustain him in times of doubt, disappointments and detours. The new believer learns he must lean on God and not attempt things the old way.

Each morning that we awake, we face a new day, a new environment. We must learn to acknowledge God's love that has kept us through the night will guide in that same preserving love each step of the day.

Talk With God:

"Today is another day in which we take a step at the beginning to equip us to face the day ahead. Therefore, touch me with Your Spirit, tell (remind) me to walk in Your Love, and Trust me to be myself as I walk in the environment of a new day. I love you and worship you. Amen"

February – Day 14

Text: John 15:13 NKJV

"Greater love has no one than this, than to lay down his life for his friends."

Thought: "Greater Love Has No Man!"

February is the sweetheart month of the calendar year. It is the time of year to prove your love for someone special. The popular and present day custom is to give a card, a box candy, make a call or send a cluster of flowers.

However, Jesus demonstrated His great and gracious love by laying down His life for all humanity. His death on the cross paved the way for man to experience first-hand the amazing grace and atoning love of God.. Such an expression of love is overwhelming both by the giver and the receiver.

As I write this, I am reminded that our anniversary is coming up this month. I asked her what she wanted. She said, "Nothing." I told her that I would be her gift. She smiled.

A sincere moment of heart-felt praise and thanksgiving to God would be sufficient to let Him know that you love and appreciate all He had done for you and all he has designed for you in the future.

Let us be challenged to share our love with our Heavenly Father and all humanity that we come in contact with this day.

On this Valentine's Day celebration, let us be reminded of the amazing love of Christ demonstrated by the greatest act of genuine love – His death on the cross.

Talk With God:

"Thank you Lord for giving us the greatest expression of love on Calvary and making it possible for us to experience it and emphasize it by our love for one another. Amen."

February – Day 15

Text: 1 Corinthians 13:7 Amplified Bible

"Love bears up under anything and everything that comes is ever ready to believe the best of every person, its hopes are fadeless under all circumstances and it endures everything [without weakening]."

Thought: "Love Is Blind"

I read an interesting and inspiring story the other day. It was about a small boy who came from a poor home. The lad was shabbily dressed: mismatched and patched. Although he liked all of his classmates and teachers at school, one of the teachers was a special favorite. When asked why, he replied, "she is so interested in ME, she doesn't see my patches."

That's the way true believers of God look at others when they really "love through Jesus." Love is blind to surface defects. Love sees beneath the surface – the hurts, the hunger, the heart.

Our text declares that the love of God is so sweet and so strong that it becomes blind to any social misfortunes, spiritual weakness, or selfish wrongdoing. Godly love has a standard that we are in this boat together and we need one another.

We must lift one another up, lighten the load of each other and lean together on the grace of God for our leadership.

Talk With God:

"Lord, I know that sometimes I see people and particular things that upset me; however, let me become blind to other's habits and hang-ups and see there hurts and hungers. And in doing so, reach out to minister to them in word or works. Help me to have a clear vision of ministry but a closed vision to those things that would hinder my growth and giving for your honor. In your name I pray. Amen."

February – Day 16

Text: Romans 1:16 KJV

"For I am not ashamed of the gospel of Christ: for it is the power of God unto salvation to every one that believeth"

Thought: "Godly Love Destroys the Myth"

A story is told of a miner recently filled with the love of God attending an effort by an infidel lecturer to explain away the existence of God as a myth.

As the lecturer finished speaking, the miner stood up and spoke. "Sir, I don't know what you mean by myth but can you explain me? Three years ago I had a miserable home life: I neglected my wife and children; I cursed and swore; I drank up all my wages. Then someone came along and expressed and explained the love of God to me. Now all is different. We have a happy home life: I love my wife and children; I pay my bills; and I have given up drinking. I feel better in every way. A new power has taken possession of me since Christ came into my life. Sir, can you explain me?"

The lecturer had no answer to give, but the miner sent people home knowing that Jesus was anything but a myth. They had seen a living demonstration of the love of God and the liberty that the Gospel brings into a life.

We should never be ashamed to stand against the wiles of the enemy and declare the work that God has done in our life. Our testimony will make us strong and cause others to search their heart.

The Gospel is a life that influences, a light that illuminates and a liberty that produces independence from sin. What power the Good News of Jesus Christ provides. Let us enjoy the blessings it brings and be examples to others that they may experience the born-again privilege.

Talk With God:

"I am thankful that I have experienced the love of God that changes a life and gives the courage and confidence to live daily in a newness of life. I wish to express God's love to those in whom I come in contact. Teach me to possess beauty and portray boldness in my daily lifestyle. Amen!"

February – Day 17

Text: Hebrews 4:12 KJV

"For the Word of God is quick and powerful and sharper than any two-edged sword, piercing even to the dividing asunder of soul and spirit, and of the joints and marrow, and is a discerner of the thoughts and intents of the heart."

Thought: "Love Makes the Impossible Possible"

The story is told of someone driving through the desert and on an occasional stop noticed a beautiful flower growing out of bare rocks. It was amazing to realize that the wind must have blown some seeds into a crack of the rocks and with a little rain the seeds grew into the beautiful flower.

God has repeatedly performed such majestic and miraculous occurrences in life. It is beyond human comprehension or capabilities.

Do your problems seem too difficult to handle or your path too dangerous to trod? Friend, God can break through the harden surface and plant a seed of love that will spring up and provide shade and soothing in the midst of every problem and along each step of our path in life.

The text declares that God's Word powered by His great love for humanity will perform a work that seems impossible. Yet, there is no impenetrable surface in the heart of man, the heat of battle or the halls of life's school that God can not pierce. He will allow His love to drive His Word into the area of our life that is dry, dead and deserted to produce beauty and provide a blessing. It is up to each of us individually as to what the Word will do for us each step of every day.

Talk With God:

"Lord, I am glad that your love for me opens the Word to me. I am glad that the same love can plant the deeper refreshing and revelation needed to walk this life. Amen.

February – Day 18

Text;   Psalms 1:1-3 NIV

"Blessed is the man who does not walk in the counsel of the wicked, or stand in the way of sinners or sit in the seat of mockers. But his delight is in the law of the lord, and on his law he meditates day and night. He is like a tree planted by streams of water, which yields its fruit in season and whose leaf does not wither, whatsoever he does prosper."

Thought: "A Love for God Is a Love for His Word"

Taking advantage of a balmy spring day, 4 ministers decided to get together for a friendly game of golf. After several really horrible holes and lots of terribly bad shots, their caddy asked,

"you guys wouldn't be ministers by any chance?"

Actually, yes, we are," a member of the group replied. "Why?"

'Because," said the caddy, "I've never seen such bad golf and heard such clean language!"

Meditating on God's Word will promote righteousness in your life and protect you from falling into sin. In fact, most people have either lost this revelation or they have never received proper instruction on living in the Word.

It is a shame that many people read the Word of God in a haste making it no more than a time of hurried commotion rather than a time of devotion. The differences lay in a love for the messenger and the message – God.

Love is the fulfilling of the Law. To experience love is to engage in the Word and enjoy the Word. To express love is to be enriched in the Word and energized through the Word's power.

Today, meditate on the scripture text and its message -- The promise of power, provisions, peace and prosperity.

Talk With God:

"I do not comprehend nor completely understand all your wonderful truths found in your Word; however, I desire to reverence, read and receive from its pages courage, comfort and confidence to live for you. Grant this desire O Lord, and strengthen me as I share the principles and promises of your living and lovely Word. Amen."

February – Day 19

Text: Ezekiel 22:30 KJV

"And I sought for a man among them that should make up the hedge, and stand in the gap before me for the land, that I should not destroy it: but I found none."

Thought: "Love Will Make up The Hedge"

Recently a Cincinnati attorney was appointed by the court to defend a man accused of burglary. Later he was given permission to withdraw from the case due to the fact that the one he was to defend was the one who broke into his own home. The court agreed with his reason and said justice would best be served if the victim did not have to defend the one accused of offending him.

When it comes to our relationship to God, however, it's a different story (and I am glad). The only one able to be our advocate is the One against whom we have committed the crime.

These words of the Lord spoken through Ezekiel to the unfaithful nation of Israel hold two messages for us today. They both are built on love and brought about willingness.

One deals with the prophetic revelation of the coming of Christ to the world who would become the One who would stand in the gap (instead of us -- He took our place by dying on the cross; innocently lay on the sacrificial altar and intercedes for us before the Father) and complete the lineage of God's people and God's plan.

The second message is to realize that through God's love we may be the necessary one to may a difference in a life who has wronged us.

Always remember the one who died as our Substitute now lives as our Advocate. And He desires that we "love one another as He loved us."

Talk With God:

"O Lord, how delighted we are to know you stood in the gap for us and made up the hedge although we were guilty of rebellion against you. And we know how difficult it may be for us to follow your example in loving one another even when they are guilty of hurting us in some way. But I desire that you move out any ill feeling, make me a vessel of love and mold me into an instrument of hope. Amen."

February – Day 20

Text: John 1335: KJV

"By this shall all men know that ye are my disciples, if ye have love one to another."

Thought: "Live To Love"

In our society we hear much about the urgency of living for the Lord. It's the theme of the Church, the theme of the Christian and the theme of the contents of God's Book—the Bible. In the church, it is echoed in the songs and sermons. In the community, it is echoed in the believer's conversation and conduct. In the confides of the heart of the believer, it is echoed in the prayers and praise of their heart.

I fully agree that this should be the goal of all people. It is the message of reality – Godliness brings about goodness and goal achievement.

However, recently, I been impressed by something even more important. Although, it is essential to stress LIVING for Jesus; we must never forget to underscore the absolute necessity of LOVING for Jesus.

The Apostle Paul says that without love our living and our laboring for Christ is worthless. Our service to humanity is useless unless we perform it and portray it as acts of love.

It is ease to love those who return love. However, loving a family member who has wronged you, loving a friend who has let you down or loving a foe who doesn't like you at all is very difficult. However, this is what God desires of each of us. It is through His love to us and in us that enables us to love those regardless of their thoughts of us. Remember, if not for the grace of God we could be the one that holds ill feelings toward another.

Talk With God:

"Lord, I am glad that your love enables me to live for you. I am thankful that you set the example and I can follow leaving a pattern for others to follow. Establish me, enrich me and enable me to love and live for you. Amen."

February – Day 21

Text: I Corinthians 13:6-7 NIV

"Love does not delight in evil but rejoices with the truth. It always protects, always trust, always hopes, always perseveres."

Thought: "Love Is Truth, Trust & Triumph"

Years ago a military officer and his wife were aboard a ship that was caught in a raging ocean storm. Seeing the frantic look in her eyes, the man tried unsuccessfully to allay her fear of the storm. Suddenly she grabbed his sleeve and fearfully growled, "How can you be so calm?" he stepped back a few feet and drew his sword, pointing it at her heart, he said, "Are you afraid of this?" Without hesitation she answered, "Of course not!" "Why not?" he inquired. "Because it's in your hand, and you love me too much to hurt me," she said. To this he replied, "I know the one who holds the winds and waters in the hollow of His hand, and he will surely care for us!"

The officer was not disturbed because he had put his trust in the Lord.

Do we trust the Lord with our circumstances that seem to be out of our control? Do we fret over conditions that we can do nothing about? Are we overly concerned for confrontations that are mere opinions? God loved us not to leave us but to live within us. It is up to each of us step by step to trust Him. With each step we grow confident in the love of the Lord. And the more confident, the easier and earlier we will confide in Him regarding our situations..

The Apostle Paul reminds us that the love of God will always protect, provide and persevere.

Talk With God:

"Today Lord, I will begin a new day and I will need you to accompany me on my journey. I do not know what I will encounter, but I know that your love will give me peace, girt me with strength and grant me power to stand and withstand the storms. Amen."

February – Day 22

Text: Song of Solomon 2:4-6 NIV

"He has taken me to the banquet hall, and his banner over me is love. Strengthen me…refresh me…with love. His left arm is under my head, and his right arm embraces me."

Thought: "Something for God to Do"

Today is a day that God is willing to handle all your problems.

If life happens to deliver a situation to you that you cannot handle, do not attempt to resolve it yourself! Kindly put it in the SFGTD (Something for God to do) box. Don't fret but allow God to do it in His time

Once the matter is placed into the box, do not hold onto it by worrying about it. Instead, focus on all the wonderful things that are present in your life now.

Solomon in the second chapter is allowing the Bride to remember her satisfaction in her beloved. Likewise with God, He loves and literally embraces His bride, the believer, and desires that she will willing be reinforced in His strength, rested in His strong arms and reassured of victory in His sincere love.

Therefore, even if you find yourself the victim of other people's inconsideration, ignorance, iniquity or insecurities; remember, things could be worse. You could be one of them.

Rejoice in having given your thoughts, your time, your talents, your trials and your temptations to one who loves you more than anyone – God.

Talk With God:

Lord, thank you for allowing me to give you my praise and my problems. I know you will be a victorious banner of love as I walk in obedience to your commandments and under your command. I accept your leadership and your love. Please accept my sincere and surrendered love in return. In your name I pray. Amen.

February – Day 23

Text: Psalms 139:3 NIV

"You discern my going out and my lying down; you are familiar with all my ways."

Thought: "Love Doesn't Forget"

Today, I heard a cute story about an elderly widow and widower who lived in a mobile home park for Senior Citizens in Florida. One evening during a community supper, the two were seated across from each other. Throughout the meal, they cast admiring glances at each other and share shy smiles. At the end of the meal, he asked her if she would marry him. Her reply was,"yes, yes, I will."

In a short while, they departed to their respectful residence. Early the next morning, the man awoke and pondered what her answer to his proposal was? He called her and she reaffirmed her positive reply to his question.

However, she stated that they both had memory difficulties. She admitted that she was glad he called, for she couldn't remember who made the proposal to her.

Friend, we may forget the promises of God's abiding presences, anointing power and amazing love; but God never forgets us. He is acquainted with all our ways and has proposed a love that will sustain us in all our conditions.

The Psalmist declares that God is aware of our every step, is acquainted with all our ways, and accepts the responsibility of keeping us along life's way.

It is possible to let a birthday or anniversary of someone we love occasionally slip by. Yet, God has never forgotten us. It may appear at times, He has; but He has never been late nor has He let it pass from His memory (exeptt our sins, when we seek His forgiveness. That He never remembers)

Talk With God:

"I am so glad Lord that you enjoy good humor and I am glad we can learn lessons of life from humor. Therefore, let me rejoice in the fact that you never will forget to watch over me, weigh my actions and walk with me on a daily basis. Thank you for that promise. Amen."

February – Day 24

Text: I John 4:18 NKJV

"There is no fear in love; but perfect love casts out fear"

Thought: "Love Overshadows fear"

Fear is a condition that exists when faith is absent.

A person may experience fear when a test or treatment has to be performed regarding physical symptoms of an illness; a betrayal by a friend; a separation from someone due to death, divorce or duty of war; failure at our workplace; captivation by habits and hang-ups; changes in one's life; lost of possessions due to economic and environmental disasters. Yet, in all these we can become like the Apostle Paul or any other believer who stands firm in the love of God.

Fear will cause pain, problems and perplexity; yet God cares about us and stands ready to erase the fear, ease the pain and give us grace to endure or escape the condition and circumstances.

Now, let me make one thing very clear; I am not condemning a person who fears nor certifying that they do not possess God's love in their heart and mind. I am saying that God desires us to trust Him and be filled with His love in order that we may know that His love will cast out fear. We must allow the love of God to work for us – by allowing our minds to conform to that reality and our heart to hold to that revelation.

Love is like a small and simple match lit in a dark cave. It makes total darkness disappear. Where no vision existed prior to the lighting of the match, we now can see clearly that we need not fear.

Talk With God:

"Yes, Lord, I know I will allow things to create fear in my life. However, I desire to become so filled with your love that the height, depth, width of your love goes, glows and grows beyond my comprehension. Fill me that I may make any symptoms of fear flee from my presences. In Your Name I ask. Amen."

February – Day 25

Text: I Corinthians 15:10 KJV *(emphasis added)*
"But by the grace *(favor, love)* of God I am what I am"

Thought: "Love Is What Makes Me"

In such a competitive world as today, it is hard to be the greater of any one thing. Although many attempts are made at being a specialist in various fields, yet not one seems to have achieved the top specialist slot in a particular field.

Yet, God calls us to be the greatest at one particular thing – being you. He desires that we wake each morning, walk each step of the day and wind up finishing the day successfully. Wow! What a commandment and what a challenge! No, I do not say that we were to have a perfect day or live a perfect life; I simply said we are to be a success at being our self – being the greatest me!

However, what does that involve? The task is an impossible one if you flounder in the shadow of others. There is always someone with better skills than yours or mine. Yet, living in the shadow of God's love, you can become the best YOU possible.

Jesus challenged us to "let our light shine that others may see your good works, and glorify your Father which is in heaven." In other words, when we are just "us" letting God shine through us, we are being the best "You" possible.

Let your goal today be to be the world's greatest "Me" by loving God and allowing God to love others though you.

As Ethel Waters use to say, "I know I am somebody cause God don't make no junk."

Talk With God:

"Wow, I can be the greatest by walking in your shadow O Lord. I can have self-worth, I am yours and I am willing to be loved and lead by you. Let me shine in your grace and share the glory of your love to others. Amen."

February – Day 26

Text: Philippians 4:13 KJV
"For we are laborers together with God"

Thought: "Labors of Love"

I recently saw an amusing comic strip in which two mules tied together by opposite ends of a short rope were striving in opposite directions to reach a pile of hay. Yet, their efforts were stalled as they pulled against one another. In the next frame of pictures, the mules are exhausted sitting staring at one another. The next shows the two mules having the same idea – they would cooperate by going to the hay pile one at a time.

Individuals are sometimes like two mules – stubborn, selfish and starving. We pull against one another to get what we want. We even pull against God's will trying to get at happiness in life. Yet we never quite accomplish the mission pulling against one another.

The Word of God tells us that we are co-laborers one with another and with God. We need God and one another to accomplish most earthly needs, eternal needs and wants.

Therefore, it should be our love for God, our love for one another, and our love to success in reaching our goals of life. It is only as we work with one another and above all else allow Him to work in us, that we can achieve that which is profitable to all (God, Others and self).

I love the message of the children's chorus "If We All Pull Together." The simple message is "how happy we'll be." As co-workers, fellow-students and neighbors; we must co-exist. However, the only way that it can be done is through the love God.

. Talk With God:

"Yes Lord, I am aware that sometimes I am like a mule – stubborn, selfish and starving (missing out on the blessing). Yet, I desire to be cooperative and considerate of my fellow man and a co-laborer with each believer and you in building the Kingdom. Give me understanding and undergird me with strength to accomplish this task. Amen."

February – Day 27

Text: Ephesians 6:13-14, 24 NIV

"Stand your ground, and after you have done everything to stand, stand firm…grace to all who love our Lord Jesus Christ with an undying love."

Thought: "Love Grants Favor to Stand Firm"

Botanists tell us that certain plants are too weak to stand up by their stems, so they must be supported by stronger plants or objects in order to grow properly.

What a marvelous illustration of the Christian life. Deep in his heart each believer must realize his own weakness and search for support and strength. Those who do not put forth the effort through prayer and personal Bible study remain undeveloped and useless in their spiritual ability to stand and be steadfast. Thus, a failure to be faithful and fruitful will result.

God has given His armor (Ephesians 6), His attitude (Matthew 7—the Golden rule), and His attributes (He is omniscient – all knowing, He is omnipresent – all present, He is omnipotent – all powerful, He is omnibus – all providing). to help us stand true to His will and stand tall in His way.

The Apostle Paul in our text challenges the Christians at Ephesus to be strong and stand firm in the doctrine of the Lord and in their devotion to the Lord. He shares with them the courage and confidence to stand stating that it is found in our personal love for Jesus

Take a moment each day to thank God for the day and get in tune with Him for His guidance and girding that you may be able to stand firm in His love and in His leadership. He loves you and desires to lift you up.

Talk With God:

"Today Lord I want to know your love so strongly that I may have a supporting pillar for building my life, boasting of your love and boosting those whom I come into contact with. Thank you for your power for today and your promise of tomorrow. Amen."

February – Day 28

Text: *Ephesians 4:16 NIV*

"From Him the whole body, joined and held together by every supporting ligament, grows and builds itself up in love."

Thought: "Love Is the Foundation & Focus for Living"

Today is mine and Elaine's wedding anniversary. We have endured many hardships and heartaches; however, God has been good to us and given a marriage based on love and appreciation. We have learned much about marriage, making a home, ministry and making ends meet. All have been possible through a keen awareness of God's presences, knowledge of His Word and kneeling in surrender of self.

I believe that God has someone for everyone. I have found that to be a truth with Elaine and me. She has definitely been the precious stone that has brought our marriage an A1 rating. And I believe she would agree that I was, am and always will be the man for her.

When you look at your marriage like this and consider the same principles, purposes and prizes for your relationship with God, you will find a marvelous and magnificent union existing. Humanity must allow their relationship with God to be a loving, living, life-long commitment. What God unites, let no one put asunder.

Begin this day with a renewed commitment to the Lord. Let bygones be bygones, and tomorrows take care of themselves. Focus on today and built the foundation and focus for real living on a holy, harmonious, and happy love relationship.

Talk With God:

"Today, O Lord, we pray this simple yet sincere prayer. It is a special day for me and everyone who comes into my life space. It is a day of renewed commitment to you and to all who are a part of my life. I desire the best for them and I determine to be the best to them. Help me to hold up my end of any relationship of which I am a part. I love your and thank you for loving me. Amen."

February – Day 29

Text: 2 Samuel 22:30 KJV

"For by thee I have run through a troop: by my God have I **leap**ed **over** a **wall**"

Thought: "An Extra Blessing!"

Not every February has 29 days. Not every year is a leap year. Only once every four years do we get an additional day in February and an additional day in the year. Therefore, if you were to keep this devotional book and use it for daily reading each year, you would need a devotional on that extra day – February 29th.

David realized that God always seem to provide an extra blessing to his life – whether it was daily provisions, divine protection, deliverance, or directions for living. In his song of thanksgiving found in 2 Samuel, chapter 22, we find gratitude for that extra touch of courage, that extra thrust of strength, that extra truth of assurance, that extra torch of visibility, or that extra thought of comfort.

I like the way "The Message" translates our text. "Suddenly, GOD, your light floods my path, GOD drives out the darkness. I smash the bands of marauders, I vault the high fences. What a God! His road stretches straight and smooth. Every GOD-direction is road-tested. Everyone who runs toward him makes it."

God doesn't wait for leap year to grant us these extras. They are repeated over and over just as this verse is repeated verbatim in Psalms 18:29, and in many other events and experiences of Scripture we see the evidence of God's extra blessings clearly.

Talk With God:

"Lord, I am so glad you go beyond what we really desire and delivery benefits and blessings to us in our walk of life, our war with the enemy of life and our worship of you in life. I desire to glorify you, grow in you and glow for you. Manifest your everyday touch to my life and overflow my life with the extras that I may be a better, bigger and bolder light for you. Amen!"

Step 3 – March
"Blowing In the Wind"

As the month of March moves in, the winds begin to kick up and blow out the coldness of the winter months and bring in the April showers. This provides for a ground breaking freshness of blooms and blossoms. Leaves sprout and lovely songs of birds fill the air. What a refreshing touch we experience.

It reminds me of the song written by Bob Dylan and made so popular by Peter, Paul and Mary. The song, "Blowing in the Wind," has been suggested to have several interpretations. One was that it was an anthem of the 1960's civil rights movement that captured the frustration and aspirations of the black people that had been voiced for generations.. Another was that it echoed the cry of God regarding humanity's rebellion and rejection of the love, the laws and the liberty of God that offered true freedom.

Friends, God has been challenging humanity for centuries to hear and heed His Word. He knows the answer to man's condition, the avenue to better life, and the anchor for a prepared future rest in Him. As He breathes His refreshing Word, His reviving Spirit and His restorative Plan of Salvation unto us, let us take a deep breathe of relief and take in the renewing breathe of life.

Let us remember that it was the breathe of God that made man a living soul in the beginning and it is the refreshing winds of the Holy Spirit that fills man with an anointing and an amazing challenge to be the son, the servant and the soldier of God.

. Stand still and speak the Name of Jesus! Sit still and soak up the truths of God's Word! Suppressed still by troubles, sense His presence real! His spirit is flowing unto humanity each day and He blows a breath of heaven sent fresh, fortifying and freeing winds of victory for each of us.

March – Day 1

Text: Matthew 8:24 KJV

"And, behold, there arose a great tempest in the sea, insomuch that the ship was covered with the waves: but (Jesus) was asleep."

Thought: "Courage Against The Contrary Winds"

Once upon a time there were three little pigs. They were concerned about security, so they went to seek their fortune. The first built a house of straw. The second built his of sticks. But the third built his of bricks. Well, the big bad wolf huffed and puffed and blew down the house of the first and second little pig. But as the story goes, the wolf could not blow down the house made securely of bricks.

Everyone is concerned about security. We live in an unsafe and unsettled society. Therefore, the concern is justified. However, I wonder how many are concerned for spiritual security. Severe weather and sickness can devastate the physical being. Financial collapse and fire can erase material matter. Yet the spiritual safety will determine our destiny. We must build a solid foundation and strong structure with the future in mind.

To do so, we must check out the blueprints (God's book), collect the material (pure heart and clean hands), converse with a reputable contractor (Jesus) and contract the work (agree and accept Christ); then we can feel safe and have a stable setting in this life.

In our text, Jesus and the disciples were crossing the lake to the other side to minister when a terrific wind storm that caused the waves to fill the boat. The disciples became shaken yet Jesus slept. When He was awaked, he calmed the winds and waves. Jesus will stand with you when it appears your boat is about to capsize due to the winds and waves of adversity. Trust Him.

Talk With God:

"Lord, it is with thanksgiving that we present our self to you this day. It is with honor that we yield our life to your keeping. There is no other foundation nor fortress to whom we can reside in than you. We love you. Amen."

March – Day 2

Text: Ezekiel 28:17 & 24 KJV

"Thine heart was lifted up…and there shall be no more a pricking brier unto the house of Israel."

Thought: "Still In the Business of Giving the Breathe Of Life"

Have you ever had a flat tire? I have. In fact, I had three in one week – it was back in the days of the automobile recap tires.

Yet, recently I had a flat tire. There were no nails, glass or other sharp objects present that pierced the tire. There was no large cut or break in the tire. It just simply became deflated. The air leaked out of the tire from a broken valve stem.

Life is sometimes like that. Most of the time, we feel full of air, frisky and fulfilling. (Now, I don't want those who know me to giggle here, when I declared to be full of air – hot air)

Yet, occasionally we go flat. We simply deflate.

Stress, sickness, sorrow, suffering, and other situations suck the air right out of our life. But our life does not have to stay flat. We can be restored, repaired and renewed.

I have a friend who is a specialist in fixing flat lives. His Name is Jesus. He is the Personal Counselor, the Prince of Peace, and the Provider of all things. He is as near as your breath, just whisper His Name and He will respond. Look Him up in the book; He is listed in the Bible. Check Him out in the community, He is found at the Church.

He has been in the business for centuries and is capable of working on any life regardless of the age or condition. He does His work free of charge and will guarantee the job if you follow His guidelines. I know you will be satisfied.

In our text, God promises Israel again that He would fix their spiritual flatness by removing the deflating substance (sin) and restore them in His beauty. God will do it again for you and me. He will fix the problem and restore us.

Talk With God:

"Thank you Lord for being available in time of need, whether it is basic salvation or the believer's stability and for being the answer to life's difficulties. I long to please you and live to promote your Kingdom. Deliver me, direct me and cause me to delight in You. Amen."

March – Day 3

Text: Psalms 27:4 KJV

"One thing have I desired of the lord, that will I seek after; that I may dwell in the house of the Lord all the days of my life, to behold the beauty of the Lord, and to inquire in the temple."

Thought: "Top Priority"

Today is a special day for a special person, the birthday celebration of our only granddaughter. I pray she will have a delightful fourteenth birthday. She enjoys spending the night with her girl friends, texting on the cell phone, surfing on the internet, listening to music, and watching television. However, there is something that ranks higher than any of these in getting her attention. You guessed it – BOYS.

If you think about it, such a criteria might apply to all humanity. The items of interest may change but I think the format is basically the same.

I wonder if mankind is not guilty of having many different interests in life, yet allowing one to be above all others. I think so.

The thing that I am concerned about is not the little interest in this life, but the major craving of our life. Is it money, material, man (or woman), mental comprehension, and masters of corporations? Or is it pleasure, power, position and possessions? Or is it sex, social success, substance abuse (drugs, alcohol, etc)? What should it be? How about sincere love for and service to the home, humanity and the Heavenly Father?

In the latter should lay our answer and our aim. God has blessed us with an opportunity to whisper, walk and work in a way that the whole world feels the winds of refreshment and real excitement. The psalmist desire was to please God by praising Him and progressing in his relationship with Him. Let such a desire motivate us.

Talk With God:

"I wish to thank you Lord for every member of my extended family (children, in-laws, grandchildren). I love my friends and fellow workers. I love my church and my country. I love you Lord. I desire only the best for each of these but I want you to use me to fan the breeze of restoration to all who have not chosen you as their number one priority of life. This I pray, Amen!"

March – Day 4

Text: Psalms 27:13 NIV

"I am still confident of this: I will see the goodness of the Lord in the land of the living."

Thought: "Resiliency"

I read a beautiful quote one day. It simply yet sincerely stated a fact of reality – "Today's tall oak tree is yesterday's nut that held its ground."

Resiliency is an important factor in living. The winds of life may bend us, but if we have resilience of spirit, they cannot break us. To courageously straighten again after our heads have been bowed by defeat, disappointment and devastation is the supreme test of character.

And that ability to spring back comes from God. Man is weak in comparison to God. Man is weak in comparison to the difficulties of life – for most of the hardships, headaches, and heartaches of life are attacks by the evil spirit to defeat us. The enemy desires to break our spiritual strongholds, bind our knowledge of God and blind us to God's goodness in life.

Yet through God we are able to rise above the situation – spring back into firmness, faithfulness and fruitfulness for God.

The Psalmist knew of the importance of resiliency. Whether wrong was done to David or David did wrong in facing circumstances of life; God was always faithful to his servant that admitted his need of Him and accepted His forgiveness and fortitude to rise from the ashes of defeat and disappointments.

We too can spring back when slapped by the enemy and sapped of strength. We simply need to accept the strength made possible through the abiding presences of the Lord.

Talk With God:

"Lord, I know the winds of adversity blow against us; but I also know that you are our stability and strength. In you we can resist the attack, ride out the adversity and reign over the enemy. Keep us and kindly encourage us Amen."

March – Day 5

Text: John 14:6 NIV

"Jesus answered, "I am the way and the truth and the life"

Thought: "Keep True To the Course of Life"

The Bible declares that many are "tossed to and fro by every wind of doctrine." It also states, as in our text, that Jesus is the Way, the Truth and the Life" which is the true doctrine of scripture and spiritual life.

I personally am convinced that Jesus Christ is the way, the truth and the life. And I also am convinced that without the way, there is no going; without the truth, there is no knowing; and without the life, there is no living.

The world we are living in is filled with chuck holes and many other hazardous conditions that will damage, detour and delay our walk with God. Yet, in Jesus we have a way that is straight and narrow and is paved with the quality of character that will insure safe driving conditions.

The world we are living is complex and at times very difficult to stand the test, trials, troubles and temptations that come our way. Yet with Jesus Christ we possess a knowledge that will enrich, equip and enable us to pass the test, possess the strength and pursue our goals.

And life at times seems no more than "being alive, existing;" however, with Christ we are able to rely on Him for a spring of joy, a standard of peace and a substance of togetherness.

God will be faithful in sending the refreshing winds of His Spirit to each of us who walk the path of righteousness found in Christ.

Talk With God:

"Today Lord, I come to you seeking to walk in the revelation and reality of the abundant life you have promised to those who believe. I believe and boldly move forward declaring that this is the day you have made and demonstrating that conviction by rejoicing in it. I love you. In Your Name I pray. Amen."

March – March 6

Text: II Samuel 22:11 NIV
"He mounted the cherubim and flew; he soared on the wings of the wind."

Thought: "He Rides the Winds"

Today is my oldest daughter's birthday. It is unbelievable that daddy's little girl is now forty years old. My, how time has flown. It seems only like yesterday that I took my wife, Elaine, to the hospital and a beautiful blonde haired, blue eyed, eight pound, two ounce girl blessed our life.

A lot of things have happened since that day. We have endured many hardships and enjoyed many happy moments. For them all I am thankful. I made a lot of mistakes (really) and learned a lot of lessons on parenthood. In fact, I am still learning.

The winds of time will continue to blow until God stands and calls a halt to the adversity, animosity, and aggravation that accompany life.

The winds of time will whirl in circles of destruction, disillusion and disappointment; but God will ride the winds to offer us His consolation, courage, and confidence to press on.

According to this verse, God is active in His intervention in times of terrible and trying winds of adversity. Even as He allows damaging winds of life to rip and roar across the land and our lives; He is always on the wings of such. He is present to grant and give us the uplift that is needed and many times the understanding essential to carry on.

Time seems to fly and situations seem to blow in bringing hardships and heartaches; but He rides the wings of the wind to strengthen us.

Talk With God:

"Lord, I do not understand why winds of devastating proportions blow into our lives; but I am thankful that in the midst of pleasure or perplexities, you are present to lift us up. Amen."

March – Day 7

Text: Ezekiel 37:9 NIV

"This is what the Sovereign Lord says, Come from the four winds, O breath, and breathe into these slain, that they may live."

Thought: "Let it Breathe on Me"

- Permit me to share with you the words of the poet, Herbert Spencer:

> "Look at the coal covered with ashes;
> There is nothing appearing in the hearth but only dead ashes;
> There is neither light, nor smoke, nor heat;
> And yet when these embers are stirred to the bottom,
> There are found some living gleams,
> Which do but contain fire, And are apt to propagate it."

Many people are like this fireplace, no life of the grace of God appears there. Individuals have yielded to temptation and become cold and dead. Yet, deep in the inner being there is a soul that cries out for the light and life of God. It searches for the warmth and welcome atmosphere of the love and life of God. The ashes simply need to be rekindled.

It is so human to allow our flame of life to die down. We become occupied with other things that rob us of our duty and devotion to God.

If your spiritual fire has died low and you desire it to be relit; talk with Jesus (in His Word or in Prayer). He is wiling to stir your soul by blowing on the embers of that childlike vision of a loving and living God.

In our text, Ezekiel was commanded of the Lord to speak to the winds to bring the breath of life to the dead, dry and desolate nation of Israel. God desired to restore the nation. God desires to restore and rekindle our numb, negative and negligent spirit (in our conscience and in our nation).

Talk With God:

"Lord, we need the warmth of your love and the light of your life; therefore, rekindle our spiritual flame. Renew our devotion to you and enable us to escape the coldness of our spiritual life. We must keep the flame burning for personal warmth and persuasion of others who are spiritually cold to join us around the fire of spiritual life. Amen"

March – Day 8

Text: John 15:16 RSV

"You did not choose me, but I chose you and appointed you that you should go and bear fruit and that your fruit should abide…"

Thought: "Happiness Is A Product Of Self-Giving"

Just as the wind blowing into our face on a hot summer day or across our body wet with sweat while performing a task on a spring morning; the winds of happiness will envelope our life as we give of our self in service to the Lord and to the living multitude around us.

It appears that some people simply have a determination and a desire to be unhappy. They are focused on self with no intent of being fruitful unto others. However, when this is the case, "there will be no happiness in Mudville today. Mighty Casey has struck out." (This cute little remark is from an old baseball story of Casey at bat).

When we pursue something demanding and worthwhile above and beyond ourselves, happiness seems to be there as a by-product of the self-giving. Happiness comes as a dividend of our investment.

A smile, a simple handshake, a sweet compliment, or sent note is all it takes to bring happiness to others and oneself. Sometimes a square meal, a sip of water, or a soft rub of the forehead will produce the comfort and courage needed. When applied, happiness springs up in the act of courteousness and comfort and floods the soul of the applier.

This is your day to experience happiness and enjoy life. Prepare for a wonderful day, for it is the plan and purpose of God for you.

Talk With God:

"It's me again Lord, facing another day. I need strength in my body, spirit in my soul, stability in my walk and sincerity in my heart. Prepare me, prompt me and pump me up for I am going to experience happiness and enjoy this day. Amen."

March – Day 9

Text: James 1:6 NIV

"But when he asks, he must believe and not doubt, because he who doubts is like a wave of the sea, blown and tossed by the wind."

Thought: "Believe and Enjoy the Wind; Doubt and Be Tossed About"

I recently read a quote that said, "The right temperature at home is maintained by warm hearts – not hot heads.

Allow me to rephrase this quote by saying, "Warm hearts and cool heads, not hot heads and cold hearts develop a great character."

Our position in Christ will make a difference in our daily life. If we are a believer and walk in fellowship with Christ each step of the day, we will enjoy the refreshing and renewing breath of life. If we do not believe and walk daily with Christ, we will be tossed about by the winds of life.

We must be determined when we awake each morning that we will declare that no problem or pressure will come our way in which we can not handle. I hope we awake each day with a declaration that if and when situations arise that buffet us, we will keep our trust in the Lord and allow Him to guide our steps and govern our spirit.

We do not know what a day may hold for us. It may be a perfect day of sunshine and safety. But if it is a day of using the sword, seeking a shelter and depending on the SONshine; then we still can enjoy the heavenly breezes that the Scriptures and the Holy Spirit will bring to our being.

So, don't doubt – don't have a double allegiance – to the Heavenly Father and the flesh, Choose to believe that God is Truth, our Tower of Strength and our Triumph.

Talk With God:

"Lord, I truly love you and desire to walk in total allegiance to you. For I know you are my Redeemer, my Reinforcement and my Refresher. Guide my steps, govern my speech and give me strength in order that my path be straight, sure and steadfast.. Amen."

March – Day 10

Text:　　Acts 2:2 Amplified Bible

"When suddenly there came a sound from heaven like the rushing of a violent tempest blast, and it filled the whole house in which they were sitting."

Thought:　　"Let the Four Winds Blow"

An old song by Fats Domino called, "Let the Four Winds Blow," comes to mind when I think of the mighty wind of the Holy Spirit coming upon the disciples in the Upper Room on the Day of Pentecost. For in this blues song, the message of strong, stable and satisfying love is expressed.

God promise of an outpouring of His Spirit to comfort, convince, convert and grant courage to every believer was delivered and demonstrated on the Day of Pentecost. It came in an amazing and attention getting wind of His love. For those who obeyed His commandment to tarry in Jerusalem to be endued with power on high, they were filled and became fit for duty. It was to others an awakening and anointing of a new birth.

The occurrence was like God had opened the windows of heaven and allowed His Spirit to flow earthward from all four directions (North, South, East, West) to that chamber.

We need a daily refilling and renewing of God's Spirit and I pray it will be a mighty gust of a heavenly breeze. Let it be a great, gracious and glorious spiritual wind gust that creates a stir for believers and unbelievers alike. Let the four winds blow.

If you considered what happened following the events of that day, you will see a spiritual revival – rebirth and restoration – changed the world and continues to change lives today. Oh, for such an event on a daily basis in our heart, our homes and our homeland.

Talk With God:

"O Holy Spirit, we need you once again to renew our lives. Give us a breath of fresh air from heaven. Stir us to examine and experience this revelation. I need a fresh touch of your love, your life and your liberty. Amen."

March – Day 11

Text: Psalms 77:6 KJV

"I commune with mine own heart: and my spirit made diligent search."

Thought: "Don't Allow a Truth to Sail Over Your Head"

In the days of Christopher Columbus, the common belief was that the world was flat. One day Columbus was sitting under a tree eating an orange. A butterfly landed on top of the orange, walked around and down the side of the orange without falling off. In his excitement, Columbus reasoned that the same force of nature that kept that butterfly connected to the underside of the orange would also keep him and his ships connected to the earth and not fall off the edge.

Now we know that the butterfly had microscopic "suction cups" on his little feet. However, such a revelation did not fly like wind over Columbus's head but set off a visual reality that produced a discovery of our homeland, America.

You know sometimes we sweep our hand over our head to signify that an idea or thought spoken or showed us totally bypassed us. It zipped right over our being never landing in our brain -- never comprehended.

We must allow the revelation of God to create within our thinking a perception that will shape our reality.

We must begin each day, pausing for a moment to meditate on the realization that God wants to reveal His faithfulness, His fruitful character and His focus for us that will light up our day, lead us in the right way and keep us lifted up in His strength to face whatever.

Talk With God:

"Lord, help me today to be still and know that you are Lord. Help me to examine my devotion to you and the day that is set before me. Help to walk in a way that will reveal your character. This I pray, Amen"

March – Day 12

Text: Luke 15: 18 KJV

"I will arise and go to my father, and will say unto him."

Thought: "Prayer Is Not a Speeding Bullet of Change"

When I was a kid, I remember that the Lone Ranger made his own bullets out of silver. It was his duty to develop a true and tempered bullet to defend the Wild West. I recall reading that it would take a silver bullet to kill werewolves. I don't believe in such creatures, but the point being there was a weapon that would destroy the evil creature.

Then the other day, I was reading an article and it mentioned that many people think that praying and Bible reading will perform change like a speeding magic bullet. We are shot by God with a silver bullet of transformation and all the evil goes away. This is not true however.

We need to have a change of heart and a commitment to do different in our conduct, go a different direction in our way of life and be different in our character; however, it will not happen by some earthly measures. It will take a revelation of the Savior, a repentant heart and righteous living.

Many people say the words of the "repentant prayer;" but fail to follow through with the dedication and duty of living the life. Oh we may begin each day by READING the Word of God, saying a prayer TO God; yet as the day goes along we do not MEDITATE on the Word read nor do we commune WITH God each step of the way.

We must arise and arrive. Prayer and Bible Study is not telling God or seeking from God things that will justify our will. We must begin the day in honest confession, and then perform our delightful daily duty of serving and sharing the Lord, who died for us, delivered us and will direct us.

Talk With God:

"It should be our delight to commune with God in prayer and Bible reading, then allow Him to speak to our heart and head before He takes our hand, and venture into the day. Amen! "

March – Day 13

Text: II Samuel 5:24 NIV

"As soon as you (David) hear the sound of marching in the tops of the balsam trees, move quickly, because that will meant he Lord has gone out in front of you to strike the Philistine army."

Thought: "Wind Signs"

Have you ever seen a wind sock? It is a cone-shaped cloth bag open at both ends. One opening is bigger than the other. It is attached to a pole or tower. As the wind blows, the sock will catch the wind and be moved by the force of the wind in the direction it is blowing. It is an instrument used at airfields in assisting aircraft landings and takeoffs.

David needed a sign from the Lord to reassure him of the timing to attack the armies of the Philistines.

You and I need to know the direction for our lives. We can search the Scriptures of God and allow His Spirit to speak to us with inner inspiration. As He does, we can have a refreshing touch of His breathe in our lives. We can know when to step out, speak up or sit still.

God has always been a God who promised direction, deliverance and divine provisions. It is up to us to be in touch with God and be sensitive to His voice in order to relieve these provisions

Talk With God:

"Lord, thank you for forgiving me and giving me signs and sounds of your girding and guidance. I wish to be a servant, soldier and son that will honor you in this life. Guide my steps, guard my mind and grant me grace. Amen."

March – Day 14

Text: James 2:16 KJV

"Be ye warmth and filled"

Thought: "Fan the Warmth of God"

I read and heard several announcements this past winter promoting a style of heater that would send a continual and considerable thrust of heat across a room creating a comfortable and commendable warm atmosphere anywhere in the room. It guaranteed a large room would not lack warmth. The quietness and quality of the fan distributed the air in all directions and at an output according to your setting.

God wishes to fill your day with His wonderful and warm love. It is His desire to make you feel comfortable and confident. When you face the coldness of life in your finances, family setting, feelings (emotions) and feeble efforts; God's warm love will thaw the chill and throw a good dose of heavenly warmth around you.

There is nothing like feeling the arms of God wrap around you and drink in the refreshing living water of His salvation and spiritual security. In this embrace, we are able to enjoy the day. The blistering winds of personal confrontations, public conflict and political correctness may blow hard and harsh; but God will switch on the turbo fan of love on our cause, condition and circumstances.

God will never speak of warmth without providing that warmth. He will never send one away without provisions. We must learn to do likewise.

Talk With God:

"Lord, it is cold in the world today. Struggles, stress, sorrow and suffering is everywhere. Folks are freezing to death in there complacency, compromise and conflicts. God, please send a spiritual heat wave to unthaw our life and our nation. Amen."

March – Day 15

Text: I Peter 2:21 KJV

"Leaving us an example, that ye should follow His steps"

Thought: "Don't Let Time Pass You By – Do Something with It"

Today is the birthday of our middle grandson, Brandon. Brandon is a fiery, feisty lad of nine. He is a lot like his dad (our son). The reason is that his dad spends a lot of time with him (wrestling around, throwing football, hunting, going to church, eating out, etc.) Brandon enjoys showing off his muscles (just like his dad use to do and like dad enjoying seeing Brandon do.) From this experience we can learn a lot.

If we spent time with our Heavenly Father, each of us can become a lot like him. We can develop our character and our conduct by interaction with our Lord. The more we enjoy doing "things" with Him, the more we can develop and be willing to show off our growth in life.

What are some things we can do each day with our Heavenly Father that will please Him and promote a happy, healthy and honorable relationship with Him?

First, we can praise Him for each day He has blessed us with.

Secondly, we can present our petitions (desires and devotion) before Him. As we do, let us seek His knowledge and wisdom to perform them effectively and efficiently.

Third, we can spend a moment interacting with Him (Prayer & Bible Reading).

Fourth, we can go throughout the day thinking of Him (meditating on His Word).

Fifth, we can share our thoughts about Him with someone.

God loves us and desires our love. And each step of each day must be built on the relationship we have with our Heavenly Father. Don't let the winds of neglect and negative attitude rob us of a warm and wonderful relationship.

Talk With God:

"God, I am proud to proclaim you as my Heavenly Father. Help me to interact with you as you attempt to interact with me. Teach me how to demonstrate my love for you and how to receive your love for me. Regardless of what happens, help me to know you care and help me to show I trust you. This I ask. Amen"

March – Day 16

Text: Ecclesiastes 1:14 NKJV
"All is vanity and grasping for the wind."

Thought: "Gone With the Wind"

The epic film based on Margaret Mitchell's novel *Gone With The Wind* opens with these lines: "There was a land of Cavaliers and Cotton Fields called the Old South. Here in this pretty world, Gallantry took its last bow…Look for it only in books, for it is no more than a dream remembered, a civilization gone with the wind."

In this epic the way of life disappears and the dreams that drive the main characters. Throughout the Civil War, Scarlett O'Hara is preoccupied with her love for Ashley Wilkes. But by the story's end, she is disillusioned.

Solomon in his writings saw the futility of seeking satisfaction in people, possessions and personal knowledge. Despite amassing wealth, achieving knowledge, accomplishing great projects, and abiding with many wives; he declared that nothing on earth satisfies nor secures man.

God created us to seek Him, secure Him and become satisfied because of Him (John 10:10). All other transitory and temporal things leave us unfulfilled. Our ultimate fulfilling comes in a relationship with God.

People and possessions come and go. But the spiritual satisfaction Christ offers sustains us in the world and will endure all situations that we encounter. Do not let this day pass you by; but leap into it with the justification (freedom of His fervent and forbearing love) and joy of the Lord.

Talk With God:

"Lord, I appreciate you for giving me something that is sure and stable, sweet and satisfying. I desire to praise you and be a personal witness for you this day. Amen!"

March – Day 17

Text: I Corinthians 9:26 Amplified Bible
"I do not box as one beating the air and striking without an adversary"

Thought: "Swinging At the Wind"

Many a boxer swings at their opponent and misses. Many a baseball batter swings at a pitch and misses. When an athlete performs such an act with all his might, he usually loses his balance and uses a lot of energy. The same is true with our spiritual bout in life.

Each believer is in a battle (II Timothy 2:3) and each believer is engaged in a bout (our text); therefore, we must know our adversary (I Peter 5:8) and make our swings count.

We are not shadow boxing or playing a game. We are involved in a daily confrontation between good and evil; right and wrong; moral and immoral. We must stand for the right and in doing so, we must engage in a battle of the mind and the morals of life.

We have to be engrafted into the Word (James 1:21) and equipped with the whole armor of God (Ephesians 6:13-18) as we engage each day set before us. It will benefit us nothing to swing at the wind, we must make contact. Contact is made when we "let our light shine before men" (Matthew 5:16).

Stay in shape, stand firm and swing with all your heart.

Talk With God:

"Lord, we do not know what lies before in this new day. However, we can know who side we are on and with whose strength we confront life. We are on your side, and we have your strength to counter and conquer any opponent or opposition this day. Thank you for saving us, standing with us and granting us success today. Amen."

March – Day 18

Text: Matthew 13:22 Amplified Bible

"As for what was sown among thorns, this is he who hers the Word, but the cares of the world and the pleasure and delights and glamour and deceitfulness of riches choke and suffocate the Word, and it yields no fruit."

Thought: "Choked By the Billows of Dirt & Debris"

I am sure each of us remembers the attack on 9/11, when terrorist hijacked several jet airliners and crashed them into designated targets. One of the targets was the Twin Trade Towers in New York City. What a sad and sickening sight it was to watch replays of the incident. The extreme heat of the exploding airliners into the structures melting the support frames causing them to collapse, fragmenting the material as they fell, forming and forcing billows of dust and debris down the streets, covering buildings, vehicles and people for blocks.

The enemy of our life, Satan, attacks every day and attempts to choke the life out of us. He causes a breakdown of our financial support, our family relations, our fleshly health, and at times our faith in God. And as we begin to feel like the wind has been knocked out of us, we must trust that God will make a difference.

It is easy to become attracted and attached to the pleasure, popularity, pressures, power and possessions of this world. When we yield to their deceitfulness (terrorist attacks), our world will crumble and collapse. Yet, in our weak, wrecked and wasted state of mind, body or spirit; we can cry out with our seemingly last breathe of air – h-e-l-p.

Therefore, walk throughout this day declaring God's glory, defending your relationship with Him and depending on His power to keep you.

Talk With God:

"What a relief to know that you O Lord are aware of our every start, every step and every stop throughout the day. What a delight to know that you O Lord care about us and stand ready to rescue us, revive us and restore us to the right relationship we need in you. Amen."

March – Day 19

Text: Ephesians 5:2 NKJV

"As Christ also had loved us and given Himself for us, an offering and a sacrifice to God a sweet-smelling aroma."

Thought: "Our Spiritual Aroma"

Have you ever walked into a home or a place of business and a sweet aroma caught your attention immediately? I am sure you have gone into a home where an aroma of a cake baking in the oven or cinnamon spiced cider was just brewed or cured bacon frying in the pan made you hungry. In a place of business, you may have entered where an aroma of a scented candle was burning or sweets were displayed or selected fragrances were sold. How wonderful the aroma.

Did you know that a life filled with the self-sacrificing love of Christ is like a sweet smelling spiritual aroma unto God and unto man? Just as Christ portrayed His total commitment to the Heavenly Father's will and to humanity need; we must be willing to be dedicated and devoted to the same. And we can if we allow the love and life of Christ to dwell within us step by step.

Imagine God, the designer and developer of our life, taking a deep breath of our conduct and character responding satisfactorily with a smile and saying, 'This is mine child in whom I am well pleased.' Wow! That excites me and encourages me.

Let us go a step further, imagine someone struggling catching a whiff of that spiritual aroma in the words we use, the way we respond, or the work ethics we possess. Would it help them or hinder them? Let us consider this as we begin our day.

Let us be determined that we are going to smell -- Good and Godly. So, walk cautiously and considerate in order not to stink up the place.

Talk With God:

"You are not deodorant but you are our delight, O Lord. Therefore, I desire to be filled with your love and follow your lead as I live this day. I want to please you and purposefully be a spiritual perfume to those around me. Amen."

March – Day 20

Text: Psalm 150:6 NKJV

"Let everything that has breathe praise the Lord"

Thought: "Don't Waste Your Breath"

If I were to scoop up a handful of dirt and blow real hard into it, all it would do is scatter everywhere and give me a dirty face. However, when God did it, He got a living, breathing human being capable of thinking, feeling, dreaming, loving, reproducing and living forever.

Sometimes I uses phrases such as "catching my breath," "holding my breath, or "saving my breath." However, these phrases describe a particular incident that occurs in my life. I cannot save my breath for a later time. If I don't use each breath at the present time, I will lose it and may pass out due to a lack of oxygen.

When God breathed into Adam, he gave more than the breath of life; He gave a reason to live. God created man to walk and worship Him each day of his life. That is why the Psalmist made the declaration he did. Man was created to talk with God and lift a testimony of praise to Him.

We waste our breath when we speak vain sayings, shout vulgar remarks or sing vile lyrics.

We cannot blow life into a handful of dirt, but we can use our breath to speak words of comfort, courage, confidence, challenge and commendation. When we use our breath to honor our heavenly Father and help humanity; we are not wasting it.

Talk With God:

"O Lord, we are grateful to you for giving us the breath of life, physically and spiritually. Enrich us with the words of life (The Scriptures) and enable us to breathe words of life (praise to you and personal love to others) unto those we come in contact with this day. Amen!"

March – Day 21

Text:	John 3:8 NJKV

"The wind blows where it wishes, and you hear the sound of it, but cannot tell where it comes from and where it goes. So is everyone who is born of the Spirit."

Thought:	"Go fly a kite"

I remember days of childhood, when we used to take newspaper, sticks, and string along with mother's home made flour paste and strips of cloth to make our kites. When it was made we would take our crude kite into the field nearby and attempt to get it airborne. Time and time again, it would nosedive into the ground. Yet, time and time again, we would lay the kite down on the ground, move a little distance from the kite and when we felt the wind blow; we would take off running lifting it up into the air and pray for the wind to keep blowing. When the wind blew, the kite was airborne and we were enjoying the time of our life.

Sometimes we need to "go fly a kite." Now, I did not say, we should go tell someone to "go fly a kite" or "just go jump in a lake." I do not mean it in that context. However, I do believe that we need to listen for the voice of God and allow His Spirit to lead us in our walk of faith. As we recall the days of kite flying and that it took the wind to succeed, so it takes the Spirit to succeed.

Isaiah, the prophet, declared "whether you turn to the right or to the left your ears will hear a voice behind you, saying, 'this is the way; walk ye in it." (Isaiah 30:21). God will lift us up and allow us to soar in heavenly places. But we must build our character (kite) according to His inspiration and instructions; then be willing to hear His voice or feel His Spirit.

As we feel the wind of the Spirit, we must obey and use the opportunity to praise Him, pump us up and persuade someone else to join in the pleasure and privilege..

Talk With God:

"Lord, what lessons we learned from childhood. Thank you for enabling us to recall and receive a revelation that would enhance our lives today. I acknowledge my need of you and appreciate your willingness to love me, lift me up and light up my life in a way that others would see in me. Amen."

March – Day 22

Text: Acts 3:19 KJV

"Repent, then, and turn to God, so that your sins maybe wiped out, that times of refreshing may come from the Lord."

Thought: "Achoo! God bless you"

How many times have you said, "God bless you" when you heard someone sneeze? Countless, I assume. Have you every thought of why you say such a phrase following a sneeze? Was it just a common response? Probably!

However, think with me for a moment. Did you know why you sneeze? I read recently that a sneeze is an attempt by the body to expel air to get rid of the irritating substances like particles of dust, pollen, perfumes, and other pollutants. Now, let me ask you, what is the greatest pollen in the entire world? It is sin!

Sin is a pollutant; an irritating and infectious pollutant. However, you can not expel sin with a sneeze; but Jesus died in order to expel sin from your life. Then, maybe our little catch phrase, "God bless you," can be a witness of the revelation of God's plan to eradicate sin from your life.

What an opportunity to speak to someone about the saving knowledge of Jesus Christ or an occasion to whisper a prayer for a revelation of God's ability to set a person free from their irritating sins.

Think about it when you sneeze. How gracious and good God is to relieve us of our wrong doing (sin) and allow us to share such a great revelation to others who are sneezing their head off.

Talk With God:

"Wow! Lord, how marvelous and majestic are your works -- Your work on Calvary and your creation of humanity, so amazingly complimentary of each other. Humanity needs Calvary's victory and Calvary needs humanity to reveal the availability of such victory. Let me take full advantage of the opportunity to share the victory of Calvary. Amen."

March – Day 23

Text: I Timothy 4:7-8 NIV

"Train yourself to be godly. For physical training is of some value, but godliness has value for all things, holding promise for both the present life and the life to come."

Thought: "What Exercise is Most Profitable?"

I know you are probably one of many who exercise daily. Right? I know I personally fall short of staying in condition physically. I attempt to do stairs and do some treadmill walking, but not on a regular basis. I know I do not exercise enough for I give out to easy when exercising. I become breathless and bored.

However, we do hear about a lot of people (athletes, actors, and anyone who is attempting to get the attention of a person (date, spouse, etc). We do hear a lot of advertisement regarding exercising and exercise equipment and exercise programs.

However, to stay in physical condition involves more than exercise. It is essential that a person maintain a proper diet, get daily doses of fresh air, enjoy the right portion of sleep and participate in a program of exercise. The combination of all these will help a person to be physically fit.

And physical fitness is important to good physical health. However, we must pay careful attention to the health of our soul also. Such care involves enjoying the Bread of life (God's Word); exhaling fear and inhaling faith; experiencing the rest and reassurance of God's peace and provisions; and exercising ourselves unto Godliness. The combination of all these will help a person to have an active relationship with God and a Godly attitude with man.

It is important that we keep fit both physically and spiritually. Let us remember that a disciplined body means physical fitness and a disciplined soul means spiritual usefulness.

It is a blessing to be both fit and fruitful. It keeps the spring in our step and the success in our day. It keeps us from becoming breathless, bored and beat.

Talk With God:

Blessed Holy Spirit, I am so glad that you are able to inspire us to maintain a right perspective in our life for true satisfaction and strength. We desire to work out daily with you as our Sponsor and Spiritual Instructor. Amen."

March – Day 24

Text: I Corinthians 15:52 KJV

"In a moment, in the twinkling of an eye, at the last trump: for the trumpet shall sound, and the dead shall be raised incorruptible, and we shall be changed."

Thought: "The Wind Of The Trumpet Echoes!"

I remember when I was in the military; I would hear the echoes of the wind of the trumpeter playing a particular song several times a day. In the morning, reveille was played calling our attention to a new day—rise and shine, fall in line. In the evening, taps was played signaling the close of another day. And on special occasions, the National Anthem would be played challenging us of a need to possess and perform our allegiance to our great nation. It would stir something within me each time the wind of the trumpeter would blow and keyed the proper sound. I was glad to be soldier in our nation's military for we were and still remain the greatest nation on the face of the earth.

Throughout the Bible the sound of the ram's horn was heard belting out signals of allegiance, attack and attention.

One day the great trumpet will sound and all of God's children will labor no more, will lay down the fleshly robe and be lifted up into the glory of an eternal God. What a sound to anticipate! When it echoes across the land, I want to feel the vibrations of His breath coming from the trumpet. I want to be prepared to stand before Him, praise Him and proclaim His King of Kings and Lord of Lords.

Therefore, today live like this could be the day of the sounding of the trumpet.

Talk With God:

"I thank you Lord for breathing into our lives and allowing us to become a living soul. I thank you for breathing into our lives pushing out the poison air of sin. I thank you for giving a new spiritual life. I thank you Lord, for scheduling a time for one more breath of the trumpet sound calling us home to glory. I love you. Amen."

March – Day 25

Text: Ecclesiastes 4:6 KJV

"Better one handful with tranquility [peace] than two handfuls with toil and chasing after the wind."

Thought: "Chasing the Wind!"

So many people are caught up in the downward spiral of depression, discouragement and defeat simply because they have chased the wind instead of learning contentment. But it is time to pause and give consideration to putting a stop to wild spending, wasted living and willful neglect of the peace and purposeful living that God offers.

So many people are unhappy. They live under a mask of contentment but are blown from side to side in their inability to remain stable.

God wishes to fill your life with His fruitfulness (Galatians 5:22-23) that provides contentment and produces Godliness. Having our life filled with His fruitfulness will establish us and give faithfulness to our being.

However, we must determine what is important in life and become devoted to what it takes to keep our focus on that one thing. And that which is most important for us is our relationship with God (Psalms 27). "For Godliness with contentment is great gain."

You do not need an abundant supply of material goods, mental knowledge, ----- but we must have a relationship with God in order to be happy with our self, live in harmony with others and have a hope beyond this life.

Talk With God:

"It is a fact that today Lord I have more than I have ever possessed. I am grateful for each thing; however, help me to resist being carried away with the wind of every whim and want of my life. Teach me contentment and complete satisfaction. Show me how I can give of any extra you have blessed me with to others that would benefit them. Amen."

March – Day 26

Text: Psalms 46:1 KJV

"God is our refuge and strength, a very present help in trouble"

Thought: "An Escape to Freedom"

The other day I heard the chirping of birds so clear that it sounded like they were in the house. I listened closely and then realized the sounds were coming from my small shop (really an enclosed patio). I opened the door from the laundry room and peeped out. Two little sparrows were fluttering around in the shop. I opened the door and went into the shop and began to whistle and talk with the frightened creatures. I moved slowly toward the exit door and opened it, then made my way along the side of the shop and starting waving my arms attempting to shoo them toward the open door. It was not long before they spied the open door and with a rapid flap of their little wings they soared outward and upward to freedom.

It is amazing how we find ourselves boxed in with no visible means of escape (or so we think). However, if we will only begin to chirp signals of help; we will soon see Him come on the scene and begin to motion with His outstretched arms of love the direction of escape (of endurance if He feels this is best).

In fact, so often we awake in the morning and feel the pressure (in our body, in our brain, in the business that awaits us) before the day really gets underway. However, a simple chirp or cry unto the Master will produce His response and His rescue.

I enjoy listening to birds whistle and produce a wing song of joy; just as God enjoys listening to the voice of His people. Whether it is a chirping of joy or a chirping of being boxed in, He still cares for us, comes to our side and causes a celebration of being restored to the liberty of life.

Talk With God:

"Today Lord, I am glad to know you are aware of our every whisper, whine and weary state of being. I am grateful that you will response, remind and rescue us. Keep us and make us keenly aware of your very present help in time of need. Amen."

March – Day 27

Text: Psalms 51:10 KJV

"Create in me a clean heart, O God, and renew a right spirit within me."

Thought: "Spring Cleaning"

Usually, when the winter is blown away by the winds of March, and warmer days begin to appear; many think of spring cleaning. It is time for sweeping the dust balls out from under the bed, switching winter linen for lighter linen, storing the blankets, shedding the house of the cobwebs, shining (polishing and dusting) up the furniture, storing or throwing away anything that has cluttered up the house over the winter months and let the sun shine in by opening the windows and doors. It is a time of high-speed action. Everyone in the house has a part.

How about spiritual spring cleaning? Do aggressive or alienated thoughts clutter up your mind? Have you engaged in activities that have become habitual and harmful to your spiritual life? Have you grown somewhat slothful and sloppy in your work and witness of God? Have you become self centered and side tracked from your devotion and dedication to God? Have you become negligent and negative about your approach to life?

If so, let us get busy cleaning out and clearing up the mess in our life. Let us apply so good old-fashioned repentance, re-establishing the Word in our heart and mind, and then allowing the winds of His Spirit to sweep into our open life bringing a refreshing and a restoring touch of spiritual aroma.

Talk With God:

"Yes, Lord, we need to evaluate, examine and do some excavation of our life. We must clean out the clutter and correct the clatter of our spiritual machinery. We need to readjust and realign our total being from time to time. Today is as good a day as any to begin. Have your way in refreshing and restoring me. Amen."

March – Day 28

Text: Luke 12:6 KJV

"What is the price of five sparrows? A couple of pennies? Yet, God does not forget a single one of them. And the very hairs on your head are all numbered. So don't be afraid; you are more valuable to Him than a whole flock of sparrows."

Thought: "What a Thought: I Am Special!"

I remember once as I was driving a bird flew right in front of me. I attempted to swerve, but I see it flip over the vehicle and in my rear view mirror hit the ground behind me. It hurt to know I killed an innocent creature on accident, but God reminded me that he hurts even greater when one of his special creations, Man, disobeys and detours his life away from safety and into the path of danger and death.

I am grateful that God considers us more valuable than the total of all other creations: the beautiful environment, the balance of the solar system, the beast of the field, the birds of the air, the big mouth bass and all other fish of the waters. Yet, we sometimes are guilty of short changing God by robbing Him of the devotion and duty assigned to us.

We are created to be smart, soul-oriented and spiritual minded; yet how often do meet the standards that God originally created for us?

It is time to take a deep breath and breathe out a loud, loving, lip praise shout of *Hallelujah* to the King of Kings for making us a special creature. He is our Lord and Master. We are to learn His Word, lean on His Spirit and light the way for others. We are special with a capital 'S'. And I don't mean selfish, slothful, or sinful; but saved, sincere, serving and satisfied.

God is good to us and His godliness is good for us! Let's be the special creation that He desires of us.

Talk With God:

"Thank you Lord for making me, Me. Thank you for allowing me to be able to know my Creator and be able to conform to His image. I love you and long to be more like you everyday. Correct me, change me and take control of my total being for I want my life to be a reflection of your life. Amen."

March – Day 29

Text: Psalm 57:5 NKJV
"Be exalted, O God, above the heavens; let Your glory be above all the earth"

Thought: "Breathless"

When was the last time something took your breath away? Was it a fresh sniff of a cleaning agent such as ammonia? Was it a frightful experience at the sight of a snake or spider? Was it a view of a majestic scene – a fresh appearance of a rainbow after a rain shower, the flight of an eagle in the sky or the face of a big buck that comes in our sights while hurting in the woods? Was it the appearance of a love one that you had not seen in years? Was it the actions of a small child in a play, at a recital or reciting poetry?

There are many events and experiences that can leave a person breathless. And I believe it all began in the Garden of Eden. God created man with His own breath, and then man became breathless when two things happen. First, I believe the goodness, grandeur and glory of the garden took the breath of man away. Secondly, I believe the fear of their wrong doing took the breath right out of Adam and Eve as they hid behind the trees of the garden.

Humanity today becomes breathless for the same two reasons. In our attempt to run and hid from God in our sins and selfishness, we pant and gasp for breath. And in our extreme awe of the creation of God, we find ourselves breathless at the beauty, blessedness, and benefits given unto us.

Therefore, let us be challenged this day not to seek our will but decide at the very beginning of the day to take a deep breath and let out a praise of appreciation, anticipation and affection to God.

Talk With God:

"When I survey all your glory on earth, and all your goodness to man; I can't help but praise you and personally serve you. Keep me this day and in kindness help me show others the way. Amen"

March – Day 30

Text: John 5:40 Amplified Bible

"And still you are not willing (but refuse) to come to me that you might have life."

Thought: "Shallow Breathing Is a Sign of Death"

Shallow breathing is associated with illness, intense pain and internal weariness. Shallow breathing is not good for it does not allow the stable air from our lungs to be exhaled and allow a full flow of fresh air to be inhaled. Stale air in the body produces carbon dioxide and fresh air produces a full flow of oxygen throughout the body for proper functioning.

When I think of shallow breathing I can't help but remember both my grandfather's and my brother's illness and death. In the late 1970's when Grandpa John (of whom I was named) was very ill and eventually died of emphysema, he would take very shallow breathes. The medical staff told us this was not good for his body and would eventually rob grandpa of his life. I had to repeat the tragic occurrence again five years ago when my brother, Bobby, breathed so shallow that he was grasping for air.

Whether or not they wish to admit it, many people are grasping for a breath of fresh air uncontaminated by sin, suffering and sorrow. They have entertained and enjoyed a lifestyle that has robbed them of an abundant life in Christ.

We must be willing to come to the Great Physician; allow him to help us lay aside the things that are destroying our spiritual health and take his advice of regular breathing treatments. The more we abstain from things that hinder our spiritual well being and the more that we sing of His promises, shout praises and speak of His precepts; the better we will feel, function and fight to enjoy our relationship with Christ.

Talk With God:

"Jesus, I know we are guilty of doing things that hinder and hamper our spiritual well-being. However, be merciful to us and help us resist the temptations, reside in your Word and rest in your love. Amen."

March – Day 31

Text: Psalms 30:5 NIV

"Weeping may remain for a night, but rejoicing comes in the morning."

Thought: "Wake to a Song of Praise"

My lovely wife use to have a poster of Garfield the cat, posted on the door of the refrigerator, that had a slogan on it that said, "Don't even speak to me until I've had my second cup of coffee." Many people do not like sounds, pleasure or problematic, first time in the morning. I love the sound of birds chirping in the early morning. I could go to sleep listening to the sounds of birds chirping and wake up with them chirping.

I remember as a kid, the one pet we could have in the 'housing project' was a bird. We had a beautiful green and white parakeet. He would whistle throughout the day until it was time for bed and we would place a cover over his cage. The next morning, I would lift the cover from the cage and he would begin whistling again. To me it was a grand experience.

God desires us to awake knowing He has sustained us and strengthen us with the essential rest for brain restoration and body renewal. As we awake, let us lift our spirit (if not our speech) in praise to His Holy Name.

As the SUN rises over the horizon with it beautiful light of day and the SON rises within our heart with His beautiful light of daily renewal; let us whistle a tune of gratitude and glory to the One Who is able to mount us upon His wings and cause us to soar in heavenly breezes throughout this day.

In our text, David was rejoicing due to the victory God had given him. Dark moments of struggle and strain caused heartaches and headaches, but God brought deliverance and delight. He is still the same God. He desires to give you a song after a time of seemingly dread, doubt and defeat.

Talk With God:

"O Lord, it me again rubbing my eyes and reaching out in faith as I begin the day. I thank you for the rest and press forward to represent you in all I do this day. Give me a song and give me the strength. Amen"

EASTER
a Time to Rejoice

Step 4 - April

"Buried, Yet Alive"

The month of April usually brings to us the recollection of the passion week of Christ and the rejoicing event of Easter – the story of the betrayal, brutal beating, bloody crucifixion, burial and beautiful and beneficial resurrection of Jesus Christ.

It is ironic that it begins with April Fool's Day--a day in which many play pranks on family and friends; or a day when one may be send on a wild goose chase looking for something that doesn't exist or a day when individuals attempt to get people to believe ridiculous things. However, there is nothing foolish about the revelation and realization of the risen Lord.

Yes, I believe that He died for the sins of humanity. Yes, I believe that He was buried to challenge each and every believer to bury their carnal desires and devotions in order to partake in the resurrected life. Yes, I believe that He rose again to signify the newness of life that we are to live because of Him.

The Word of God declares in the Apostle Paul's letter to the Romans (chapter 8), "Therefore, we are buried with Him by baptism into death: that like as Christ was raised up from the dead by the glory of the Father, even so we also should walk in newness of life. For if we have been planted together in the likeness of his death, we shall be also in the likeness of his resurrection: Knowing this, that our old man is crucified with Him, that the body of sin might be destroyed, that henceforth we should not serve sin. For he that is dead is freed from sin. Now if we be dead with Christ, we believe that we shall also live with Him"

When we "bury the hatchet" – the wrong we have committed, the wrong others have committed to us, the wrong we allow to be harbored within our heart -- will bring peace, a personal fellowship with God and man, and allow us to posses the promise of an abundant life. This is what Easter is all about. This is what the month of April is all about – planting that we may reap in harvest time (For the old saying is…the best time to plant is on Good Friday—the day of the burial of Christ).

April – Day 1

Text: I John 1:8-9 Amplified Bible

"If we say we have no sin – refusing to admit that we are sinners – we delude and lead ourselves astray, and the Truth [which the Gospel presents] is not in us – does not dwell in our hearts. If we, [freely] admit that we have sinned and confess our sins, He is faithful and just [true to His own nature and promises] and will forgive our sins (dismiss our lawlessness) and continuously cleanse us from all unrighteousness – everything not in conformity to His will in purpose, thought and action."

Thought: "Foolish Yet Forgiven!"

Today is my dad's birthday. I can recall some moments of compassion and celebration that we enjoyed together. However, during his life, he did many foolish things. (Haven't we all)? Mom and dad divorced when I was but a lad. Yet, in spite of the lonely moments, the lack of a daily fatherly love, the lapse of fatherly instruction and loss of daily inspiration by him; I never allowed my love for him to diminish or die. I do not feel, in his own mentality, he believes he abandoned me or ceased to love me. I have discussed and debated many an issue with Him. Many times the issues were resolved and at other times they were rejected. Yet today I hold no grudge or ill will against him. I have forgiven him of any blessing that could have been ours but did not materialize. I will do anything for him and I believe he would return the favor.

What about our relationship with our Heavenly Father? Do we play the fool? Are we forgetting to fulfill our purpose in the relationship? Do we forsake our duty and fail to enjoy the delight of togetherness?

You see, God never forsakes us (Joshua 1:9), forgets us (Psalms 8:4), fails us (II Timothy 1:12) and will never cease to forgive us (I John 1:9). It is up to us to keep alive the warm, wonderful and welcome fellowship that is available. We must not play the fool and fail to engage in, be enriched by and enjoy our relationship with the Heavenly Father.

Talk With God:

"Father, it is a joy to know that you love us just as we are. It is a delight to know that you have already forgiven us even before we ask. It is a blessing to know that you desire to walk in fellowship with us each step of the day. Thank you for this awareness and now I make myself available to enjoy this day in cooperation with you. Amen."

April – Day 2

Text: Mathew 28:20 Amplified Bible

"I am with you all the days – perpetually, uniformly and on every occasion – to the [very] close and consummation of the age Amen."

Thought: "He Is Present"

In our text, the life on earth for Jesus in the physically form is about to end. He is giving instructions to His disciples of the work that needs to be done and the necessity to remember one important thing – He will be with them.

Friends, God is aware of each step we take but He aggressively pursues and awaits the privilege of walking side by side with us in fellowship. He calls us, convicts us, and challenges us with His love to acknowledge Him, accept Him and abide with Him. It is our choice.

And experiencing God's presence is not as complicated as it may seem. For you see, in our human relationships, we cultivate intimacy with others by spending time with them. We talk with them, listen to what they have to say, learn from them, and labor to do what please them. In these ways, we are present with them developing our relationship. The more time you spend with them the more you get to know them. The more you know them, the more frequently you think of them and desire their presences. It is basically the same with Jesus. The more you spend time with God (in prayer, Bible study and worship) and develop your relationship with Him, the more you will come to recognize His presence in you life.

As we take steps in the journey of life, we become aware of His presences. And in His presences we are aware of His character (His power, promises and personality – love, joy, peace, patience, kindness, goodness, faithfulness, gentleness and self-control). In His presence, we CAN face any person, any problem, any persecution, any pleasure, any pressure, any pain, and any purging (correction).

Talk With God:

"I dedicate my life anew to you this day O Lord. I invite you to dwell in my life and help me to develop a daily pattern of building our relationship by spending precious moments with you and communing with you on the path of life. I need you in times of pleasure and problems. Thank you for being near. Amen."

April – Day 3

Text: John 17:4; 19:30 NIV

"I have brought you glory on earth by completing the work you gave me to do. – It is finished"

Thought: "From the Shadow of Death to Sunshine!"

We are told that the Birmingham, Alabama, city art gallery displays William Hunt's famous picture of "The Shadow of Death." The artist has portrayed Jesus as a youth in Joseph's carpenter shop. The sun is sinking in the western sky sending its slanting rays through the open door of the carpenter shop. Jesus has gotten up from his work bench and is stretching out his tired arms. As He does, the setting sun casts a shadow on the wall behind Him, creating the appearance of a man on a cross.

This picture portrays a great truth about Christ – He lived with the consciousness that Calvary was the ultimate will of God for His life. In fact, our Lord came into this world for the express purpose of dying to save sinners like you and me (John 3:16-17).

Yes, Christ braved the shadow of eternal death to bring us the sunshine of eternal life.

Because He willingly faced death to give us access to His throne (Hebrews 4:14-16), let us approach the presence of God with our petitions, our praise and our personal acceptance of His call on our life. Let us accept the fact that we are born with a purpose just as He was born with a purpose.

Jesus did not stop until the job was finished. We must never slow down, slumber nor stop living a life of honoring Him in our personal conduct, conversations, countenance and our personal concern for others.

Talk With God:

"Thank you Lord for knowing the plan, walking the path and fulfilling the purpose of your life on earth. Thank you for making me aware that I have a purpose in life also. Help me now to experience and express that purpose lovingly. In Your Name I pray. Amen."

April – Day 4

Text: I John 3:20 NIV

"God is greater than our hearts and He knows everything"

Thought: "His Hand Is Bigger and Bigger is Better"

Back in the days when raisins were sold unpackaged, a storekeeper told a little boy he could take a handful of the tasty little treats. When he hesitated, the grocer put his own hand into the box and insisted that the lad take what he offered him. Later someone asked the boy why he was reluctant to help himself when the man told him to do so, he replied, "His hand is bigger than mine."

We might question the youngster's motive, but his reply suggests an important truth for you and I. It's much better for us to let God choose what is best than to take what we want. When we think of the limitless bounty of His goodness and grace, how foolish to desire anything other than what comes from His hand.

John the Beloved declares in our text that God is greater than everything including our own being. He knows us and knows what we want and need. Therefore, we must learn to let Him nourish our life and we will see how much greater and more glorious the blessings and benefits will be.

As the little song says, "He's got the whole world in His hands;" His hands are big enough to hold me, my problems and my plans. I must trust Him to work out His will for my life.

Talk With God:

"Lord, thank you for allowing me the pleasure to partake of your blessings. Thank you for the privilege of knowing that trusting you above my own understanding and unique abilities bring heaping handfuls of benefits that enrich my life. It is my desire to be blessed and be a blessing. This I ask in your Name. Amen."

April – Day 5

Text: Philippians 1:21 Amplified Bible

"For me, to live is Christ – His life in me; and to die is gain – [the gain of the glory of eternity]."

Thought: "Choose To Live!"

All men die. This is a universal experience. One man, however, did not have to die. Yet, He did so anyway—not out of necessity but by choice. The eternal Son of God, recognizing the plight of man, voluntarily left the glories of heaven to become one of us and "to give His life a ransom."

In this season of Easter, as we celebration both His resignation to die and His resurrection to life; let us remember that it was a decision of sincere devotion to humanity and a dedication to pave the way to life eternal.

Because of His love for us, He came into this world with a death plan—a plan that provided us with forgiveness, freedom and a future.

Christ chose to die—that we might have the choice to live.

Through this day, keep in mind that your choices will make a difference. You can choose to smile or put on a sour face. You can side step some issues or step right into them. You can walk on the waves or be washed away by them. You can stand firm in your beliefs or flounder in your doubts. Christ came to make a difference. Let Him!

Let our desire in this life be to live for Jesus, experiencing and expressing Him in every way possible. Then, when this life comes to an end, we have everything to gain because of His promises.

Talk With God:

"Lord, today, is either the first day of the rest of my life or the last day I will experience life. Therefore, allow me and anoint me to live in a way that will be pleasing to you, preparation for me and an offer of a promise to others. Amen."

April – Day 6

Text: Joshua 24:15 NIV

"But if serving the Lord seems undesirable to you, then choose for yourselves this day whom you will serve, whether the gods your forefathers served beyond the river, or the gods of the Amorites, in whose land you are living. But as for me and my household, we will serve the Lord."

Thought: "Choose You This Day!"

One wonders how many who enthusiastically cried, Hosanna! on Palm Sunday were shouting Crucify Him, Crucify Him a few days later. Some people must have been disappointed, even resentful that Christ didn't overthrow the Roman government and set up His Kingdom.

Over the centuries the issue has not changed. If we follow Christ solely because we think He'll deliver us from life's hardships, heartaches and headaches; we are headed for disillusion. Being His disciple means renouncing sin, raising His standard of righteousness and resign oneself to follow wherever He leads—in perplexity and in pleasantness; in poverty and in prosperity; in problems and in peace.

He is the calm in the midst of the storm if we will yield control to Him.

We can not serve two masters (Matthew 6:24). You can not put off forever your choice (I Kings 18:21). You must decide.

Joshua told the children of Israel that you have a choice. You can become disgusted with the way things are going and want to receive directions from another source. You can be tired of certain rules and regulations and decide to do it your way. You are about to enter a whole new experience (occupying the Promised Land), a rededication is a must.

So it is with us today. God doesn't want weekend visitation rights; He wants full custody. Surrender and serve Him wholly and holy. Joshua's words in the preceding verse of our text said, "[reverence] the Lord and serve Him in sincerity and in truth " (Joshua 24:14).

Talk With God:

"Today, I make a choice. I will surrender my life to serve you. I will honor you by honoring others. I will lift up your Name as I lift up others. Amen."

April – Day 7

Text: Philippians 3:8 Amplified Bible

"Yes, furthermore I count everything as loss compared to the possession of the priceless privilege – the overwhelming preciousness, the surpassing worth and supreme advantage – of knowing Christ Jesus my Lord, and of progressively becoming more deeply and intimately acquainted with Him, of perceiving and recognizing and understanding Him ore fully an clearly. For His sake I have lost everything and consider tit all to be mere rubbish (refuge, dregs), in order that I may win (gain) Christ, the Anointed One."

Thought: "Losing To Win"

A large poster on the gym wall read, "When all of life is over and the great judge calls your name; it will matter not whether you won or lost, but how you played the game." Wanting to win is not wrong. But when it comes to real success, it may be necessary to experience some lessons to gain God's approval later.

Look at Christ, for example. His supporters wanted prompt, political and personal victory over the Roman government. But Jesus was committed to doing the Father's will—no matter what the cost. His attitude and action led to what looked like sure defeat, yet to each one who has experienced His touch of renewed life knows better. It proved to be the right plan and paved the way to a righteous victory.

There are no losers with Christ. If we are willing to submit and surrender, we will eventually be raised to victory.

The Apostle Paul declared that everything of this life is of little importance compared to the challenge of Godly living and the Godly rewards of eternity. What is most important is our Godly lifestyle that honors the King of Kings.

Talk With God:

"Lord, the wins of this life soon fade away and the losses hopefully have taught us humility. If we get so caught up with secular and social celebrations that it overshadows our spiritual goals of life – forgive us and free us from such thinking. Help us to keep our focus and faithfulness centered on you. Amen."

April – Day 7

Text: Psalms 42:5 NIV

"Why are you downcast, O my soul? Why so disturbed within me? Put your hope in God."

Thought: "Victor Or Victim?"

Most of us don't need to be reminded that we live in a time of crises. Problems exist on every front. Baffling situations constantly confront us, casting us sometimes into doubt and despair. How we react to these difficulties makes the differences.

As a believer, we should be able to engage in battle, endure the conflict and erupt in celebration that God has kept us true or brought us through.

Are you a victor in life or a victim of life? Do we feel our world has collapsed or that we have only engaged in a confrontation that will soon past? Do we cringe and cry out the old saying, "What I have done to desire such as this?" or do we shout and sing knowing "He will work all things for good."

The Word of God says, "Let not your hearts be troubled; we have a high priest that is touched with the feelings of our infirmities; be still and know that I am God; in all thy ways acknowledge Him and He shall direct your paths."

We will overcome and gain the opportunity to celebrate, when we fix our focus on Christ (Hebrews 12:2) and built our future on faith (I John 5:4-5). He came to earth for this purpose—to express His supreme love and explicitly demonstrate His supernatural liberty.

Our only hope in this life is found in our relationship with Jesus Christ! For it is in Him that we are clothed in the character of His love, concealed in the protective power of His grace and content with abiding provisions and presences.

Talk With God:

"Lord, I am glad that you are aware of our every condition, circumstances and concern. I am grateful that you care regarding our situations and will response with tender compassion, correction and companionship. I love you and need you each step and every day. Amen!"

April – Day 8

Text: Ecclesiastes 3:12 NKJV
"Nothing is better for them than to rejoice, and to do good in their lives."

Thought: "Today Leads To Tomorrow"

I do not know if it is me growing older and my body has become more susceptible to the chill of winter or if this winter was just extra cold. I believe it has been a little of both. However, I am eager for warm weather. I welcome the spring of life – green grass, glowing sun, going outdoors (to walk, to work and to enjoy the warmth). I welcome the resurrection power of earthly life and eternal life found in our Creator and Lord.

But let us be careful that we don't rush away moments that will provide the blessings for tomorrow. In longing and looking for better days ahead, we forget that every day – regardless of the weather or whatever – is a gift from God to enjoy, to experience and to enrich us for tomorrow.

If we are attempting to achieve the will of God for our lives, we are exactly where we need to be and experience what we need to experience to learn that we may be able to endure and enjoy the days ahead.

Regardless of the season of life, there is always a reason to rejoice and render praise to the Creator of every day. We must be challenged to find that blessing and that benefit that will cause us to content, comforted and challenged.

Talk With God:

"Today may be cold or it may be full of critics and complainers; but I will feel your warmth, O Lord, and I will be content to live for You. I will attempt to spread good cheer and face each challenge knowing where I am and who I am following. This is my prayer dear Lord. Amen!"

April – Day 9

Text: Luke 1:37 KJV

"For with God nothing shall be impossible."

Thought: "Miracles Are A Blessing From The Miraculous God!"

Some skeptics say, "Oh, the miracles, I can't accept miracles."

One may drop a brown seed in the black soil and up comes a green shoot of vegetation. You let it grow and by and by you pull up its roots and find it red. You cut the red root and find it has a white heart. Can any one tell how this comes about—how brown cast into black results in green and then in red and white? Yet, you eat radishes without troubling your mind over the agriculture miracle.

Miracles do occur. And the greatest miracle is the conversion of a soul. How the shed crimson blood of Christ on Calvary applied to the blackness of sin can transform a hard hearted sinner to become soften to walk a different trail, talk with a different tone, view life with a true perspective and have a renewed promise of tomorrow.

A miracle is when the impossible happens. Miracles take place everyday. Sometimes they're very subtle and subdued. Other times, it's very profound and public. It can happen to anyone.

Miracles occur when God wishes to reveal Himself or when God wants to get your attention. He never displays His miraculous power to gain approval of man, gain acceptance by man or give personal favors to man. He bestows miracles on man to intensify His glory for man to behold; intercede in prevention, protection and provisions for man, and incite interest in the heart of man to be born again.

Talk With God:

"I am glad that I serve an Omnipotent (all powerful) God. I am glad that You are able to do the impossible. However, never let me expect, experience or enjoy a miraculous event for personal satisfaction or success. Always help me to trust you with my personal life and my prayer life, believing that a miracle can be a response of your care and concern for me. Amen."

April – Day 10

Text: II Corinthians 5:17 KJV

"Therefore if any man be in Christ, he is a new creature: old things are passed away; behold all things are become new."

Thought: "Renovation Is His Job"

If an iron worker has a statue corroded by rust and age, creased and crumpled in many places; yet desires to salvage it, he will create a form from the image of the old. Then, he will break up the damaged statue and place it into a furnace. After melting it, he will retrieve it and pour it into the cast made. When it cools, he removes the cast, sands and shines the new image until it appears more beautiful than ever.

The dissolving in the furnace was not a destruction, but a renewing of the statue; so is the death of our sinful nature. It is not a destruction of our life but a renovation of our life. We are still human with the same natural abilities and appearance; yet with a renewed foundation and focus for living.

Does your life need a renovation by the Master Craftsman? Are you weary, worried, worn, warped out of shape and wasted? Jesus invites you to come unto Him and He will make you over again.

Humanity attempts to transform his life by changing his name, changing his environment, changing his appearance, changing his philosophy, or changing his priorities. However, these things will give us a new nature compliant to the will of God. However, each of these things is affected when we truly allow Christ to create within us a newness of life brought about by His life, love and liberty.

As we begin this day, we need to allow Christ to melt us, mold us and make us a fresh, fruitful creation.

Talk With God:

"Lord, I am glad that I have a Savior who is willing to refresh, refurbish and renew my life every day. I am glad that I am able to experience You in a forgiving, fortifying and fresh touch. Amen."

April – Day 11

Text: John 8:12 NIV

"I am the light of the world. Whoever follows me will never walk in darkness, but will have the light of life."

Thought: "Light Brings Life"

A story is told about a potato bringing a message of new life. It went like this. A young lady had lost her husband and it seemed all was gone. Yet one day as she was going down the basement steps, she noticed a large white thread-looking vine. She picked it up, and followed it to its source. There was one potato that she had missed when she brought the last ones up. She turned and followed it in the direction of the window. There it had put out several small leaves to make a new start in life.

She stood transfixed. It had not been easy for the eye of the potato to reach the light and begin development, yet it did. Then and there a new effort was made within her to begin anew.

And friend as you turn to the light of Jesus Christ you will find a new beginning.

The world is filled with darkness -- the darkness of sin, self and satanic presences. The darkness robs man of light, life and liberation. However, God who is light draws us to Himself where we are able to grow in the SONshine of His love. As we grow we are able to catch the attention of others who may be wandering, worrying and wasting away, with no hope or happiness.

Let us realize Christ is the light of the world and receive Him as our light; then allow Him to reveal a newness of life to others who are separated from Him, suffering without Him and searching for something to bring a ray of hope to them.

It is up to you to light up your life and let others see Him (Matthew 4:16).

Talk With God:

"Lord, I need your guiding light to lead me in the darkness of this life. I want Your Word to be a lamp unto my feet and a light unto my path. I want to what I am, who I am and where I am. I can if I live in your light. In Your Name I pray. Amen."

April – Day 12

Text: John 14:19 KJV

"Because I live, ye shall live also."

Thought: "He Is The One Who Lives!"

In a glass casket in Red Square in Moscow lays the embalmed remains of Lenin. The inscription on the casket says, "He was the greatest leader of all peoples, of all countries, of all times. He was the lord of the new humanity. He was the savior of the world."

Did you notice that everything said about Lenin is in the past tense? He "was," but he is not now. He has passed forever from the scene of the living. The followers of the world's religions can take us to the grave sites of their leaders and tell us what a great leader Buddha or Confucius or Mohammed was. They were, but they are no more.

But we need a leader, a savior which lives. One who abides with us and is acquainted with our ways. Praise God, there is One—He is Jesus! He is Lord! He Lives! Let your heart rejoice and be reassured in the fact that you can have a living, ever present, leader who cares and is in control.

He is one who hears our praise and petitions, then responds in compassion and concern.

Jesus died and was buried. Yet He rose again and ever lives to make intercession for us. He has conquered the enemy of death, controls the outcome of life and constantly speaks to the heart of man to trust Him. All other philosophies, plans, programs and personalities that attempt to teach us the way to success and satisfaction will fade, fail and fall short of the ultimate goal designed for man. Only Christ is the Living Source of Life.

Let us be engrafted into His Word (James 1:21), be enhanced by His love (Ephesians 3:19) and be established in His grace ((Hebrews 13:9).

Talk With God:

"Lord, I know humanity has made a fool of themselves in trusting earthly leaders and trying philosophies, plans and programs that offer no real hope for today or tomorrow. Enable me to lean on You, learn from You and be led by You. Amen."

April – Day 13

Text: Acts 17:28 KJV

"For in Him we live, and move, and have our being...for we are also His offspring."

Thought: "He Gave His All and Expects No Less from Us"

Dr. J. B. Chapman used to tell of an Indian who related his experience in consecration: "brought my pony and put him on the altar. But no blessing came. I added my blanket and my tepee; still there was no blessing. Then I added my squaw and my papoose; and there was no blessing yet. But when I cried, And this poor Indian too, Lord! – The blessing came.

God can use your possessions, positions, personalities; yet He is most concerned for you -- the individual. All earthly things shall pass away, yet we must give account of our personal dedication and devotion – whether it is to the will of the Savior or the will of self.

To yield oneself to God is to trust completely the One Who is too perfect to do wrong and too powerful to fail. To yield oneself to God is to become a channel through which He can pour His blessings and portray His benefits to a needy, neglected and numb world.

God has given humanity the privilege to become the children of God (Philippians 2:15). However, in order to be His children, we must be willing give our total being (Heart—our spirit, hands—our works, head—our mind, and our hungers—our desires) completely over to God. We must lay it on the altar of sacrifice, surrender and submission. He gave us His all and we should expect to give Him no less.

As we do, the blessing of life, love and liberty will come and the ability to light up the world for Him will constrain us. What a pleasure! What a privilege! What a purpose!

Talk With God:

"Lord, again I says thank you for claiming me for your own, cleansing me from sin and choosing me to do a work for you. I love you and desire to live for you even as you live within me. I surrender all to You. Amen."

April – Day 14

Text: Psalms 32:5 NIV

"Then I acknowledged my sin to you and did not cover up my iniquity. I said, "I will confess my transgressions to the lord –and you forgave the guilt of my sin."

Thought: "Forgiveness is Available to Whosoever"

Did you know that the population of the world is numbered in the billions; yet each individual is unique and unequivocally different (what a relief in knowing there is not another me). No two people are exactly alike in every way. Some may appear to be twins in appearance, others may appear alike in voice or tone, and still others may be very similar in bodily expressions.

However, there is one need that is shared by every person – the need for forgiveness. No matter how different we may be in other respects we have all sinned. (Romans 3:23). And we all have the need to be born again – we need a Savior (John 3:3).

The good news of the Gospel is this: forgiveness is available! It is offered to the little fellow who steals an apple form the corner fruit stand. It is extended to the hardened criminal who may have raped or repeatedly stabbed or shot someone to death. It is available to the crooked politician or cheating spouse. It is provided for the embezzling employee and evil gang member. It is presented to the abusive spouse and alcoholic individual. It is also for the good community minded person who is attempting to live on his own merits rather than a relationship with God. On and on we could illustrate areas of wrong doing; however, the point is – forgiveness is yours for the asking. A remorseful, repentant and righteous-seeking heart will receive the blessing and benefit of forgiveness; and be restored to a right relationship with God.

If your wrong doing was a criminal act, you will suffer the consequences of your action on this earth; but the deed is forgiven and that is recorded in heaven and will not be held against you at judgment. Jesus has paid the supreme price for the penalty of sin by His death on the cross.

Let not His death be in vain. Permit Him to forgive you and permit yourself to accept His forgiveness. Be willing to forgive others also.

Talk With God:

"Lord, I confess my sins before you. I am sorry for my failure and I sincerely ask for your forgiveness. Cleanse me and create within me a clean heart. Amen".

April – Day 15

Text: I Peter 2:21 KJV

"Leaving us an example, that ye should follow His steps"

Thought: "Is God our Pilot or Co-pilot?"

I have read several times a bumper sticker that stated, "Jesus is my co-pilot." I understand what the sticker means – I allow Jesus to give me the information that will navigate the course of life. However, it has troubled me each time I read it.

For you see, I believe Jesus should be in the driver's seat of my life. The Apostle Peter declared that we are to follow Him. He is the One leading. He is the Pilot of the ship of life. He has designed the plan of successful, satisfactory and spiritual living; It is His death that brought fulfillment to the plan; and it is His divine daily direction that will lead us in the right path of true living.

When Jesus is in the driver's seat, the detours, delays and destinations do not become a hassle of a hindrance to enjoying our journey in life. If we allow Him, He will keep us away from dead-end streets of stress, strife and sarcasm.

We must allow Him to drive and define your life. There will always be bumps and bounces in the road of life; but you can believe in, buckle up and bear the conditions knowing who is doing the driving. As Greyhound Bus Lines motto use to be: "Take the bus and leave the driving to us."

Jesus is certified to drive and committed to the task; let Him drive.

Talk With God:

"O lord, I do not want to dictate to you as one would a chauffeur; but I desire for you to be my pilot in the drive of life. Whether on land, air or sea; pilot me safely over the course please. Amen."

April – Day 16

Text: Galatians 3:12 KJV

"Christ hath redeemed us from the curse of the law, being made a curse for us."

Thought: "Bury the Hatchet"

Have you ever heard someone say, "Let us just bury the hatchet?" Did you know what they meant? To "bury the hatchet" is an phrase borrowed from the Native Americans. The phrase comes from an Iroquois ceremony in which war axes, tomahawks, were literally buried in the ground as a symbol of newly made peace.

Did you know this could also symbolize the burial of Jesus? He came to war against the satanic forces (Ephesians 6:11-12) and provide peace (Job 22:21). In His fulfilling this, He died and sin's curse (weapons of war and wickedness) were buried with Him. In His resurrection (results of His deed), he declared peace to all who would accept the plan (His death, burial and resurrection).

Bury the hatchet also means we are willing to forgive any wrong that one may have against us and any wrong that we have against someone. We are letting the past be the past and moving forward with no animosity or aggression. As one little preschooler said, "Forgive us our trash baskets (trespasses) as we forgive other who put trash in our baskets (trespasses against us)."

We no longer live by the law "that I want my way" and "you are wrong." We must come to a mutual understanding and accept the plan and path that is most beneficial for all (Micah 6:8)—do justly, love mercy and walk humbly with the Lord God. We are to live by faith in the person, plan and purpose of Christ.

Talk With God:

"Lord, I would never be able to live in harmony with man, have a healthy relationship with You or possess hope beyond this life; if I did not believe that You 'buried the hatchet' for mankind and make it possible to be at peace with You, have peace with man and possess peace within my own being. Thank you. I love you. Amen."

April – Day 17

Text: Matthew 7:21 KJV

"Not every one that saith, unto me, Lord, Lord, shall enter into the kingdom of heaven; but he that doeth the will of my Father which is in heaven."

Thought: "Christianity Is More Than Saying There Is a God"

Many people agree it is foolish to try to account for the universe without God. I am one of such inclination. And if this is a truth and we believe it; what effect does it have upon our lives?

The Bible teaches that God revealed Himself in creation (Colossians 1:16-17), in circumstances of life (Isaiah 43:2), and in the coming of Jesus Christ of Nazareth (John 3:17).

Therefore, when Jesus died on the cross for our sins, do we accept it as truth and trust in Jesus as the Redeemer of life? Do we learn about His character and attempt to live in His character? Do we allow His will to influence our walk, our words, our works and our will?

Unless His righteousness, the reflection of His love, and the reality of His truth is evident in our lives daily; we are practically atheist, not far behind the fool who says in his heart "there is no God;" even if we acknowledge the supernatural formation of the universe.

I doubt those that are reading these pages would ever dare say, "There is no God." However, I ask, do we live consistently in devotion and dedication to God? Do our lives betray any daily commitment to God?

That which does not start with God and become sustained by God, will end in guilt.

To walk in a daily relationship with God is more than acknowledging that there is a God. It is accepting Him as your Savior, acknowledging Him as Lord of your life and anticipating Him to come as the King of Kings.

Talk With God:

"Lord, I not only acknowledge that you are God; but I gladly accept You as my Savior, my Shepherd and my Soon Coming King. Help me to keep your commandments, Keep my commitments to you and keep communicating Your message of hope to a lost and dying world. Amen"

April – Day 18

Text: Romans 6:11 NIV

"Count yourselves dead to sin but alive to God in Christ Jesus."

Thought: "The Buried Burst Forth In Beauty!"

I read once a line of poetry that stated these words,

"What whispers to the bulb, 'Tis spring?'

Behold this shriveled, wrinkled thing—

It stirs and grows, bursts into bloom;

Its fragrance perfumes all the room."

God does amazing things with the coming of spring. He refurbishes the ground with the coldness of winter; then allows the sunshine and spring's warming temperatures to start the birthing process of bulbs, buried seeds, and broken bits of plants. They grow and give off a sweet fragrance (flowers and blooms) and satisfying taste (vegetables and fruits).

Not only do we experience nature glorifying God, but humanity expresses His glory in being reborn in the newness of life.

It is when we allow the spiritual rain of God's righteousness (Hosea 10:12), the sunshine of God's love (II Corinthians 4:6) and the surgical work of the Word of God (Hebrews 4:12) to penetrate our deadly, damp and dark condition; that we are able to erupt from the coldness of the sinful nature to the enjoyment of a brand new life. It is a newness of life that is displayed with an aroma and attractiveness of God's character.

Death is identified by coldness, colorlessness, and calmness (no movement). However, God wishes to give life – filled with warm and wonderful color demonstrated in a wave of praise and a walk of faith. Let us come alive with Jesus for Jesus!

Death (to sin and self) must occur for us to enjoy the beauty, the blessedness and the bountiful life of a relationship with you

Talk With God:

"Lord. I t is my desire to shake the chill of the coldness of life to enjoy the satisfaction of that which you would have me to become—a new creation. Amen!"

April – Day 19

Text: Philippians 3:21 KJV

"Who shall change our vile body that it may be fashioned like unto His glorious body, according to the working whereby He is able even to subdue all things unto Himself?"

Thought: "Changed!"

In Oberhofen, Switzerland, simple engraved brass markers are set upon the graves in the churchyard. However, one particular grave displayed a wooden board at the head of a grave. It bore the name and dates of birth and death of their loved one on it. Over this simple marker they build a little protective wooden roof. In time a caterpillar fastened itself on the underside of the roof. There it passed through the death-like state of a chrysalis, and ultimately emerged as a beautiful butterfly, leaving its former corpse-like abode behind.

What a beautiful picture of the resurrection. Christ will come and change our vile bodies that they may be fashioned in the liberty and loveliness of Him.

I am sure the loved one of this particular person was poor and limited in their personal resources to provide even the simplest grave markers that others had displayed. However, it matters not what one may possess materially, monetarily or mentally. It is our moral makeup that makes the differences.

We all have existed as a caterpillar (a worm that damages and destroys living and lovely plants. Yet, if we yield to the plan of God and allow our self to be covered (wrapped in His love, life's blood and life changing power) we shall emerge one day in a glorified and grand display of His holiness What a promise! What a power! Changed!

Talk With God:

"Lord, I am thankful for the change you have brought about in my life already. You have wrapped me in your love and caused me to be separated from that deteriorating creature I was before. I am thankful that I can look forward to a day when I will enjoy my greatest change – a true beauty of your holiness, a true liberty of your freedom and a true display of your transformation—perfection. Amen"

April – Day 20

Text: Galatians 2:20 NIV

"I have been crucified with Christ and I no longer live, but Christ lives in me. The life I live in the body, I live by faith in the Son of God, who loved me and gave himself for me."

Thought: "Yielded and Yoked With Christ!"

Writer Cliff Cole once said, "Christianity demands the homage of the intellect, that the truth be believed; it also requires the homage of the heart, that truth be felt; and of the life, that truth be obeyed."

What is this quote saying to us? It gives us a three-fold message.

One, Christianity depends and demands that the mind acknowledge and accept the truth regarding Christ. The mind must honor the reality that Christ is Who He says He is (Romans 12:2). He is the Son of God (John 6:69)! He is the Savior of the World (Mathew 1:21)!

Two, Christianity must be sincerely believed and seated in the heart (spirit) of man.(Hebrews 10:22). When this occurs, our senses will respond in our relationship with Christ. We may shed tears, spontaneously laugh, shout, sing or speak. We will feel His touch and find His presence real. We will listen and learn. We will develop a vision of His plan and purpose and view His glory in all things.

Third, Christianity must be a duty and a delight. The will of God must be followed. The way of God must be walked. The Words of God must be kept. The work of God must be done. Our life must be in harmony with His life (Galatians 2:20).

He created us with the privilege of being intellectual creatures, emotional beings, and living beings with a will to choose. In the natural setting of our life, we will be unable to yield these aspects of our being to Him and honor Him by them. However, Jesus died on the cross to bridge that gap and make it possible. And in that plan, we are able to be yielded unto Him and yoked with Him

Talk With God:

"Lord, I want a belief that I can know is a solid foundation, a sure-fire good feeling and a standard of truth that I can live by. I have it in You. Amen!"

April – Day 21

Text: Isaiah 64:8 NIV

"We are the clay, you are the potter; we are all the work of your hand."

Thought: "Christ Is My Weaver!"

Let me share with you a poem I read once. Its author had to be God, although it is listed as unknown. It is titled, "The Weaver!"

"My life is but a weaving between my Lord and me,
    I cannot choose the colors, He worketh steadily.
Oft times He weaveth sorrow, and I in foolish pride
    Forget He sees the upper and I, the underside.
Not till the loom is silent and the shuttles cease to fly
    Shall God unroll the canvas and explain the reason why.
The dark threads are as needful in the weaver's skillful hand
    As the threads of gold and silver in the pattern He has planned."

How true such words are! He is in control of life in general. And if I am His child, He is in control of my life personally. And He will make my life what it ought to be according to His plan and purpose.

I may not understand every way that I am directed. I may not even agree with every wish that he speaks to my heart. However, if I will only learn to allow the One that has freed me from sin, to feed me and teach me to follow Him, I will find that the end product of the Weaver will be worth it all. The obedience of my Spirit, the opportunities of my life and the overcoming of self will enhance my daily life and enable my devotion in life to fit the plan of God.

Let us be reminded that He is the Potter and we are the clay. This day, let us allow Him to mold us, make us and minister to and through us.

Talk With God:

"Today, Lord, I look to you and lean on you; and in doing so learn from you that I may live for you. Let me be your image and your inspiration to others this day. Amen"

April – Day 22

Text: Jeremiah 29:11 KJV

"For I know the thoughts that I think toward you, saith the Lord, thoughts of peace, and not of evil, to give you an expected end."

Thought: "He Makes the Dream Come True"

When God created the universe and uniquely formed man from the dust of the earth, He had a plan and purpose for Adam and each individual thereafter. God has declared that all humanity is absolutely a wonder beyond compare and is created with a definite reason for being. His death on Calvary and His resurrection proved it even further.

He knows everything about you and has a personal mission for you -- establishing and extending His Kingdom on earth; bringing glory to His Name and grace to your life; allowing you to have peace of mind and power to prevail against every circumstance you encounter.

God will prepare you for each day's experience. He will allow people, problems, pressures and personal delights to crowd your path of daily living; however, nothing you encounter will be by accident. The Lord is your Shepherd. He is your Standard of Life. He will lead you, love you and lift you up.

So prepare yourself to have a wonderful day – it is the day that the Lord hath made. Plan to rejoice and be glad within it. Purposely live in a way that when it is finished, you can shout, Hallelujah, what a day!

With this disposition and dedication for each day, you will touch someone's life with the beauty, the blessings and the belief that serving God is a dream come true. We must gently receive each new opportunity, grab hold of each new challenge and greet each new day with eagerness and expectancy of what God has for you.

Walk With God:

"O Lord, I am glad you made me a unique individual, understanding every circumstance of my life and undergirding me to succeed each day that I live. I want to know that I have a purpose in life and that you have a plan for my life. Teach me to tune in and trust you each day. Amen!"

April - Day 23

Text: Numbers 6:24-26 KJV

"The Lord bless thee, and keep thee: The Lord make his face shine upon thee, and be gracious unto thee: The Lord lift up his countenance upon thee, and give thee peace."

Thought: "Because Of Calvary & the Resurrection, We Appear Beautiful!"

We have been told of a story regarding one who was walking in Westminster Abbey. As they paused, they noticed an appearance of the pavement near where they stood. A beautiful many-colored light rested upon it, and gave it an awe that caused one to linger, look and lavish the glorious colors. The cause was apparent. A painted window above explained the reason and expresses the radiant multi-colored light. The pavement had no color in itself. The painted window above gave the pavement it beautiful hue.

When you pause and ponder how lives can be filled with a beauty, so bold and so blessed; it makes you wonder, how is it possible? How does a life become like the pavement at Westminster Abbey? It should be apparent! We are but a reflection of the multi-color light of a gracious and glorious God who loved us, lay down His life for us and left an empty tomb to make Himself available to shine unto our path and in our person.

You are encouraged to stand still each morning and catch a glimpse of the beauty that God has revealed and reflected to you in His Word. He desires to cause you to stand in awe at His presence His peace, His power and His potential through you. Then as you go throughout the day, He will enable others in their walk of life to pause when they see God's glory radiant through the window (words, works, and walk) of your life.

In our text, The Lord has directed Moses to reflect His blessings upon the Hebrew people. Because of the Lord's desire and devotion to man, humanity becomes blessed with His beauty.

Talk With God:

"Lord, I am glad you made it possible at Golgatha and in the garden for me to experience and enjoy a relationship with you, a reflection of your life through me and a response of praise to you. Amen."

April – Day 24

Text: Psalms 51:10 Amplified Bible

"Create in me a clean heart, O God, and renew a right, preserving and steadfast spirit within me."

Thought: "Clean Hand & A Clean Heart"

Recently, due to the fear of the H1N1 flu threat, the place where I work installed portable hand sanitizers that hang on the wall in the hallways of each floor. The emphasis was on keeping down the spread of germs by keeping clean hands. With over five hundred people coming into the building on a daily basis, prompted such action. Cleaning our hands with a sanitizing lotion will purify our hands of 99.9% of germs (or so the advertisement says).

However, I wonder how many of us attempt to keep our hearts clean? Do we use the right sanitizer that will eradicate the spiritual germs and purify our hearts?

Jesus died on the cross and shed his cleaning blood in order to provide the right ingredient for spiritual sanitation. However, just as we have to place our hand under the container hanging from the wall in the hall and push up on the base of the container to receive the sanitizing potion; we must make an effort to receive the spiritual cleaning agent for our life.

How is this done? First, we must acknowledge that there is a threat against us – germs of sin has contaminated our life. Second, we must believe the plan God has designed and demonstrated on Calvary in the death of His Son Jesus Christ. Third, we must confess our need and commit to receiving the solution. Fourth, we must declare that it is a done deal – Christ has cleansed us and created us anew.

Don't enter this day with germs of disappointment, defeat, downheartedness, disgust, and in dire need of being cleansed. Let Jesus sanitize your life with His wonderful plan of salvation and His willing promise of renewal – mind, body and soul.

Talk With God:

"Today, Lord, I have need of you to cleanse and consecrate me to your way of life. I want to walk with you each step of the day. Forgive me, fortify me and let me follow you. Amen"

April – Day 25

Text: Nehemiah 12:27 KJV

"And at the dedication of the wall of Jerusalem they sought the Levites out of all their places, to bring them to Jerusalem, to keep the dedication with gladness, both with thanksgiving and with singing."

Thought: "Day of Celebration"

Today is a very special day. It would have been a celebration day between my mother and me. It is her birthday. Although, she is gone; her memories live on and her motherhood contributions yet remain. She instilled in me an inspiration and instructions that gave me help, hope and happiness even today.

Each birthday, I would get up very early and drive home (regardless of the distance or the duty I had at church or work) and take her out to eat and then buy her a nice gift (usually an outfit). I usually drove back home later that same afternoon or leave once again early the next morning.. It was difficult but well worth the celebration.

Several special qualities identify my mom. She was always available, approachable and accepting. She cared, had compassion and enjoyed your company.

This is like the Lord God! He attempts to instill within us the justification, the jubilation and the justice of living daily with Him. He is available, approachable and ready to accept us just as we are. He enjoys our fellowship. He commends our faithfulness and our fruitfulness. He loves us, lifts us up and lights up our pathway with His Word. He causes us to know His power, His peace and His promises. He delivers us, defends us and delights in us. He forgives us, fortifies us and fights our battles. What a mighty God and what a day of celebration in walking hand and hand with the King of Kings and Lord of Lords.

Just as Nehemiah had directed the rebuilding of the wall, and now desires to dedicate the wall -- He wanted God's people and priest to participate in the celebration. Therefore, join in the celebration of God's daily restoration of your life and make it possible for others to celebrate with you as you fellowship with them.

Talk With God:

"Thank you Lord for special instructions and spiritual inspiration to celebrating this day you have given. Lead me, love through me and let me honor you with praises. Amen."

April – Day 26

Text: Philippians 2:5 Amplified Bible

"Let this same attitude and purpose and (humble) mind be in you which was in Christ Jesus – Let Him be your example in humility –"

Thought: "The Mind of Christ"

A beautiful poem by Kate B. Wilkerson titled, "The Mind of Christ in Me," is worth sharing with you. Allow the poem and the purposes of it challenge, comfort and give you courage and confidence to live for Jesus throughout this day.

"May the mind of Christ our Saviour, live in me from day to day,
>By His love and power controlling all I do and say.

May the Word of God dwell richly in my heart from hour to hour,
>So that all may see I triumph only through His power.

May the peace of God my Father rule my life in everything,
>That I may becalm to comfort sick and sorrowing.

May the love of Jesus fill me, as the waters fill the sea,
>Him exalting, self abasing, this is victory.

May I run the race before me, strong and brave and face the foe,
>Looking only unto Jesus as I onward go.

May His beauty rest upon me as I seek the lost to win,
>And may they forget the channel, seeing only Him."

Talk With God:

"Lord, I do not have any idea as to what may come my way today. I can only imagine the routine that I will take. However, enable me to trust you; enrich me to know that all things will work together for good; and equip me to tackle any situations with confidence. Amen."

April – Day 27

Text: II Corinthians 4:7 NKJV

"We have this treasure in earthen vessels that the excellence of the power may be of God and not of us."

Thought: "The Treasure Within!"

It has been said that the Great Roman Empire ran on olive oil. It was used in cooking, cleaning, care of the sick, ceremonies, choice oil for lamps and cosmetics. For decades, olive oil was shipped to Rome in large clay pots. Once the oil was taken from the shipping containers – clay jugs – they were discarded. In fact, they were broken up and eventually piled near the Tiber River in Rome. Soon a man-made hill was created from the estimated 25 million pots discarded in this single location. However, the treasure within the pots became a commodity of great important to national survival.

I am convinced that this is a perfect illustration of the Apostle Paul's writings in our text. He attempted to emphasize that our bodies are expendable, yet our spirit is eternal. And when our spirit is inhabited by the life of Christ, we become a prized creation. It affects our entire life -- Our conduct, our conversation, our countenance, our conscience, our challenges and our consequences.

We must not fill our life with substance that is temporal, tasteless and not provided true blessing in life. We must allow the character of Christ – perfect love, perpetual joy, peace, patience, personal gentleness and goodness, perceiving and preserving faith, pure humility and power of self control -- to be an anointing, an attitude and an action of our daily life.

Let this day be a day in which the true YOU – the true God given treasure of your life – is demonstrated and displayed for all to see, scense and be sweeten and strengthen by.

Talk With God:

"O Lord, I am aware that one day this physical body will fade away; but I am glad to know that the presence of you within it will last forever. No matter what conditions or circumstances I face today, enable me to rely on you which will cause me to rejoice. Amen!"

April – Day 28

Text; Isaiah 7:14 NIV

"Therefore the Lord himself will give you a sign; the virgin will be with child and will give birth to a son, and will call him Immanuel."

Thought: "God Is With Us!"

A mother received a phone message from her son's school to pick him up at the principals' office.

When the mother arrived, the principal was startled to see her wearing pajamas and with curlers in her hair. "Why are you dressed like that?" the principal asked.

"I told my son that if he acted up at school one more time and embarrass me, I would embarrass him back," she said. "So, I've come to spend the day with him."

Although God died on Calvary, one of the greatest revelations of the Easter event is that He lives—not to embarrass us to enrich us. Isaiah prophesied that this was one of the signs of the coming of Christ in human form. He would be named Immanuel, which means "God with us." To all who receive Him, He is ever present in our human form.

One of the most effective techniques and ever available devices in problem solving is the simple realization and revelation that God is a partner with us. The Bible bears this out: He is our companion (Matthew 28:20), our co-laborer (I Corinthians 3:9), and our constant friend (Proverbs 18:24). His name bears this out.

The Word of God teaches us that in all the difficulties, decisions and directions we encounter in this life, God is close by. We can lean upon Him, listen to Him, learn from Him and be lifted up by Him. He has an interest in us, an investment in us and desires to inspire us.

In the midst of the night, the morning hours or the mid-day moment, God is available to us (Psalm 55:17). He is present with power, promise and provisions for our life. He is present to enable us to endure or end the assault of the enemy. He is present to grant comfort, courage and confidence. Trust Him and tune into His presence!

Talk With God:

"What a privilege and pleasure to know you are as close as our heartbeat. What an assurance it is to know you are real and reliable. Therefore, I shall praise you this day and move forward in a positive and pure conviction that victory is mine. Amen!"

April – Day 29

Text: Philippians 3:13 KJV

"This one thing I do, forgetting those things which are behind and reaching forth unto those things which are before."

Thought: "The Past Is Dead"

Just as winter is now past, and spring has sprung; we move on to greener and more glorious things. If this is true in our natural setting; how much more should it be true in our mental and moral setting?

You cannot bring back the deeds or doings of the past. Yesterday is gone. It is dead! It is over! There are several lessons to be learned from this great truth.

Lesson One: we cannot relive the past. It is gone forever. No word or work, debt or doubt, action or attitude can be redone or relived.

Lesson Two: we must make ever attempt to live and love in a way that we hurt no one, harbor no regret nor hinder anyone from a positive and pure view of Christ.

Lesson Three: we must forgive ourselves of the wrong, wayward and willful way in which we may have hurt, hindered or hid the truth of our ill feeling toward another.

Lesson Four: we must forgive others of the malice, mischievous deeds and manipulation that they may have conveyed in our relationship with them.

Lesson Five: we must accepted God's forgiveness. He has eradicated sin and selfishness from the record when we accept Him and acknowledged Him as our Savior, Shepherd and soon coming King.

Lesson Six: we must learn from our mistakes and walk more tenderly and in touch with the Counselor of Life. He will help to guide us, govern us and guard us.

And Lesson Seven: we must move on. There will be seasons of heat and harvest ahead. We do not have time to consider the past failure, frailty and faults. We must stay inspired and involved. We must be alive, active and alert. The past is dead.

Talk With God:

"Lord, it is so hard at times to let go of the moments we cherish; as well, as the times we may have collapsed. However, help us Lord to turn to you, trust you and thank you for your amazing grace and anointing love. Teach us to learn from our mistakes. Amen."

April – Day 30

Text: Proverbs 12:22 NKJV

"Lying lips are an abomination to the lord, but those who deal truthfully are His delight."

Thought: "Day of Honesty"

I recently read that April 30th is National Honesty Day in the United States. The news was a surprise and a shock. For our times and territory has become everything but a land of honesty.

I found out in my research that author M. Hirsh Goldberg established National Honesty Day in the early 1990s as a way to honor the honorable and encourage honesty. He said that April 30 was selected because "April begins with a day dedicated to lying [April Fool's Day] and should end on a higher moral tone."

And I find that National Honesty Day is a good day to review and remind ourselves of the value of this quality of character. It should be the goal of every believer to live honest. The Bible is filled with challenges and commands of the importance of being honest. However, I find the greatest reason is that it exemplifies the very character of God Himself. He is truth and to live in His truth, we must be truthful or honest. God hates lying (Proverbs 6:16-19 and 13:5).

Lying and living a lie is the work of the enemy, Satan. It is the lifestyle of the sinner. It is the character of the ungodly. And I have heard many times the expression, "Liars are fryers," meaning that the consequence of lying is frying in the flames of hell.

Let us not just end the month of April with Honesty Day but let us strive and succeed in making every day a honorable day by living honestly in thought, talk and our walk.

Talk With God:

"Today, Lord, it is my desire and delight to honor you and to live a honest life. I pray that I will share your truth in living the way of truth. Amen!"

Step 5 – May
"Basic Leadership"

The month of May revolves around Mother's Day. Mothers are God's special creation for humanity. They are the helpmate of their spouse, the honorable channel of procreation and the holy image of the love of God. They provide the basic leadership for all humanity – for mankind does not come into existence full grown, but as a baby needing to learn the how to and whys of life.

A mother's love is present prior to the birth of her children. She has a God given ability for the creation of her child within. She has a love to commit herself to the continue growth of her child once that child reaches certain stages of life (and even sometimes before they reach that stage—believe it or not, children are sometimes stubborn). Likewise, God's love for humanity exists prior to coming into being. He is our designer and developer of physical life and is ready to continue that growth once we reach the stage of commitment on our part –and again we must agree that sometimes man is stubborn when God attempts to aid in his development.

Just as mothers teach us how to take steps in our learning to walk and teach us to speak words, then phrases in our learning to talk; God considers us children also and teaches us how to walk the path of righteousness and speak words pleasing unto Him.

During this month, we shall consider the basic leadership of God for mankind. We will attempt to share the rights, relationships and responsibilities of man to His conscience, His Creator, His community and His country. We will consider God's desire, delight and duty to build His Kingdom using sinful and self-centered man.

We have learned that most mothers are always aware of their children's circumstances and ever available to meet their needs. We must learn that God is very much aware of the conditions of our life and is a very present help in time of need.

Let us be thankful for the devotion, duty and delight that mothers have for their children. Let us be grateful to God for His devotion, determination and delight that He has for humanity. Therefore, let us possess humility, honesty and honor toward God in learning the basic training we need to become what we need to be.

May – Day 1

Text: Jeremiah 33:3 KJV

"Call unto me, and I will answer thee, and [share with] thee great and mighty things, which thou knowest not."

Thought: "His Line Is Never Busy"

Let me relate a story with you. It is told of a young child learning the numbers and ABC's. She would dial numbers from the phone directory. On one occasion, she came to her mother very much upset. She told her mother that she had dialed Jesus' number and the line was busy. What had occurred was that she found a picture of Christ in a funeral home advertisement and had called the listed number.

Well, the mother explained to the child that Jesus is not called on the telephone, but from our heart with our thoughts. She also explained that His number is never busy. He hears every call made to Him and responds accordingly and appropriately.

Friend, have you attempted to call upon Jesus today or do you think He's too busy to answer your call.

If anyone is too busy, it is usually us.

Take time to talk with Christ today. He is awaiting your call and He is concern about you.

If we were to be still and meditate (answer His call) on His Words and Works, we could hear Him speak to us with words of encouragement and enrichment.

He is ready to reveal His Person, His plans and His purpose for each of us. He is ready to prepare you for this day and promise you His power, His peace and His pleasure.

Talk With God:

"Lord, I have to admit that sometimes I call and it seems I get a busy signal or I am put on hold. However, I know you are aware of my petition and have given an answer to the plea. I thank you for your constant awareness and continual availability. Amen."

May – Day 2

Text: Philippians 3:15 NIV

"All of us who are mature should take such a view of things. And if on some point you think differently, that too God will make clear to you."

Thought: "Making the Point Clear"

So often, we do not understand fully the plan and purpose of God. As the song written by Kris Kristofferson says, "I'm only human…help me to today…show me the way. Help me believe…give me the strength…teach me to take one day at a time."

The Apostle Paul in our text was declaring that he had not yet achieved the spiritual goal of eternal life; therefore he made a dedication to press forward living in a matter that would assure the reward.

The same is true for each of us daily. If we awake each morning in this life, we have not achieved the ultimate goal of heaven; but still must keep our nose to the grind stone and walk consistently and committed to the will and way of God. We must read His Word, render praise to His Name, reserve moments to talk with Him (prayer) and refrain from doing things and having thoughts that would negate a pure relationship with Him. In doing this, we receive and retain His plan and purpose for our life. We learn to react and respond Godly in the confrontations and circumstances of life to learn

Mothers are God's tool for helping us to understand the point and get the picture. Ladies be sure to paint the picture of God clear and colorful for your children and grandchildren to enjoy and be enriched in the plan and purpose of God.

And let each of us learn from the compassionate teachings of the Holy Spirit. He will daily instruct and inspire us on the will and the walk of God.

Talk With God: "Lord, I know there are times that I do not have a clear picture of the plan and purpose of my life on a daily basis. Therefore, I call on you this day to show me the way and help to be all that I can be as I pursue that heavenly reward. Amen!

May – Day 3

Text: Jeremiah 31:3-4 NIV

"The Lord appeared to us in the past, saying: "I have loved you with an everlasting love; I have drawn you with loving-kindness. I will build you up again and you will be rebuilt"

Thought: "His Inspiration & Instruction Will Rebuild Us"

So often my mother would share with me words and warm hugs which would build a fire of restoration and renewal in my self-esteem and spiritual life. Her true compassion and tender touch would heal the wounds and give hope to the situation. Not only as a child but many times since I've climbed the ladder to adulthood.

God is even greater at this! He appears to us in our sinful nature and draws us to Himself and rescues us from the bondage of sin. He appears to us in our slips and slides of daily living and instructs us and inspires us to pick ourselves up and go again. He appears to us in situations that we struggle with and gives us a boost (and sometimes a good boot to jump start us). He appears to us when it seems the supports have collapsed and the walls have been broken down. He begins to design, develop and does a great reconstruction of our lives.

Friend, God has, does and will continue to prove He is an available aid to us in life. We must call on Him, consider His response and continue on in His loving-kindness and leadership.

No matter what the situation was yesterday, or will be today or will be tomorrow; the presence of God will prevail if we will trust Him with our love and life.

Therefore, trust Him and tune in to His inspiration and instruction.

Talk With God:

"Lord, I have learned to draw on your loving-kindness and dwell in your ever-influencing love. Help me to respond to your love and with love. Amen!"

May – Day 4

Text: Psalms 1:1-3 NIV

"Blessed is the man…his delight is in the law of the Lord, and on his law he meditates day and night. He is like a tree planted by streams of water, which yields it fruit in season and whose leaf does not wither. Whatever he does prospers."

Thought: "The Bible Is More than a Catch-all!"

A little boy once took the Bible from the center-table of the living room at home and turned its dusty pages and said, "Mother, is this God's Book?" "Certainly," was the mother's reply. "Well, I think we had better send it back to God, for we don't use it here," said the little boy.

This is a fair picture of many homes and the way the Bible is treated. The center-table Bible (family Bible) is a catch-all. It is a place for past relics, personal notes, poetry and pressed flowers. However, God has revealed to us words of facts and favor, and like David, the Psalmist; we should meditate upon His Word day by day.

The Scriptures are sufficient to make us wise unto salvation and fill us with wisdom to succeed in life.

I am grateful for a Mother who read God's Word daily and revealed the truths of God's Word to us on a daily basis. It established my life and ensured me a satisfied life. Her inspiration and instruction gave me a desire and a determination to learn and live a live dedicated to God.

But what do you do with God's Word? Do you grab its truth and give life your best shot or do you allow it to become a grab bag to stuff personal keep sakes? The choice is yours. It could change your life.

Talk With God:

"Lord, your Word is life to me. I desire to read, reminisce, and rely on your Word. Help me to hid it in my head and in my heart and not forget that in the Truth, I am able to enjoy the earthly life and experience the eternal life. Amen!"

May – Day 5

Text: I Kings 10:3 KJV

"And Solomon told her (Queen of Sheba) all her questions: there was not any thing hid from the king, which he told her not."

Thought: "Heaven Is Our Hope in Honoring God!"

Have you ever wondered whether it pays to honor God? The Queen of Sheba did. In fact, she had to find out the answer to that question for herself. She had heard of the wealth and wisdom that had been granted Solomon because of his honor to God. However, she went to meet him and as a result, she was totally amazed.

Serving God is always profitable. Although we may not possess the wealth and wisdom of Solomon, God will meet our growing needs and grant us a peace and a perpetual joy. In fact, the Psalmist David declares that our life can overflow with His presences, peace, power and prevailing joy.

Wealth should not be measured by earthly means for wealth is temporal; therefore, the goal is possess the pearl of great price (Matthew 13). Wisdom is not earned by mere mental knowledge but by application of knowledge to life through the omniscients of God. He is all-knowing and knows how to precisely and practically apply knowledge to us in order that we benefit from the circumstances and condition that prevail in the path of our life.

That sounds a lot like mothers. I have heard my daughter tells her son many times, "I am the adult and you are the child." Mothers do have a knowledge that far exceeds the learning knowledge of a youngster. And mothers, most of the time, knows what wealth is – not abundance but the necessities. For in all reality, we are wealthier than most if we have adequate food, alternating pieces of clothing, available shelter and accommodating transportation. And of course, having a mother that loves you regardless of the conditions or circumstances is a pearl of great price in the earthly scene.

God has already given us His very best—His Son, Jesus Christ. Let Him continue to supply your daily needs as you devote your total being to Him.

Talk With God:

"Lord, thank you for the pleasure to honor you with my life. Help me to yield to your wisdom and know true wealth; and in possessing both, let my life honor you. Amen!"

May – Day 6

Text: Psalms 31:20 NIV

"In the shelter of your presence you hide them from the intrigues of men; in your dwelling you keep them safe"

Thought: "The Hiding Place!"

Several years ago, I had the opportunity to go to The Netherlands (Holland). While there I visited several interesting sites. However, a special place was an old three-story house in Haarlem. It looked like most of the other houses on the street. Yet it was different because of what took place within the structure.

The building had a watch shop on the first floor and an apartment complex on the upper two floors. It was a small building with small rooms. On the third floor, at the back of a room, there was a secret chamber behind the clothes closet. Because of this secret place, Corrie ten Boom and her family were able to help many Jewish people find a hiding place from the Germany army as it rolled through the country of Holland.

We have a spiritual enemy who goes about as a roaring lion seeking to devour us. When Satan hounds and hunts us, we can find a hiding place in God. In His secret place, we can find the provisions of escape from the enemy and enter the freedom of life.

When the storms of life strike and attempt to shatter our health, happiness and hope; we have a storm shelter – a hiding place in God. When the streams flood and the possessions of this life are lost to swollen, swift and spreading paths of destruction; God is able to move us to higher ground and provide a hiding place. When the fiery darts of life strike us leaving burns and bruises, we have a haven in God (place of healing and help).

For God is a rock -- a safe place of hiding for the soul. Therefore, today, trust Him and He will grant you the provisions necessary for safe passage in the journey of life.

Talk With God:

"God, I know you care about your people. I know you have and will always make a way for each of us. Therefore, enable us to trust you regardless of the conditions or circumstances of life.

May – Day 7

Text: I Corinthians 15:58 KJV

"Be ye steadfast, unmovable always abounding in the work of the Lord, forasmuch as ye know that your labor is not in vain in the Lord."

Thought: "Consistency Is A Must!"

A story is told of a mother watching her son over the fence walk along the sidewalk. She worried for a moment when she saw his head bob up and down as if he was limping. As he rounded the corner, she saw him in full view and realized he was walking with one foot on the curb and one off.

Most people will admit that God is worthy to be worshipped. But friend, if God is worthy of our worship; then He is worthy of all our life – physical body, perception of the mind, personal soul, personality and power or strength. It is impossible to have peace, perpetual joy and power unless we consistently walk with God. The secret is total commitment – keeping both of our feet on the level ground of obedience to God's Word.

A firm conviction of Christ's Lordship is essential. We must place all our confidence in Jesus Christ. We must allow Him to be our Creator, Counselor, Comforter, Confidence, Courage and Commander-in-Chief.

Today is a day for you to try again to walk on level ground and honor the Lord with a consistent life style. Let the failures and faults of yesterday be gone and walk in true devotion to the Lord one day at a time.

Talk With God:

'Lord, I am so grateful that you watch over us and keep us steadfast in our walk and work for you. It is our delight and duty to worship you with a consistent lifestyle without wavering. I want you to keep me in tune and keep me true to your will and way. Amen!"

May – Day 8

Text: 2 Corinthians 13:14 NIV

"May the grace of the Lord Jesus Christ, and the love of God, and the fellowship of the Holy Spirit be with you all."

Thought: "Triple Treat of God"

When I was a teenager in the southern town of Waynesboro, Mississippi, we had a cool meeting place for teens called the Triple Treat. It was a nice corner drive-in soda and sandwich place (something like Sonic, McDonald's or Burger King today). It was known for its milk shakes, hamburgers and fries – triple treat.

We didn't have much growing up, so I didn't get to visit the Triple Treat very often; however, mom would always provide a triple treat for us every Sunday – southern fried chicken, mama's mashed potatoes and homemade chocolate fudge cake. My, my – it would make your tongue beat your brains out getting to it.

Well, did you know that God has a triple treat for us? As we journey throughout this life, we need rescuing, reinforcement, restoration and refreshment every day. It is found in the gracious favor of the Lord Jesus Christ, the glorious love of the Father and the genuine fellowship of the Holy Spirit.

As we enjoy these treats and experience their blessings and benefits, we are able to rejoice, resist and be refreshed each step of the way. We are able to sing, "Praise God from whom all blessings flow; praise Father, Son and Holy Ghost."

Talk With God:

"What a delight it is Lord to know that we have a triple blessing that awaits us each day. What an honor to be favored, forever loved and enjoy fellowship with you each step of the way. Keep me safe, let me sing and enable me to share your grace, glory and gift of eternal life."

May – Day 9

Text: Jeremiah 31:28 NIV

"So will I watch over them, to build, and to plant, declares the Lord"

Thought: "Thank God for His Peace and Provisions of Safety!"

Little chickens find a place of security under the wings of the mother hen. Hawks often hover high overhead, their piercing eyes searching for an unprotected victim. If the hawks glide too near the mother hen gives a particular call used only in time of danger. Immediately those baby chicks run to the safety of the mother's wings. If one fails to heed the call he may be carried away by the powerful talons of the chicken hawk. God has given every creature a means of self-preservation and security.

Mothers are individuals who are in constant watch over their children (in fact, some have been known to be over-protective). A mother is concerned for the well-being of her children. Yet, each child must learn to respect the knowledge of the mother's advise and respond in obedience.

Throughout this year in our day-to-day activities we often will feel the need of a refuge. And friend we can hear the warning call of the Savior and need to heed that call in order to be protected and preserved.

It is through daily prayer and daily devotions in God's Word that we can receive and response to the warning signal of God. He is in constant watch and is ready to warn in times of distress and danger. Let us be willing to hear and heed the call.

The personal security for today and tomorrow is dependent on your willing to be safe and your willingness to honor God's supreme knowledge.

Jeremiah the prophet declares in our text that God is a God who sees our downfall (due to sin and selfishness) yet he also sees our desire to be reestablished. If we heed His call, we will find shelter, safety and shall be restored.

Talk With God:

"Thank you Lord for your peace and the safety provisions given me in your Word. Help me to be obedient to your words and your will for my life. Amen!"

May – Day 10

Text: II Peter 1:19 Message

"You'll do well to keep focusing on it. It's the one light you have in a dark time as you wait for daybreak and the rising of the Morning Star in your hearts."

Thought: "The Light Of Rest!"

A story is told of a mother and her 4-year daughter who were preparing to retire for the night. The child was afraid of the darkness. So, the mother, alone with the child, felt fearful also. However, when the lights were turned out, the child caught a glimpse of the moon outside the window. "Is that God's light shining," she asked? "Yes", the mother replied. "Will God blow out His light and go to sleep" the daughter asked? "No, God never goes to sleep and His light is always shining!" was the reply of the mother. Then the child in simple faith said, "Well, so long as God is awake, I am not afraid."

How often have we allowed the fearful darkness of setbacks, of suffering, of sorrows, of sickness rob us of our rest and reassurances.

The answer to fear is knowing that God is with us every moment of the day and in the darkness of night (whether night hours or dark conditions of life). He knows what we encounter and knows how to handle the situation. He will grant to us the light of His Word to comfort us and give us courage.

Embrace Him each morning, enjoy Him during the day and experience Him in the dark times.

Remember the commercial about Motel Six – "we'll leave the light on for you". God will leave the light on for you.

Talk With God:

"Lord, I am glad that your light is on and rest can be mine regardless of the circumstances. Your peace and provisions are mine to embrace and enjoy. Amen!"

May – Day 11

Text: Psalm 144:15 KJV

"Happy is that people, whose God is the Lord"

Thought: "If You Are Happy Notify Your Face!"

"You always help me start the day right by your cheerful face." The clerk said to Mrs. Thomas as she was doing her morning shopping. The clerk was surprised when Mrs. Thomas told her she had not always been a cheerful person. Many years before, she had been on a sickbed for an extended period of time. During the time she was bedridden, God dealt with her soul. In the process, she acknowledged her need of Jesus and surrendered her life to Him. When she accepted Jesus, she found a joy that was undeniable and unexplainable. Her life began to bubble with the joy that was full of glory. She had the joy of the Lord because she now belonged to Him. God's blessings were hers because she had been obedient when he called.

Obedience to God's Word will always result in a justified and jubilant life. Disobedience will bring sorrow and sourness that is evident in a lifestyle. People can recognize the fruit of our internal spiritual commitment by looking at a person's face. If the person is a joyful individual or a sour puss depends on his relationship with God.

My wife often reminds me, "If you're happy, notify your face." An internal Godly contentment will produce an external joyful continence.

Therefore, let us get into the Word of God on a daily basis, grow in His grace and glow in His happiness. It makes others wonder what you have been up to. If they ask, you have an opportunity to share the message of Jesus as the happy customer did in our story at the beginning.

Talk With God:

"Lord, I realize that with the restlessness of our world today, no man can have the power to beg, borrow or buy happiness. It comes only from you. We open our heart and allow you to make your home within in order that we may rejoice externally. Let our delight in you be a means of touching another person for your glory. Amen!"

May – Day 12

Text: I Kings 18:21 KJV *(italics personal)*

"How long will you waver between two opinions? If the Lord is God, follow him; but if *(not follow whom you will)*?"

Thought: "Decisions! Decisions! Decisions!

I read a cute but curious story of a small lad in a candy store. The young boy was wandering from candy case to candy case, studying each assortment with deep seriousness. His mother, tired of waiting for him to make a decision, called to him, "hurry up, son, spend your money, we must be going." To this the lad replied, "But mother, I've only one dollar to spend, and I've got to spend it carefully."

Friend, you and I have but one life to live. Do we live it cautiously, taking each step with deliberation and determination? Do we have a plan and a purpose for our life?

The Bible says, "Lean not upon your own understanding, but in all your ways acknowledge God." God will be patient yet persistent with us. We must not waste time but use it wisely. The prophet Elijah in our text challenges the nation of Israel to quit stalling and make a decision regarding serving God or serving Baal.

During this day's activities, let us make our decisions cautiously and correctly -- in getting ready for the day, in going to our secular job, school or social setting, and in grinding out the duties and delight of the day's activities. Let us listen to the authority of God's voice (His Spirit and His Scripture) as He blesses us with His riches and behooves us to use it wisely.

The Lord wants us to enjoy and be enriched with the decisions we make in life; but we must move on with the plan and purpose He has for us in our daily lives.

Talk With God:

"Lord, thank you for every blessing you have distributed to us. Thank you for giving us the time to enjoy the blessing. Thank you for allowing us the ability to make decisions based on being caution and being correct. Yet help us to remember that there is much to be accomplished in such a short time and not to waste time in personal choices that will delay your work. Amen!"

May – Day 13

Text: John 8:7 KJV

"Neither do I condemn thee; go and sin no more."

Thought: "God's Word Suspends the Sentence!"

Many years ago a man was condemned to be hanged. While on the scaffold, he asked for a drink of water. His request was granted, but his hand shook so much that he could not drink it. "Take your time," said the king, who sat by to see the end of the law, "you will not be hanged till you drink all of it." In a moment the culprit dashed the cup from him, saying, "Well, I'll never drink it, so I can never be hanged." He took the king at his word, and his life was spared."

Friend, we may be guilty of sinning against God and desire to be punished; however, the King of Kings Jesus Christ has declared that by accepting Him we can be set free. Take Him at His Word.

In our text today, God was confronted by the scribes and Pharisees regarding the judgment of a woman taken in sin. Jesus knew their hearts. They were not concerned about what the law said nor what Jesus would say; they simply wanted to entrap Him... However, he turned the table on them.

We are not to judge the sinner for we all have sinned. However, Jesus declared the woman forgiven and free to go but forbade her to continue in her sinning. His Word is strong, straight and will set one free. We must take Him at His Word.

Talk With God:

"Lord, thank you for your willingness to forgive our sin, forget our punishment and frees us from the prison of bondage and the penalty of death. Thank you loving me and accepting my love and appreciation to you. Amen!"

May – Day 14

Text: Matthew 14:27 KJV

"Be of good cheer; it is I; be not afraid."

Thought: "All Is Well!"

Robert Louis Stevenson tells the story of a ship at sea in time of storm. The passengers were in great distress. After a while one of them, against orders, went up on deck and made his way to the captain. The seaman was at his post of duty at the wheel and when he saw the man was greatly frightened, he gave him a reassuring smile. Then the passenger turned and went back to the other passengers and said, "I have see the pilot and he smiled, all is well."

This story takes my mind back to childhood, when the weather was stormy. Mom would get up and gather all four of us in her bedroom and whisper scriptures to us. Although the storm may have raved all night, we were soon sound asleep knowing we were in the presence of our mother who loved us and cared for us. Her presence was our reassurance that all was well.

When our small boat of life is storm-tossed and our hearts are fearful, we may push through the storm to our Pilot, who is in total control, and when we hear his voice speak peace to us, we shall know that all is well.

Today may be a day in which storm clouds will hover over your life and you may face situations that will produce distress and disturbance. However, never forget that God is near and will give you hope, help and happiness in the mist of any storm. Just as Jesus in our text, came unto the disciples tossed in the stormy sea, and calmed the wind and waves.

Talk With God:

"Jesus, thank you for the promise of being with us in our daily journey. Thank you for settling our hearts of fear, steering us safely through and at times stilling the storms of life. Amen!"

May – Day 15

Text: Ephesians 5:26 KJV

"That he might sanctify and cleanse it with the washing of water by the word."

Thought: "Are You Washed Or Licked Clean?"

Recently I received an email that I thought was cute. I had heard a similar story before. But here goes, John went to visit his 90 year old grandfather in a very secluded rural area of Saskatchewan, Canada. After spending a great evening chatting the night away, the next morning John's grandfather prepared a breakfast of bacon, eggs an toast. However, John noticed a film like substance on his plate, and questioned his grandfather asking, 'Are these plates clean?' His grandfather replied, 'They're as clean as cold water can get em. Just you go ahead and finish your meal, Sonny!" For lunch the old man made hamburgers. Again, John was concerned about the plates, as his appeared to have tiny specks around the edge that looked like dried egg and asked, 'Are you sure these plates are clean?" Without looking up the old man said, 'I told you before, Sonny, those dishes are as clean as cold water can get them…now don't fret, I don't want to hear another word about it!" Later that afternoon, John was on his way to a nearby town his grandfather's dog sniffed him and started to growl, and wouldn't let him pass. John yelled and said, 'Grandfather, your dog won't let me get to my car.' Without diverting his attention from the football game he was watching on TV, the old man shouted! 'Coldwater, go lay down now, yah hear me!"

Mother would have a fit if she ever knew such a condition prevailed. Mother's are very picky about cleanness. Grandmother would have never let such a thing occur.

What about God? Do you think He does things with a spiritual wash over by carnal means? No way! He shed His own blood to cleanse us from the fleshly contaminations. Do you think He expect us to keep our life clean by it being licked clean with just another physical contaminate? I don't think so! He desires for us to wash our lives each day with the cleansing Word of God.

Talk With God:

"Thank you, Lord, for providing a true cleansing agent for our lives. Thank you for making available to us your Word that will purify us as we start the day. Keep us in all our responsibilities and relationships. Amen!"

May – Day 16

Text: II Samuel 7:10 KJV

"Moreover I will appoint a place for my people Israel, and will plant them, that they may dwell in a place of their own, and move no more."

Thought: "Replanted to Live!"

I read a story about a one-year old male cat named Simon. Simon was the joy of a grandmother's heart. She rescued him from the animal shelter and raised him almost like a child. Simon was different. He didn't eat the leaves off the plants nor dig around them. He would simply knock off the stems of the grandmother's favorite jade plant. However, instead of becoming irritated at the cat, the grandmother learned a great lesson. She would replant the stems broken off and the new plant was more beautiful and bigger than the original one. Therefore, instead of wrecking havoc on the flora, the cat's action wrought a heavenly blessing.

You know sometimes, we need a fresh start.. God may allows things to happen to our life that we feel are not beneficial but are dangerous, damaging, destructive or detrimental to us. However, this is not God's plan. He will never harm, hurt or hinder us in any way; but does allow things to come into our path that will cause us to pause, ponder and prepare for greater growth. He may allow a 'Simon' to lob off some of our branches (earthly benefits, blessings and beauty) that will kill off the old plant and allow us to be replanted. As we take root in Him we begin to flourish and produce branches with eternal benefits, blessing and beauty.

David desired to enter a new covenant between God and the Jews. He dreamed of erecting a house for God. He determined to establish the nation.

Many people feel abandoned, alone and in need of agape love (consecrated and complete love). Their branches have been lobbed off and they are shriveled and starving to death. Let us feed them with the letter (Word), the love and the life of God. Let us pray for them, plant words of encouragement and enrichment, and prepare them to be transplanted by the hand of God.

Just as the grandmother used tender loving care for the plant and understanding love toward the cat; let us allow God to use us in care, not criticism.

Talk With God:

"Lord, I want to view every condition of life through your eyes. For it is only then, that I can allow you to work in me and through me. Fill me with courage not criticism; happiness not hopelessness; gratitude not grief; and satisfaction not stress. Amen!"

May – Day 17

Text: I Samuel 15:17 NKJV

"So Samuel said, when you were little in your own eyes, were you not head of the tribes of Israel? And did not the Lord anoint thee king over Israel?"

Thought: "Consequences Occur when we Hesitate to Obey!"

I remember an incident as a young lad of ten, when my mother had asked me to run to the store (just across the street from the housing project) and get a bag of sugar. She wanted me to do it quick for it was about to rain. I hesitated, then it began to rain, and I remember her request and took off to the store. The rain was coming down hard when I left the store, and I dashed from back porch to back porch of each apartment. When I jumped from the last porch, my foot landed on the bottom of a broken soda pop bottle (and I was bare footed). When I arrived at home with the sugar, I apologized for waiting till it began to rain. But the first thing my mom noticed was the blood spilling across the floor from my foot. Instead of an angry outburst or a slap on the rear end, she took my hand and led me to the bath tub and began to doctor my injury. When the medical task was finished with proper treatment and prayer, she thanked me for getting the sugar she requested and told me she loved me. I was wrong for my delay and deserved punishment.

So often we forget to follow the Godly suggestions of the Lord. We know what choices we need to make; however, we want to do our own thing first, then if there is time, we will perform the other obligations of life, particularly obedience to God's Word. However, when we fail to act accordingly, we suffer. We miss a blessing, we make a mess of what we are doing or we might suffer consequences for the delay.

Just as Saul suffered consequences of his disobedience and deliberate self action, we too will experience suffering when we fail to obey God and forsake the opportunity to humble our self and honor God.

Talk With God:

"Lord, I wish to obey you and use every opportunity to praise you and perform my daily task with purpose. Guide my and govern my responses. Amen!"

May – Day 18

Text: John 10:14 KJV

"I am the good shepherd, and know my sheep, and am known of mine."

Thought: "Thank God He Knows!"

The story is told how a certain man on a sheep farm in Australia saw the owner take a little lamb and place it in a huge enclosure where several thousand sheep who's bleating, together with the shouting of the sheep-shearers, was deafening. Then the lamb uttered its feeble cry, and the mother sheep at the other end of the enclosure heard it and went to find the lamb.

"Do not imagine that you are beyond the reach of the Good Shepherd." He has his eyes on you, He hears you, and He has knowledge of your habits and every secret longing.

Not every person is in the sheep fold of God; yet every person is a creation of God and He is concerned for each one.

Are you concerned about yourself? Do you not want to be in the fold of God?

I heard T. D. Jakes say one time, "Often when I pray I simply cry Baa! Baa! For in me, I feel like a wounded, weary and wayward lamb and I am trying to attract my Shepherd." In fact, one night as I dismissed the service, I simply cried Baa! Baa! It was not a cry of desperation but of exaltation. For God had truly been touched in our praises and had tremendously touched his people in their petitions that particular night.

What a privilege it is to be able to know the Savior of the World, the Shepherd of life and the Soon Coming King of Kings. What a pleasure it is to be known by the Great Physician, the Gracious Lord and Glorified Christ!

Talk With God:

"Lord, I love you and lean on you daily as my foundation, focus and future. I am grateful for your love expressed by your death, at the dawning of each new day and the direction you give along the way. Amen!"

May – Day 19

Text: Daniel 4:3 KJV

"How great are his signs? And how mighty are his wonders? His kingdom is an everlasting kingdom, and his dominion is from generation to generation."

Thought: "Watch For The Sign!"

Have you ever overlooked a posted sign – keep out! or speed limit or yield – only to have someone stop you and ask, did you not see the sign? How about an officer with a ticket book in his hand? Or maybe when you made a wrong turn and your spouse reminded you in certain terms that I told you left not right? Or maybe when your stomach growled when you had just missed an exit marked food while traveling the interstate?

Mother's give signs also. She may point her finger and say go to your room. She may say its meal time, come and eat. She may say its bedtime, get some sleep. She may say it's time to get up and get ready for school, church or travel.

Signs are helpful when we heed them. How distressing and difficult life can be when signs are inconsistent or when we ignore them.

God is always faithful to post signs of correct directions, comfort, cheer, courage and challenge. Whatever we may need along life's roadway, God's Word gives us signs of warning, welcome and the way.

Daniel interpreted the dream of Nebuchadnezzar to verify that God is all-knowing and all-powerful and validate the signs giving unto the king regarding his kingdom.

The main challenge for us is in paying attention to those signs from God – remembering what they indicate and initiate what they say. As we do, we will soon discover that the signs God provides always point to His faithfulness, fruitfulness and fervent love.

Talk With God:

"Lord, I love you and desire to watch for signs of direction, deliverance and discipleship. I will search your Word and speak with you daily in order to be strengthen and sober in my drive through life. Amen."

May – Day 20

Text: I Samuel 3:4 KJV

"Then the lord called Samuel; and he answered, here am I."

Thought: "Do We Have an Ignore Button?"

I recently read that many cell phones today have a nice little 'ignore' feature that allows users to put off an incoming call if they are to busy to take the call or simply don't want to take it at all. The article stated that the 'ignore button' forwarded calls to the person's voicemail.

I am glad that I don't have such devise on my cell phone; for I know I would feel guilty if I used it. But I wonder if I am not guilty sometimes of using ignore buttons when it comes to answering God's call to me.

Now, we all know that God doesn't use cell phones; but He does call us. What about interceding for someone in prayer in the middle of the night? What about an opportunity to witness to someone we are talking with? What about doing a particular deed that would help someone. What about giving a little extra in the offering?

We may feel we are too busy, too beat, too burdened, and too betrayed to answer Him when He calls. However, what if God didn't have time to answer our call, anoint us, and attend to our need.

In our text, the small lad Samuel, Hannah's son, heard the voice of the Lord; however, he thought it was Eli the high priest. Soon, though, Samuel learned it was not Eli, but the Lord speaking to him. From that day forward, Samuel was always open to the calls of the Lord on his life. He knew he could call on the Lord and would receive an answer; therefore, he felt it was only right to be available to the Lord's calls.

Hannah, Samuel's mother had earnestly prayed for a son and promised God she would give him back to the Lord for His service. Such open dedication and devotion kept the line open for communication between God and Samuel.

Talk With God:

"Lord, I do not want to ignore your call on my life nor to my life as I journey here below. I want to be available to hear from you and heed your call for a blessing, for bracing against the storms of life and for the benefits of others. Amen!"

May – Day 21

Text: Matthew 5:16 KJV

""Let your light so shine before men, that they may see your good works, and glorify your Father which is in heaven."

Thought: "Whose Work Is Being Done?"

Winona Carroll once wrote this beautiful dialogue: "From time to time I felt it necessary to speak with my new cook when he was preparing a meal. However, with increasing frequency he would interrupt with the remarks, I'm sorry, I don't have time to listen now, and I'm busy! Finally, I stopped him and asked him, whose work are you doing? The answer was obvious, and he was silent. Well, if you're doing my work, I said, then please stop long enough to learn how I want it done."

Think about it! Who is the master and who is the servant? Who is the employer and who is the employee? Do we find ourselves feeling we can do the job our own way without doing it the way that is expected?

In the military, the old saying was, "There is the right way, the wrong way and the military way. You will do it the military way.

I imagine God often must yearn to say the same to us when we become so preoccupied in life. When we are busy doing 'things,' that we forget we learn how to do them by giving time to His instruction and His inspiration.

We must listen, learn and live the way that is best for all involved. God knows what's best is for us, what is most beneficial to the Kingdom and what will bless others. Therefore, let us establish our work, express our will in our work and exemplify our worth through our work. God will honor and be honored.

We have been blessed with another day. Let us walk in such a way, that others will see our good works and worship the Lord."

Talk With God:

"Lord, I want to be your personal servant and perform the work assigned me in such a way that your will be honored, I will be happy and others will be helped. Amen.!"

May – Day 22

Text: II Peter 1:5-7 NIV

"Make every effort to add to your faith, goodness and to goodness, knowledge; and to knowledge, self-control; and to self control, perseverance; and to perseverance, godliness; and to godliness, brotherly kindness; and to brotherly kindness, love."

Thought: "Godly Beauty is More Than Skin Deep"

You know we sometimes think that dressing up the outside enhances our worth and makes us well liked. No don't misunderstand me, I'm not saying it is wrong to dress fashionably, deck out ourselves with exquisite jewelry or display a beautiful face made possible with the correct makeup. I sometimes wish certain folks would fix up a little.

However, no amount of external application will give a lovelier, lasting appearance than the application of a right and righteous attitude. If the qualities of a Christ like character are lacking; no amount of outward adorning will change the selfish pride that cries out for constant recognition.

My wonderful wife is a certified cosmetologist. She is certified in the field of cosmology and as an instructor. She has performed and personally taught body care and beautification from the feet to the head and from finger tip to finger tip. However, she has also informed her students that beauty is only skin deep. It takes the right attitude, particular a Godly attitude, to obtain true beauty.

If we want to gain the Savior's approval and be accountable (and we will be held accountable for our appearance and our attitude), we will want to accept and apply these characteristics to our life: strength, smartness, self-control, steadfastness, spirituality, and sincere love. It's the Spirit of God in the heart that produces the appropriate external and eternal adorning.

Remember: Righteousness in the heart produces real beauty in the human character.

Talk With God:

"Lord, I am glad you have given us instructions and inspiration on how to adorn our self for your glory and our beauty. As I prepare for this day, I want to look good in my physical state of being; but appear beautiful in my Godly character. Amen!"

May – Day 23

Text: Romans 8:29 KJV

"Be conformed to the image of his Son"

Thought: "Let us be Imitators!"

Children love to imitate their parents. Little girls enjoy dressing up in Mother's clothes, classic high heels and cosmetics because they want to be "grown up." Boys like to mimic the mannerisms of their fathers because they want to be "just like dad." Adults, particularly parents, influence their children in many ways – mentally, morally and materially. Children enjoy imitating adults, particularly their parents and grandparents.

God desires us to influence, inspire and instruct us in the manner and matter of life. God desires for us to imitate Him. And there is no greater, grander, gracious or more glorious role model for living than Jesus Christ.

God wants us to be like Him. He wants us to think like Him (Philippians 2:5); talk like Him (Colossians 3:16); trust like Him (II Timothy 1:12); try (work) like Him (Colossians 3:22-23) and triumph like Him (Philippians 4:13). His ultimate purpose is for us to be conformed to His image and confident of His influence.

There are so many influences in the world today; yet none like the compassionate, caring and courageous Man of Galilee, Jesus Christ. I am glad there is an influence in life that is not of this life. An influence that is well versed in the ways of this life but not wayward like this life. An influence that is worth imitating in my life and worth initiating before others.

Let us be an instrument of God, influenced by God and inspiring others for God. Let us become imitators' everyday – imitators of God!

Talk With God:

"Lord, I enjoy being enriched by the lives of others and even initiating qualities of character that I note worthy. However, I am glad that the more I expose myself to your Word and experience our character; the greater I feel about myself. Thank you for that. Amen!"

May – Day 24

Text: II Peter 3:18 KJV

"But grow in the grace, and in the knowledge of our Lord and Savior Jesus Christ."

Thought: "We Must Grow!"

A mother gazed lovingly at her newborn child and exclaimed, "He's perfect!" He certainly seemed to be. Two years later, however, that same child would be a disappointment to his mother if he were still a baby. However, humanity in general has quit advancing in the maturity process. It appears man has ceased to grow.

How often must God be disappointed with His creation? The way we have allowed our minds, our manners and our maturity to be darken, derailed and detoured; humanity has become stunted in the purpose and plan God originally designed. Our responses, reactions and relationship in life fail to provide evidences of any progress or purpose.

Now I am speaking in general terms and not including the entire human race with the reality of our indecision to become like our Creator, which is the case of most children within a home.

If we are not growing, then how do we grow? It is through our knowledge of Christ. He is our Creator and as we learn of Him, from Him and with Him; we grow like Him. The knowledge of Christ comes to us from the Scriptures harbored within our heart, the Spirit dwelling within us and the service opportunity of worship and work. Just as a child become familiar with the people he associates with (family and friends), the place of his abode, and the particular things he does; so it is with our relationship with our Creator.

Let this day be a day of growth. Let us become devoted to the task and determined to be triumph in our efforts. Let us prove by our walk, our words and our will that our mind is set on becoming like Jesus.

Talk With God:

"Thank you for forgiving me my faults and flaws and fortifying me to mature. Keep working on me throughout each step of each day. Teach me and train me to know your will for my life. I love you and desire to live for you. Amen!"

May – Day 25

Text: Hebrews 12:2-3 NIV

"Let us fix our eyes on Jesus, the author and perfecter of our faith…endured the cross, scorning its shame, and sat down at the right hand of the throne of God. Consider Him who endured such opposition from sinful men, so that you will not grow weary and lose heart."

Thought: "Weary, worn yet a winner!"

There is a true story of a woman who was weary of her circumstances in life. She dreamed she was in a room filled with large crosses where an angel told her she must choose one. She chose a dainty cross of gold set with precious jewels. When it was fastened on her back she fell to her knees because of the weigh of it. She then chose a cross entwined with beautiful roses. But the thorns from the roses pricked her back so painfully, she cried out for it to be removed. Finally, a plain white cross was chosen. Turning, she realized it was her own cross she was currently carrying.

Following Christ does not mean we will have no problems, no pain, no pressure, and no personal crosses to bear. It means we are to take up our trials, troubles, temptations, tribulations, thirst and terror; then turn them over to Jesus. Yes, we may feel the sting of the hurt, the spirit of heaviness, and the shame of the cross; but we can also know the strength of the Savior, the salve of His anointing and the sufficiency of His grace.

God is not interested in changing circumstances, but God is interested in changing us in the midst of our circumstances giving us the ability to experience, endure and eventually escape the cross. As we learn to cope with one cross, we are able to carry another until one day we finish our journey and lay down all our crosses and take up a crown.

Friends, don't fret the circumstances, carry the cross and receive a crown. In doing so, we are able to grow, glow and glorify Him.

Talk With God:

"Thank you Lord for bearing the cross in order that I may be able to accept the burdens that come my way. Help me to endure and even enjoy the privilege. I want to be a willing servant, a witness and a winner for your glory. Amen!"

May – Day 26

Text: Romans 12:1 KJV

"Present our bodies a living sacrifice holy, acceptable unto God, which is your reasonable service."

Thought: "Back Up Your Lips With Your Life!"

An old poem talks of a family of children who all declared that they loved their mother. Yet one neglected his work around the house, another fussed continually, while the other pitched in and helped her with the chores. However, at bedtime they all said,"I love you, Mother." Then the pointed question is asked, "How do you think the mother guessed which of them really proved their love to her and proved they loved her the most?"

The answer to the question seems simple – the one who helped her without complaint.

God experiences a similar situation. There are many who declare their love for God, yet when it comes to doing it without complaint; the number decreases greatly.

If you were asked if you loved God, what would be your answer? Usually someone who reads a daily devotional book has a love for God. However, do you life a life of obedience expressed in true dedication to God? Does your life exemplify a life that has an allegiance to God and an alienation from godliness? Does your life bear pleasant fruit of love, joy, peace, longsuffering, goodness, gentleness, faithfulness, meekness, temperance and patience? Does your life perform task of labors of love and works of faith?

Although it is my pleasure to be a writer, yet words are cheap without a dedication to support them. Therefore, it should be mine and your desire to live in such a way that our walk and our words go hand and hand.

Let us back up our words with a will, a walk and a work for God.

Remember: One picture is worth a thousand words.

Talk With God:

"I do love you O Lord and I do want to live in a way that is pleasing to you and proves my devotion to you. Love me, lead me and let me spread your love in the steps I take, the speech I say and the story I tell with my life. Amen!"

May – Day 27

Text: I Peter 5:7 Amplified Bible

"Casting the whole of your care – all your anxieties, all your worries, all your concerns, once and for all – on Him; for He cares for you affectionately, and cares about you watchfully."

Thought: "Worry!"

Many say worry is a common experience of humanity. I have heard my mother and have caught myself saying on occasion, "I just can't help but worry." Worry is "to fret over a matter." And yes, humanity is guilty of worrying.

I know that it is a free country and you can worry if you want too; but it doesn't change a thing. Worry has never offered health to the afflicted, given hope to the heavy hearted, extended a hand to the helpless, provided a help to a dying business, or produced a harvest in a drought. It just can not do it. It will hinder growth, harm physical health and heighten anxiety.

There's no need to worry. The Heavenly Father knows all about our problems, our perplexities and our positive efforts. He will handle every situation (family, financiers, fear, etc) if we give them to Him. While it is a fact, we can't ignore our circumstances; we can have faith by casting them on the Lord.

Don't lock your troubles up in your mind. Bring them out in the open, tell God all about them and let Him give you grace to cope with them as He confronts them Himself.

Friend, we have to realize that God doesn't want weekend visits with us but full custody, which means He is willing to take all our headaches, heartaches and hardheadedness. He knows our struggles with things like worry, but let us try Him out and trust Him. .According to His Word, He will prove true to the test.

Talk With God:

"It sounds easy to say it and to write it; but to do it takes a lot of courage and confidence. But Lord, I know you are able to sustain me, support me and swing me to your way of thinking. Help me this day to believe that you are working in my behalf. Amen!"

May – Day 28

Text: Psalm 19:8 KJV

"The commandment of the Lord is pure, enlightening the eyes."

Thought: "Clarity Of Vision!"

A story is told of a young lady who was amazed at the bold, beautiful and brilliant landscape while touring the countryside for the first time after being fitted with special eyeglasses. She was focusing on beauty beyond anything she had ever seen.

So often, life is blurred, botched and broken. It seems distorted and disfigured as if our vision is growing weak. However, if we would focus our attention for a moment on the Person and promises of Jesus Christ; we then would be able to filter out that which distorts the magnificent and marvelous view of life that He has designed for us. His amazing grace and anointing glory would enhance our vision. Our lives would become uplifted and undergirded with the strength and sight we behold through His lens of love.

If sorrow, sadness, stress, sickness or self-centeredness distorts our vision; let us visit the office of the Great Physician who is able to grant clear, clean and correct focus of life's treasures (Hebrews 4:16). He is able to apply drops of His cleansing blood and cleansing book (Bible) to our spiritual vision.

God's Work on Calvary and God's Word on companionship will enlighten and enrich our life for greater enjoyment.

Let the Lord perform a daily checkup on our view of life and make the necessary adjustments for clearer vision.

Talk With God:

"Lord, I will admit that my view of life is sometimes distorted and damaged with sin; however, I ask you to apply your anointing and make your adjustments in order that I may see clearly and celebrate the vision you give. Amen!"

May – Day 29

Text: Psalm 139:2-3 NIV

"You know when I sit and when I rise; you perceive my thoughts form afar. You discern my going out and my lying down; you are familiar with all my ways."

Thought: "God Knows Each of Us Individually!"

Two twin boys, Ted and Tom, were looking at some pictures of themselves. Ted stated, "When we look at these pictures of us I can't tell who is who." The twin boys were identical and yet, Tom was slightly taller than Ted. Ted was more aggressive than Tom. The boys had identical genes and nearly identical environments (friendships and fond places of enjoyment and entertainment). Each boy greatly influenced the other. Nevertheless, each felt his own feelings, thought his own thoughts, and made his own choices. Each boy was unique in his own way. Their mother knew them regardless if they were alone or together. For seven years now, she had watched them develop and help to direct their lives. She had taught them and trained them to obey her and be open with her.

This is true with humanity. God creates us with a unique likeness but with diverse characteristics. He allows us to take on our natural heritage – size, shape, speech, sway and skin color. Yet, He has allowed man to be individuals also – drives, desires, devotions, duty and dedication.

Just as Ted and Tom's mother gave them the choice to develop their likes and dislikes; God gives us the choice. He grants us the power to choose to obey Him and use the opportunity of life to develop our God-given talents and abilities for His glory. We can resist the idea and reject His will or we can receive His direction and respond in devotion.

The Psalmist in our text declares that God is acquainted with us personally and is aware of our every move and motive. Therefore, let us trust Him Who has designed us, to develop us and direct us.

Talk With God:

"Good morning Lord! I thank you for another day and making me special in every way. I am grateful for the night's rest and the golden opportunity to live for you today. Lead me, love me and let me shine for you. Amen!"

May – Day 30

Text: Zechariah 4:10 KJV

"For who hath despised the day of small things? For men shall rejoice"

Thought: "Little Is Much When God is In It!"

Mother Teresa once said, "We cannot do great things on this earth. We can only do little things with great love."

How true such a statement is! We can't change the world, but we can make a difference. All those little acts of kindness will grow into larger and lovelier deeds that will carry weight in providing a better place to exist.

Little acts of kindness demonstrate our love for God and God's creation. Consider with me for a moment the many little things that a person can accomplish that will make a difference. We can paint a house, pick up litter on the street, prepare a meal for someone who's hungry, plan a time of fellowship with an elderly person, pat someone on the back who has been downhearted, put a smile on someone's face by a pleasant word, plant a seed of comfort with a hug, pause a moment to listen to a hurting heart or pray a prayer for those struggling with sin, self and stress of life.

Now, if we focus on instant results we will most likely become disappointed and discouraged. Yet, it is usually the little things that bring true satisfaction and tend to establish great works.

Just as Zerubbabel, an unknown, rebuilt the city of Jerusalem; so may each of us perform the simple privileges that arise before us for His glory and honor.

Talk With God:

"Isn't it wonderful, Lord, how many little things can be done that most of the time we never think of until the opportunity presents itself? Therefore, Lord, I desire that you develop within me the ability to discern the little things of life that will demonstrate how big of a God I serve. Amen."

May – Day 31

Text: I Corinthians 4:2 KJV

"Moreover it is required in stewards, that a man be found faithful."

Thought: "Fundamental Requirements!"

As we conclude the month of May and get ready to move into the month of June, let us consider certain fundamental requirements that mothers and fathers must provide according to God's Word.

One requirement is to protect our children from dangers and damage they encounter or could experience in life. As parents we are to protect them from personal rebellion peer pressure and problems they may encounter which may hinder their mental, moral and material state of being.

A second requirement is to provide for their needs and at times their notions. Stomachs (food), shelter and schooling head the list.

A third requirement is personal identity. It is the job of parents to explain and encourage personal identity – the rights, relationships and responsibilities of the child;

What a job assigned to parents! But did you know that God has the same responsibilities toward us as His children. He desires, delights and is determined to share with us and school us in the revelation of His willing to protect, provide and develop personal identity.

God has His marvelous grace, His majestic Word and His miraculous mercy in example and expression for us to learn from, lean on and live in.

Just as God is faithful, let us be found faithful in accomplishing our assignment. Just as God is worthy of trust, let us be trustworthy.

Talk With God:

"Lord, I do trust you to do what your Word declares of you. I want to be filled with your love, your law and your light; that I may be able to experience and exemplify to my family and friends your grace, your glory and your gladness. Amen."

Step 6 – June
"Begotten Of God"

The month of June holds two very important events, one occurs on a particular day and the other may occur any day of the month. The first event is the celebration of Father's Day on the third Sunday of the month. The other event is a Marriage Ceremony, for the month of June is known for being the bridal month of the year. Both of these events usually focus on the father of the home.

Father's Day is a day of honor for all dads. It is the duty of every dad to make stable provisions for the growth and development of the children in a home. It usually is the delight of each day to give his daughter away (as a bride) to another (the groom) to care for her. The father must not take his responsibility lightly but fulfill it with respect and rejoicing.

The Heavenly Father has given His Son, Jesus Christ, to take the church as His bride. The begotten of God assumes full responsibility for establishing a relationship and erecting a residence for the bride. Jesus Christ does not take that responsibility lightly but with sincerity and strict devotion, He carried out His duty on the course of earthly life, the crucifixion, and the continued daily care of humanity and the coming reign of His Kingdom.

It is up to each of us daily to dedicate our being to His cause and develop our being to fulfilling that purpose in life.

June – Day 1

Text: Genesis 1:2-3 KJV

"And the Spirit of God moved upon the face of the waters. And God said, Let there be…"

Thought: "A Shout of Permission for a Power Display"

I have found myself saying a lot of times during prayer: "O Lord, let me be used of you; let me feel your presence; let me know your purpose; let me see your power." But then, today, I was reading and came across a quote by author Harold Hill that stirred my soul and brought insight to my words and phrases used in my prayers. He said, "**Let** is a word of tremendous faith with volumes of meaning poured into it. It assumes the total love and good will of the Father. It assumes that heaven is crammed with good gifts that the Father desires to give His children."

In the beginning, God made the declaration, "Let there be…" before each creative act. It was a deliberate yet dedicated act.

It is a deliberate act of faith when we speak to God and say, "let me be totally consecrated Lord to thee;" or "let your will be done;" or "let your Word be manifested in this work."

When we whisper with love during our communion with the Heavenly Father, we are surrendering our life as a vessel to be filled and fortified with His person, His principles and His Promises. We are giving God permission to touch us, transform us and teach us His way of life.

God doesn't need permission to do anything except in building a relationship with humanity. For he created man with a free will to accept or alienate. Therefore, when man says, "Let" to God, he is inviting God's presences, power and promises to become a living reality in his life.

Talk With God:

"Lord, it is my prayer that every step of the way I make myself available to you and 'let – allow' you to fill me, flow through me and forever praise you. It is my desire to be a vessel meet for the Master's use. Amen."

June – Day 2

Text: I Timothy 6:17 Amplified Bible

"…set their hopes on…God, Who richly and ceaselessly provides us with everything for [our] enjoyment."

Thought: "Is Life Too Busy For Enjoyment?"

Does your life seem like an endless cycle of activities? Does each day seem to be a dread to face because of the multitude of things that must be done, whether at home or work? Do you ever wonder if the spin of life will ever come to a halt allowing you some rest and relaxation?

I am sure if you are like every other person, you are caught up in the cycle of life – do this, go here, be there, get this, don't forget that.

While it is true, life is a continual cycle of events and experiences. God did not create us to fall apart and wear out prior to having an enjoyable and enriching experience in life itself.

But we must remember two very important things: God is our Wonderful Creator and He is our Wise Counselor. ONLY as we accept Him as our spiritual Creator and acknowledge Him as our success Counselor, will we find the time, true peace, thrill and triumph of life?

The time that you seem to be flying in the wind, enjoy the experience and do the best you can to stay on course; then when you land momentarily, apply the spiritual oxygen of renewal and refreshment from knowing God loves you and lives within you. He will renew your strength and grant you readiness for the next run.

In our text, Paul challenges the rich not to be proud and pious in their possessions, but realize that God has provided everything for our delight. God will direct our steps in the areas of life that is beneficial and a blessing of joy.

Talk With God:

"O Lord, I do feel at times I am caught up in a whirlwind and have become so weary of life. But I look to you for guidance and Godly counsel. I know you care and that you have given us life to be productive in our task, to be people of relationships and to be prepared for tomorrow. Keep me busy, but let brotherly love and bubbles of joy fill my life. Amen."

June – Day 3

Text: I Corinthians 3:9 KJV

"For we are labours together with God"

Thought: "If We All Pull Together, How Happy We'll be"

I'm reminded of a story about a father and his son who together carried a heavy weight. One was carrying a heavy basket, when the other asked to assist him. "Well, how is that possible when the handle is so short on the basket?" the other wanted to know. The one asking to help suggested, "Let us cut a stick longer that the one we have and put it through the handle and then we each can carry an end of the stick balancing the basket in the middle."

So they cut the stick and did accordingly as discussed. The one carrying the basket to begin with took the stick first, then the other picked up the other end, and together they proceeded to their destination.

Friend, sometimes we attempt to struggle alone, trying our best to balance the load. However, we grow weary, worn and whipped. We need the help of another to aid us in carrying the heavy burdens of our life. And not just anyone will know how to help. But Jesus is always a kind Friend who is keenly aware of our situations and knowledgeable of the right solutions for the situation. He knows how to make our burdens light. He became human to personally acquaint Himself with our circumstances, pay the supreme price and prepare Himself to be an eternal intercessor for us.

We must also keep in mind that God has placed many in the field of life who labor for the same harvest that we do. Therefore, we must learn to trust God to show us those whom we can lean on in times of need – those of whom we can trust to pray for us, prompt us to stay true, pick up part of the load and help us carry it, or simply pour a rich blessing of reality into our cup of life. Then in turn we can do the same unto them. Together we make it happen and become happy doing it.

Talk With God:

"Lord, I believe you will lead us personally and at times point us in the direction of others. I am convinced that I can assist others in walking through this life and I must be confident that others will assist me. Thank you for this revelation. Amen."

June – Day 4

Text: I John 5:4 NIV

"For everyone born of God overcomes the world. This is the victory that has overcome the world, even our faith."

Thought: "You And God Are A Majority!"

I recall reading a story of a young lad and his father walking into the harvested corn field with the intent of clearing the field of the standing stalks stripped of the ears of corn and plowing them under as they cultivated the soil of the field. As they walked toward the tractor with the disk already attached and ready to prepare the field for another crop, the small lad paused and pulled at a tall dry cornstalk. He was having trouble pulling it up. However, his dad turned to see what he was doing and saw the predicament the boy was in. He walked over and wrapped his arms around him and placed his hands on the stalk and together they pulled the old cornstalk up from the ground. The young boy jumped with joy and shouted, "The whole world was pulling against us dad, but we beat it."

Friends, we face a lot of situations where we find it almost impossible to conquer, contain or correct. However, we must realize there is a Heavenly Father who is ever present to make the impossible possible. He has the size, the strength and the willingness to come to our rescue.

A believer and God make a majority. When we are at rest in the Lord and rely on His ability, we are able to accomplish any task and achieve any goal.

Therefore, as I walk this day, I desire you to accompany me and help accomplish within me the purpose of your will for my life.

Talk With God:

"Thank you Lord, for including me in your plans and purpose of life. Thank you for allowing me to walk and work with you. Thank you for giving me hope and helping me accomplish the task assigned me in life. Lead me this day. Amen!"

June – Day 5

Text: Psalm 91:11 NKJV

"For He shall give His angels charge over you, to keep you in all your ways."

Thought: "Control!"

You can't control the length of your life – but you can control its width and depth. You can't control the contour of your face – but you can control its expression. You can't control the weather – but you can control the atmosphere of your mind.

So, why worry about things you can't control when you can keep yourself busy controlling the things that depend on you.

God will give you the strength to control your life: its experiences, its expressions and its expectations.

Let's get busy in the cooperative effort of controlling that which is depending on our faithfulness and fruitfulness.

The Heavenly Father knows our weakness, our wants and our willingness. He will honor our capabilities, our commitments and our consecrations to accomplish His purpose in our life. He is able to grant purity, peace and purpose to all we are and all we do in life. Therefore, let us commit to doing what we can control and not worry about what we can't control –that is His job.

God is in control and give clear instructions to His heavenly host to protect, provide and perform His will in the life of mankind.

Talk With God:

"Control is one area in life that every human needs assistance. Our walk, our words, our wandering thoughts and our will becomes influenced and infected by the atmosphere and actions of a sinful world. Therefore, O Lord, create within me a clean heart and a clear conscience and give me the help and hope to learn from and lean on you. This is my sincere prayer. Amen!"

June – Day 6

Text: Exodus 13:18 KJV

"So God led the people about, through the way of the wilderness of the Red sea: and the children of Israel went up harnessed out of the land of Egypt."

Thought: "The Power Of Being Harnessed!"

It has been said, "No horse gets anywhere till he is harnessed. No stream ever drives anything until it is confined. No Niagara is ever turned into light and power until it is tunneled. No life ever grows great until it is directed, dedicated and disciplined."

And how true those statements have been proven. A life must be brought into focus with reality – sin, suffering and sorrow exist. A life must be firmly grounded to principles that will accomplish the mission of life – purified from sin, made partners with Christ and promised a future. A life must be disciplined daily in respect, responsibilities and relationships.

Yes, in order to truly grow great and graciously, we must be led by Christ, learn to yield to the lessons of His Word and live according to the rules of righteousness.

In our text, God gave specific instructions to Moses regarding the deliverance of the Hebrew people from Egypt. God marshaled them, marched them and managed them in a way that was beneficial for a consecrated and complete victory over Pharaoh and the Egyptians. This term "harnessed" did not mean that they were bound. They were being delivered from bondage.

He will do the same for us today. We must heed His command to obey His Work, His will and His way of travel in this earthly environment if we are going to succeed in the victory of life. Our daily routine must make time for real communion with God – His Word, His Way and His Will.

Talk With God:

"Lord, I know sometimes, my thoughts run wild – thinking thoughts that will condemn me and need correcting. Lord, I know sometimes, my trail in life runs crooked and is allowed to grow up in thorns and thistles. But, O Lord, be merciful to me and correct my thinking. Allow me to be mindful of you and your love for me. Amen!"

June – Day 7

Text: I John 1:4-5 NIV

"We write this to make our joy complete. This is the message we have heard from him and declare to you: God is light; in him there is no darkness at all."

Thought: "The 24/7 Light of God"

The story is told of a young child who saw a firefly making a path of light as it flew. He inquired of his dad how the firefly was able to glow. His dad caught one and showing it to his son explained, "See, he carries the light in his tail – just like backup lights on an automobile. And then the son exclaimed, "I wish I had a light wherever I went."

Did you know that the Heavenly Father has given to each person who desires a light, a light that will expose who he is, where he is, and where he is going?

Jesus Christ is the light of the world and He desires to be a light unto you, before you and within you.

In the midnight hour of crises, in the mid-day confrontation of dark storm clouds, and in the moments of triumph, God is the light of glory and grace. His light will make all darkness flee and cause delight to prevail.

Our text written by John declares that the light of God is ever available, never to be extinguished. In this light, fear is evicted and joy is evident.

Talk With God:

"Let me see the beauty of your light shining in little things that I come in contact with this day. Help me to look for the bright moments of life and lift up your Name for providing such enrichment and encouragement during the day. If storm clouds gather, give me your light to eradicate the fear of the enemy, the environment and everyday encounters. Amen!"

June – Day 8

Text: 2 Timothy 2:15 Amplified Bible

"Study and be eager and do your utmost to present yourself ot God approved (tested by trial), a workman who has no cause to be ashamed."

Thought: "A Called Third Strike!"

In the game of baseball, a batter doesn't worry when the umpire signals "strike one." In fact, the batter doesn't become too upset if he swings and misses and the umpire calls "strike two." However, when the umpire yells "strike three," the batter knows he is out and his chance of getting a hit, scoring a run or driving in a run has failed. It could cost the team the game.

Does the situation of your life appear to be ready for a third strike?

Have you swung and missed in your attempt to solve a problem, serve a need, or simply answer a puzzling question?

If so, maybe additional training and toughening will enable us to do a better job. Greater application of the knowledge of the game and available practice will aid us in making contact on the ball.

Let us face it; we will not succeed every time. We are subject to an occasional failure. However, let us never go to bat anticipating a strikeout. No batter is judged by his one mistake or misfortune at the plate, or in the field or on the base path. An athlete is considered good or bad by his overall stats at the end of the year.

We must realize that "the Lord is our strength and in His wisdom we can accomplish the task over the long haul. At the end of the game of life, we will receive the championship ring if we have applied our self to the plan, purpose and preparation.

The writer of our text is challenging Timothy (and all believers) to apply themselves to the principles, the practices and the performances of the plan and purpose of God (found in His Word). He exhorts all to succeed at proving themselves worthy of the walk and the work of God.

Talk With God:

"Lord, don't let me strike out in life. I want to receive your instruction and I want to take the initiative to develop my skills and abilities for your glory. Teach me and train me in your way. Help me this day to prepare and practice living for you. Amen!"

June – Day 9

Text: Matthew 6:8 NIV

"Your (Heavenly) Father knows what you need before you ask Him"

Thought: "Jesus Is A Specialist!"

We live in a day of specialization. This is especially true in the medical profession. There is a specialist for almost every part of the body. Families must depend upon several physicians to meet their medical needs.

Dads are just the opposite. They are a jack-of-all-trades, but a master of none. (Or so is the case with me).

Yet, the Heavenly Father is the master of every situation. You might be able to say, He is the master of all trades. Why shouldn't he be? He is the creator of all things.

And we must accept this reality; He is never limited or lists a change in His abilities. He does not profess that a particular task is harder to accomplish than another yet He does prefer a particular task above another – the salvation of a soul over physical healing, personal intervention, pain removal, problem solving or patching marriages. He is concerned for humanity's every situation but above every thing, He desires and delights in redeeming man.

Jesus never turns anyone away. He is ready to minister to you. We must learn to lean on Him, listen to His advice and live in dedication to His will.

There is no malfunction of the physical, moral dilemma or mental incapacitation, that he can't administer aid too. He is the master of all. He is the Great Physician.

God knows our every need and is available and able to supply your need regardless of what it may be. He is a specialist.

Talk With God:

"Jesus, I am glad to know that you are a specialist in every field. You are acquainted with all my ways and know how to guide me in the path of life, gird me with strength to do your will, and guard me from all harm and hindrances that I may encounter. Amen!"

June – Day 10

Text; Haggai 1:5 Message
"Take a good, hard look at your life. Think it over."

Thought: "Think About It!"

I am a dad that is constantly pulling pranks and practical jokes on my family members and friends. However, if I am so willing to dish it out, I must be willing to take it. Which reminds me of an email I received from my youngest daughter one day? It was a simple yet silly IQ test – you have gotten them before.

Here's a one-question IQ test to help you decide how you should spend the rest of your day… There is a mute who wants to buy a toothbrush. By imitating the action of brushing one's teeth, he successfully expresses himself to the shopkeeper and the purchase is done. Now, if there is a blind man who wishes to buy a pair of sun glasses to hide his eyes, how should he express himself? (Think about it first before finishing this paragraph). He opens his mouth and says I would like to buy a pair of sunglasses. Then the email read: If you got this wrong, please turn off your computer and call it a day. I've got mine shutting down right now. You know you missed it too, so shutdown your computer.

Many of us never stop to think what God is saying to us. He is not a practical joker (although I believe He has a sense of humor for His Word says 'a cheerful heart is good medicine' (Proverbs 17:22 NIV). However, I am referring to the reality of life. God doesn't joke around about the commandments, the choices and the challenges He issues. We must learn to consider our responsibilities and our relationships to the Heavenly Father and to humanity.

God loves us and doesn't want us to linger and lose an opportunity to be the best we can be in life. Therefore, THINK!

As our text declares, we must think – consider – about our walk, our words, our ways. Are they pleasing to God, positive and pure? If not, do something about it.

Talk With God:

"Lord, you have created us with the ability to think; therefore, enable us to consider your will, your word and your way of life. Help us to walk daily according to your plan, your purpose and your prize for us. Amen!"

June – Day 11

Text: Luke 5: 24-25 NKJV

"He said to the man who was paralyzed, I say to you, arise, take up your bed, and go to your house. Immediately he rose up before them, took up what he had been lying on, and departed to his own house, glorifying God."

Thought: "You're Responsible!"

The CEO was scheduled to speak at an important convention, so he asked his assistant to write him a punchy 20-minute speech.

When the CEO returned from the big event, he was furious.

Cornering his assistant, he didn't hold back. "What's the idea of writing me an hour long speech?! Half the audience walked out before I finished."

"I wrote you a 20-minute speech," the assistant replied, baffled. "And I also gave you 2 extra copies you requested."

(Now we know why it took so long to present the speech.)

God has given us inspiration and instructions in His Holy Word. He has made it available in a variety of paraphrases and styles (for clear understanding); yet it is up to you and I to read and react. It is our responsibility to learn the Word and live the Word according to His plan and purpose.

Seek God's Word and Wisdom in order to convey the proper message in simple yet sincere means. When God gives us specific guidelines to follow and to faithfully obey, we must give allegiance to His will and adhere to His word.

It is our responsibility to respond and His righteous will to render.

Talk With God:

Heavenly Father, we are glad to know that you have given us the privilege to be in charge of our life. It is our responsibility to accept your instructions and acknowledge your inspiration for our life. Therefore, give me the courage and the confidence to learn your Word and lean on you for guidance.

June – Day 12

Text: I Peter 5:7 NIV
"Casting all your anxiety on Him because He cares for you."

Thought: "There Is An Avenue Of Hope!"

The story is told of a father who approached a friend concerning a loan for medical purposes. Mr. Evans listened sympathetically to the anxious father. Without several thousand dollars for needed surgery his son would die. "Can you help me?" he asked. "No, I can't", replied Mr. Evans, "but the foundation which I represent can."

Friends, I nor your friends nor your family can rescue and redeem your life from sin and give you eternal life. However, I and maybe a family member or a friend can reassure you in a foundation that can come to your aid. Its founder is Jesus Christ. He is the solid, sure and spiritual foundation that can reach out to you in your need of love, liberty, leadership and life everlasting.

What a delight it is to know that God cares about our every need and has heaven's resources at His disposal for distribution to the hungry, hurting and helpless of this life. He is ready to minister unto you in your dire secular and spiritual condition.

And what is more delightful is the fact that I, as a believer and a beholder of His blessings, have the pleasure and privilege to recommend others to Him. Therefore, as I have been told of Jesus, I will tell others of Him.

Talk With God:

"I am glad that I was told about you, O Lord. I am glad that I talked with you and now testify of your hope that you shared with me. I glad that I can share the truth that is available to all who are hopeless and helpless – that is You care! Amen."

June – Day 13

Text: Matthew 11:15 KJV

"He that hath ears to hear, let him hear."

Thought: "Listen & Receive!"

A story is told of a group of applicants waiting to be interviewed for a job as a wireless operator. The paid little attention to the sound of dots and dashes which began coming over the public address system. Suddenly one of them rushed into the employer's office. Soon he returned smiling. "I've got it!" he exclaimed, "I've got the job." "How did you get ahead of us?" they asked. "You might have been considered if you hadn't been so busy talking that you didn't hear the manager's coded message" he replied. "It said, the man I need must always be on the alert. The first one who interprets this and comes directly into my private office will be hired."

The lesson is clear: too many are not really tuned in to God's channel. Therefore, they fail to hear God's directive. The Bible declares that we have been blessed with a natural hearing device and challenges us to hear and heed the call of God unto our lives. In fact, we are declared his chosen ones when we heard and heed the voice of the Almighty.

It is our choice each day to tune in and truly listen. In doing so, we are able to receive inspiration, instruction and an invitation to greater service for His Kingdom.

Talk With God:

"Lord, I want to awake each day with an ear tuned in to your voice. I desire to prepare for the day, perform the day's activities and feel pleased at the end of the day that I have obeyed your call. Guide me and give me the strength to do your will. Amen!"

June – Day 14

Text: Galatians 6:7-8 NIV

"A man reaps what he sows."

Thought: "Preparing for Reflections in Life!"

The world is a looking glass, and gives back to every man the reflection of his own face. Frown at it, and it in turn will look sourly upon you; laugh at it and with it, you find a jolly and gentle companion.

The relationships we have in life are very important. As we are in our relationships of life, so will be our reflections.

Together, our view of ourself and our value of our relationships with others, will determine the happiness and harmony of our life.

However, if we allow God to enter the picture and help develop our view of self and help develop valid relationship; our life will be more enriched and enjoyable.

This is why it is important for us to look into the mirror of God's Word each morning and make any adjustments (in our conscience, countenance and conduct) necessary for a happy, helpful and harmonious day.

God loves us and lives today to provide us with the essentials elements of a grand and glorious day. Determine in your will and demonstrate in your way that you desire to please God and walk in partnership with your family, friends and fellow-workers.

Talk With God:

"Today, Lord I have risen to ride the waves of life like a surfboard. I will ride the crest professionally and if I get wiped out, I will personally try again. I know you will prepare me for what may come my way. Amen!"

June – Day 15

Text: Ecclesiastes 3:1 KJV

"To every thing there is a season, and a time to every purpose under the heavens."

Thought: "God is Good!"

This date holds mixed emotions for me. In 2002, it was a day of destruction, deliverance and delight all in one. First, it was the day after a tornado had hit our town. The roof of the church was damaged, a tree lay across one of the church vans, and many homes were destroyed or damaged across our town. However, it was a day of deliverance, for only one person was seriously injured and no deaths were reported. When the storm hit, almost a hundred children were inside the church (we were in the midst of our annual Vacation Bible School). They were scared but were safely cuddled in a place of protection and in the palm of God's hand. Thirdly, our oldest daughter, who was pregnant with her second child, was trapped in her trailer surrounded by fallen trees. We got her out with no harm, but the emotional crises caused her to go into labor and we rejoiced in the midst of all the devastation the birth of our second grandchild, Brandon Heath.

Folks, we never know what a day holds, but we can know who holds the day. In the midst of any day, we may encounter multiple experiences that will produce a variety of responses and reactions. This is why we need a Friend like Jesus. He is the Master of wind, waves, and ways of life. He knows how to give protection, provide peace and carry us progressively forward, regardless of the circumstances of the day.

Therefore, today, start your day with an inventory of who walks with you, what disposition do you have and what is your goal of the day.

God has declared through His writers of the Scriptures that God does not allow anything to happen that will not prove to be for good; for He is the giver of good.

Talk With God:

"Lord, I know I have never walked through this day before; but I know that you are by my side. I thank you for that confidence. Grant me the courage to stand with you and stand for you in spite of the conditions that may develop throughout this day. Amen!"

June – Day 16

Text: Psalms 36:9 KJV

"For with thee is the fountain of life: in thy light shall we see light."

Thought: 'The Fountain Of Living Waters!"

A story is told of four men in a mighty auditorium. Each man stood in a corner of this huge building. These men desired to come together, but neither would make the first move. In the center of the vast room was a beautiful fountain, spouting forth a stream of water ten foot high into the air. Finally someone proposed that they all meet at the fountain in the middle of the auditorium. One by one, they moved toward the fountain. As they came closer to the fountain, the nearer they came to each other. At last they reached their destination and clasped hands around the sparkling waters of the fountain.

Jesus Christ is the great fountain of life, liberty and love. He was at the center of attention on Golgotha and was lifted up high on Calvary's tree. He desires to draw each of us together for a life of hope, happiness and harmony.

Regardless of our co-existing in a particular setting – home, business, school, shopping and church; God desires that we come together in the realization that we need each other. And this can occur only as we visit the fountain of living waters – Jesus Christ.

Talk With God:

"Lord, give us a thirst to co-exist and comply with each others. Let us drink from the fountain of life and delight in our fellowship with one another. Amen!"

June – Day 17

Text: II Corinthians 12:10 Amplified Bible

"So for the sake of Christ, I am well pleased and take pleasure in infirmities, insults, hardships, persecutions, perplexities and distresses; for when I am weak (in human strength), then am I [truly[strong – able, powerful in divine strength."

Thought: "In Our Weakness, We Know His Strength!"

Tears streamed down his face as Billy struggled to lift the leg that pinned his dog, Towner, motionless form against the earth. "I can't lift it," he sobbed. Suddenly, the load felt light as his father's hands reached down and lifted with him.

"Daddy, "he said excitingly, as he felt the puppy's warm tongue licking his cheek, "I didn't know you were so strong until I found out I couldn't do it by myself."

Friends, do you so vainly try to accomplish successful living alone – by yourself. You will never be able to do it. So, don't try.

God stands near by to extend His hand of assistance. He is ready to delight you with His demonstration of unbelievable strength. It is only when we acknowledge our weakness can He display His strength.

Regardless of the circumstances you faced yesterday or that you may face in your path today; God waits near by and is willing to respond with His omnipotent (all-powerful) influence and impact.

What a declaration by the Apostle Paul in our scripture text today,. Yes, we may have to endure many things, but endure we shall because of the strength and stability of God's presence and power.

Talk With God:

"Today, O Lord, I will put my trust in you and will walk faithfully knowing I have a friend that will come to my rescue if anything befall me that I can not handle. Amen!"

June – Day 18

Text: Romans 6:16 KJV

"Know ye not, that to whom ye yield yourselves servants to obey, ye obey; whether of sin unto death, or of obedience unto righteousness."

Thought: "Who Leads Our Life?"

Two bowling teams chartered a double-decker bus for a weekend tournament in Atlantic City. On their first ride, the Brown team rode inside the bus and the Blue team rode outside on the upper deck. The Brown team members were loudly whooping it up when their team captain realized it was awfully quiet upstairs. She decided to go up and investigate. When the Brown team captain stepped out on the upper deck, she found all the members of the Blue team clutching their seats in sheer terror. "What is going on up here?" she asked. "We're having a great time downstairs!"

To which the Blue team captain replied, "Yeah, but you've got a driver."

Dumb, I know, but who leads your life?

Let me make a simple but sincere declaration about you. You are important! Yes sir! Yes Madam! You are important because you are capable of making decisions that will govern your life. Others may give input but you make the decision.

To be successful in business, to make a sweet and happy marriage, to develop a super personality or just have a standup day depends on you. You hold the key.

However, the greatest decision of which success or surrender pivots is the choice of leadership. The Bible declares that we are lead by a supernatural God or self.

Jesus Christ is the One which guarantees success. Self is frail and has a track record of failure. With Christ at the helm we can ride out every storm and rest in the times of smooth sailing.

Whether you are successful or not depend primarily on your spiritual decisions. In whom do you trust? Self is important because we must make the choice. We must decide if it is more valuable to us to "do it our way" or to "trust in a God who cares and is in control."

Our choice results in death or delight.

Talk With God:

"What a delight to walk hand and hand with the almighty God. I am convinced that I will be successful and safe with you by my side. Amen."

June – Day 19

Text: Romans 6:1 KJV

"Shall we continue in sin, that grace may abound?"

Thought: "Consequences With Come!"

The story is told of Ralph, a growing boy, whose main temptation was playing with fire. It was such fun for him to watch paper and wood go up in flames. Many times his father had told him, "Ralph, I don't want to ever see you playing with fire again. You could be severely burned or even killed." But Ralph continued sneaking around alleys and playing in burning trash barrels. His father's warnings went unheeded. Finally one evening when Ralph, his brother and his cousin were playing with fire, Ralph's dad caught them in their mischief. The boys had to suffer the consequences of their actions. They were punished.

In our world today it may seem easy to hide our actions, thinking no one will find out what we may have said or done. But sooner or later our deeds will catch up with us. And usually it comes at the most inopportune moment – when we least expect it or when we are in the presence of someone we hoped would never learn of it.

Each day let us ask God to forgive us the errors of our way – the sins of commission (what we have done wrong) and the sins of omission (what we fail to do right). Let us approach His throne and seek His grace and guidance to help us stay close to Him.

The Apostle Paul declared to the Romans that the desire to sin should not continue to exist in our lives just because we have a loving Heavenly Father who is full of grace.

Talk With God:

"Lord, today, I need a fresh touch of your cleansing presence and claiming power. I want to overcome my sin and give occasion to fulfilling my duty to you. Share with me your love and show me your way. Amen!

June – Day 20

Text: John 14:6 NIV

"Jesus answered (Thomas), "I am the way and the truth and the life."

Thought: "Talk With The Master Of Life!"

If we wish to know a particular subject, we seek someone who is an expert in that field; whether by an article on the internet, a book in the library or a conversation with an individual.

If we wish to know something about bridges, we go to a construction engineer. If it be medicine; we go to a physician, a pharmacist or a chemist at a pharmaceutical company. If it is law; we speak to or search out information from an attorney or a judge. If it is agriculture; we seek a common or commercial farmer, or a member of the farmer's co-op.

Why not follow the same rule in the investigation of how to live a good and gracious life? Jesus is the author and authority on faith and faithfulness; therefore, as we search His experiences, His expertise and His expositions on life; we will find the knowledge, kindness and keeping power to enjoy life.

Jesus is the creator of life, the caretaker of life and the controller of life. You can find essential information regarding His plan, His program and His purpose of life by a personal chat with Him or by checking out His Words or reviewing His works. You can enter into His worship, walk with His followers or willingly meditate on His truths; and in doing so learn that He knows what is best for everyone who desires to be enriched by life and enjoy life.

Talk With God:

"You are the Master designer of life O Lord. You are the Master developer of life. You are the Master on which we can depend on in life. I will look to you for knowledge each day and walk in keen awareness of your ever abiding presence. Amen!"

June – Day 21

Text: Revelation 3:20 KJV

"Behold, I stand at the door, and knock: if any man hear my voice, and open the door, I will come in to him, and will sup with him, and he with me>"

Thought: "You Hold The Key!"

It has been said, "If you kicked the one responsible for most of your troubles, you wouldn't be able to sit down for six weeks."

If this statement is true, and I feel that it is; then it is saying that each of us holds the key to a better life.

Each of us has many keys of which we use to open doors of benefits and blessings in life. I know I have several keys myself. I have a key that allows me to step into our home, a key to start the engine of our vehicle, a key to a storage building, a key to the switch of our riding lawn mower, a key to the sliding glass doors of the deck, and a key to the security office where I work.

However, in reference to life and the rich experience we can enjoy there is only one key. When man turns to a greater source of wisdom, power and strength than himself, he begins using the key to unlock a better life. And no greater source exists than the ever abiding presence of Jesus Christ.

When He is invited to abide with us, we will abound with resources capable of handling any situation we encounter. He will enrich us, encourage us and enable us to become a life overflowing with His love.

Talk With God:

"Lord, I am glad that you have given each of us a key to better living. It is used when we seek you in prayer, praise and practical application of your Word. I desire that you remind me of my potential, power and pleasure in unlocking the spiritual instruction, inspiration and influence available to me. Amen!"

June – Day 22

Text: II Timothy 1:12 KJV

"For I know whom I have believed, and am persuaded that he is able to keep that which I have committed unto him against that day."

Thought: "Strengthen and Secure!"

The test of life is to make us, not break us. Trouble may demolish a business, but develop his character. For the blow at the physical man may be the greatest blessing to the internal purified man.

For in the midst of storms and stress, we seek calmness. And the greatest calm comes in a peace of mind, positive assurance, and the personal knowledge of knowing someone cares and is with us. That someone can only be Jesus Christ, the grand Prince of Peace, that glorious Blessed Assurance and the great I Am!

Are you battling against conditions, circumstances and confrontations alone? You don't have to. There is a courageous, comforting, confident companion and champion seated on the throne in heaven. He rules, He reigns and He is ready to respond to us.

As we allow Him to work on us and in us, we become an instrument of light, love and laughter. We are able to be an overcomer and an opportunist for Jesus.

However, as Paul said to Timothy, we must commit our total being unto Christ. He takes us and shapes us into a powerhouse that can endure the trial of life and express the truth in the triumphs of life.

Talk With God:

"Thank you Lord for loving me enough to engraft your Spirit within me making me what you would have me to be. Teach me, train me and trust me to step out on faith and strife in faithfulness. Amen."

June – Day 23

Text: John 15:5-6 KJV

"I am the vine, ye are the branches: He that abideth in me, and I in him, the same bringeth forth much fruit: for without me ye can do nothing. If a man abides not in me, he is cast forth as a branch, and is withered; and men gather them, and cast them into ht fire, and they are burned."

Thought: "A Dependable Resource!"

Have you ever thought how difficult it would be to operate your vehicle without a battery? What about trying to operate one of your home appliances without electricity? Or trying to listen to the radio or watch television without a station to tune in to.

So many items in our everyday life would be useless without dependable resources to make them worthwhile.

Your life may be wasting away, incapable of providing enrichment, enjoyment or enablement – if you don't have Jesus Christ. You see, He is the source of our potential, pleasure and purpose.

The Bible says, "Abide in me and I in you, and ye shall bear forth much fruit." That means with Jesus your life produces a virtuous, valid and victorious life. You are able to understand and be undergirded and useful for the glory of God.

Christ is a dependable and daily resource of power and peace to energize our being. As we face difficulties, He is our wonder-working power. As we face decisions, He is our all sufficient knowledge. As we face detours and delays, He is our peace and personal guide. He is our dependable resource and daily reassurances.

What a friend we have in Jesus!

Talk With God:

"Lord, I am grateful for your dependable devotion to each of your children. Thank you for caring. Show me your way each day and help me to share with someone else the way. Amen!"

June – Day 24

Text:　　John 15:4 KJV

"Abide in me, and I in you, as the branch cannot bear fruit of itself, except it abide in the vine; no more can ye except ye abide in me."

Thought:　　"Let the Lord Grow in Your Life!"

Have you ever seen a cucumber inside a bottle with a small neck? Strange as it may sound, I have and it puzzled me at first. I wondered how in the world a full size cucumber could get in there. The bottle was not cut, then glued back together either. I soon learned that a small cucumber still on the vine was pushed into the bottle and allowed to grow inside the bottle.

Some people have harmful habits, and in all probability the habits grew in them while they were young or in the early stages of trying something just for the sake of doing it.

Just as surely as a little boy grows into adulthood; so does a wrong habit or a little sin grow when tolerated? Like small stones, they build up until a high, strong wall of separation exists between God and themselves.

However, that wall can be broken by an honest confession and a confident faith in God.

It is puzzling to me how God can forgive us of wrong doing, free us of the binding habits of sin and fortify us in His strong and stable love. But He can, for I once was blind but now I see. I once was lost, but now I am found. I once was bound, but now I am free. And the more I allow God to grow in me, the greater His presence will be in my life.

Each day I want others to see the growth of God in my life. I want others to wonder how is it possible, then inquire and find out how marvelous the work of the Lord is.

Talk With Him:

"Lord, I want you to empty my life of habits and hurts that may have accumulated over the years. I want you to fill me with your presence and allow your Spirit to grow in my life. I want to be an amazing example of the abiding presence of God. Amen!"

June – Day 25

Text: Matthew 7:7 KJV

"Ask, and it shall be given you; seek, and ye shall find; knock, and it shall be opened unto you."

Thought: "He Is Our Power Booster!"

I read a story the other day that I liked very much. It told of a little boy whose father found him trying to lift a heavy stone. The youngster pushed, and pulled, yet had a problem trying to get the boulder to move. Then as he was just about to give up, his dad said, "son, are you using all your strength?" "Sure am," he answered. "No, you aren't," the father responded. "I've been standing here all the time and you haven't asked me for help."

This reminds me of the attitude of man. We so often try to do things without availing ourselves of God's resources. Now, I understand that God wants us to exert our energy, enthusiasm and enlightment to achieve many of our goals and accomplish many of our purposes. However, once we have expended our own energies or realize from the beginning we can not tackle the situation without extraordinary assistance; we must call 911 in heaven's directory. No task is insurmountable, no temptation irresistible or any trouble inescapable with the Lord aiding us.

We should never toss in the towel, throw our hands up in despair or tell God "why me?"
We are not doing everything possible unless we are drawing upon the pure potential of His prevailing power.

So, as another day arrives, do your best then give Him the rest? Call on the Lord for additional assistance, advice and assurances. You have that privilege.

Talk With God:

"I have found out that I can not do certain things that must be done in living the life for the glory of God. I have learned that your grace, goodness, gladness and great strength has provided the additional power I need to live victorious. Thank you for your fresh and free fortification in dealing with sin and situations of life. Amen!"

June – Day 26

Text: Luke 12:20-21 KJV

"But God said unto him, thou fool, this night, thy soul shall be required of thee: then whose shall those things be, which thou hast provided? So is he that layeth up treasure for himself, and is not rich toward God."

Thought: "Don't be a Fool, Have Faith!"

A story is told of a rich man as he lay on his death bed. His little girl could not understand why her strong father seemed so helpless now. She asked, "Daddy, are you going away?" "Yes, honey," he replied, "I'm going away, and I'm afraid you will never see me again." The little girl was quiet for awhile, and finally she asked one more question. "Daddy, have you got a nice house to go to?" The wealthy dad who had popularity, possessions and plenty of money in this life considered her question and began to cry, "What a fool I've been," he exclaimed, "I have a great business here on earth, I have acquired a bundle of wealth, I have lived in one of the biggest and most beautiful mansions you could build; but I will be a pauper in the next life!"

Our life on this earth is very short when it is compared to the endless ages of eternity. Yet many spend all of their hours, their health and their hopes for this life with no thought for the next.

So, I ask, what on earth are you doing, for heaven's sake?

Today is a golden opportunity for us to examine our lives and evaluate our devotion in life. Are we preparing for the end of the earthly journey or simply enjoying the earthly journey without consideration of the eternal destination?

Talk With God:

"Lord, I want to enjoy this life but not at the expense of missing the blessings of the life to come. Therefore, love me, lead me and let me honor you with my whole heart, head and hands – help me to consecrate myself to you, keep constant thought of you and have a compassionate and charitable life style. Amen!"

June – Day 27

Text: I Peter 5:6 KJV

"Humble yourselves therefore under the mighty hand of God, that he may exalt you in due time."

Thought: "Submissive Will Bring A Salute!"

"Don't let him treat you like that?" "What are you, his servant?" "Show him who the boss is?" These and similar statements exemplify the secular idea of manhood. It seems to be one of self-assertion – being able to impose one's will on another.

This is the disposition of our modern society. It is a Burger King mentality, "Have it your way." (I am not criticizing the slogan of the hamburger enterprise -- Burger King is home of the Whopper and I like the Whopper with an order of those small onion rings and a milk shake.) However, everyone seems to assert their "personal rights" without giving consideration to the rights of others.

Unnecessarily giving deference to others is often viewed as weakness or at best a lack of self-confidence.

However, the spiritual idea of manhood possesses the quality of Godly character of surrender and submission. Being willing to yield in order to gain is a noble jester. It is not taking the position of inferiority but possessing gentleness for cooperation, commitment and comradeship.

Do we possess an attitude of humility? Christ did and desires that we do likewise.

As the Scripture text shares, when we are humble, God promises that there will come a time to be exalted, whether in this life or the life to come.

Talk With God:

"Today Lord, I want to walk in your spirit of humility and express happiness and hope to all I come in contact with. Regardless of whom I encounter or what I experience, I want to exemplify you. In your Name I pray. Amen!"

June – Day 28

Text: Amos 3:3 Amplified Bible

"Do two walk together, except they make an appointment and have agreed?"

Thought: "Working Together!"

I wish to refer to a comical thought I read the other day. It told of a little boy asking his father for assistance in repairing his broken wagon. When the job was done, the boy looked up and said, "Daddy, when I try to do things by myself, they go wrong; but when you and I work together they turn out just fine."

It was cute, yet very meaningful.

And it is that way in real life. If we try personally to repair our failures and faults it may turn out worse than when we began. However, if we will allow God to help us, "all things work together for those who are called according to His purpose." In being partners with God, life becomes a mighty fine experience.

Why don't we turn to Jesus Christ today and ask His help in fixing our problems, forming our attitudes and focusing on achieving His purpose of life?

He is ready if you are willing!

When we agreed with God's plan for our life, He will work out the details and enable us to fulfill our duty to Him.

Talk With God:

"This is the day that I will determine to work with God and work with others to achieve the purpose you have for my life. Lord, I ask for your favor, your faithfulness and your fortitude to achieve this goal. Amen!"

June – Day 29

Text: Psalms 138:7 KJV

"Though I walk in the midst of trouble, thou will revive me: thou shalt stretch forth thine hand…and thy right hand shall save me."

Thought: "Waste Not Time Nor Talent!"

Wheels spun on the ice as a frustrated motorist tried in vain to drive up the slippery hill. The smell of rubber clung to the cold night air. The goal was unattainable – until the driver allows his vehicle simply drift to a lower spot and tried again. Then with a steady speed the care moved past the troublesome path of ice and on to its destination.

Imagine the energy we waste "spinning our wheels" over problems God desires to solve for us. Many times the best solution to an impasse is to retreat to God's presence and simply let the matter rest. As we release the situation to divine wisdom, we find the peace, the power and the purpose to continue on safely, stable and successfully.

Fretting, fussing and becoming fearful about the situation will not accomplish anything; it will only make it worse. To get over the hump, the hindrance, the hill; we must put our trust in the God. He will provide the grace to endure or the gallantry to escape.

I don't understand some of the problems I encounter nor do I see any benefit from them; however, the experiences of life I am faced with I will accept them believing that there is a God-ordained reason for them. Many I may have caused myself and need to learn from the consequences. Others may just be life itself; in these I must learn to trust in God. Whatever, the case, each of us must accept life and acknowledge the Lord to guide us up the path of life.

Talk With God:

"Lord, I admit that I may encounter situation that I cannot tackle; but I will trust you. You are my song of deliverance and my strength for deliverance. In you I abide, I adore and I ask to lead me through. Amen!"

June – Day 30

Text: Romans 14:6 Amplified Bible

"He who observes the day, observes it in honor of the Lord."

Thought: "Today Will Bring Trials, Troubles & Triumph!"

Well, today is another of those special days. Although every day is a special gift from God, on this date, God blessed us with a special gift – our first grandchild, Johnathon. "Jack," as I call him, has since graduated, has a steady girlfriend, holds a good job and is in college. He is a handsome young man who has a strong and sincere love for God. He has experienced and endured much sorrow in his brief life span: the separation by death of both his brother and his dad; the serious illness of his mother emotionally and physically; and self struggles that encounter most growing children in our society. Yet, he has seen the hand of God at work in his life by granting him peace, protection, provisions and prevailing joy.

Friend, God has made each day for you and I to experience, enjoy and be enriched in and by. Let it be a time that we make every effort to offer praise unto Him our Keeper and our King.

Today may bring trials, troubles and temptations; but as we walk with God, it will bring trust, true fellowship and triumph. We find before each day an opportunity to prepare our self for the day by renewing our relationship with God. We find during each day an open door to obey the voice of God in directing our steps of life. At the close of each day, we find the occasion to praise God for His abiding presence that has given us guidance and grace for the day.

Talk With God:

"Lord, today I will to thank you for the power of your Word that will guide, govern and give me strength for this day. I wish for you to uphold me that I may be used of you to touch a life for eternity. This is my prayer, Amen!"

Step 7 – July
"Battle Scars & Victory"

July is a month of bittersweet memories. We celebrate our national independence; however, it came at a cost of thousands of lives and many more wounded physically and psychologically. But as the little chorus says, "you will never know the victory till after the fight." Battle scars are the negative side of victory.

Not only do we enjoy the liberty of living in a democratic nation because we have fought and won the victory; we live in a country that is "one nation under God." Our motto echoes the reality of spiritual liberty based on the fact "In God we trust."

Thank God that we have forefathers who defended these liberties through the decades. My only hope is that the present and future generations will take a stand and protect the standard of righteousness and a rich heritage of democracy.

The future looks dark and dim in respect to the continued enrichment and enjoyment of our way of life; however, a dedicated body of Christ (the Church) must unite in prayer and personal demonstration of godly living to halt the rising waters of compromise and complacency.

We must be willing to voice our opinions at the polls, in the prayer closet and in our personal walk with God. We must be willing to maintain our liberties and muster together our country for the good of all.

The great Apostle Paul declared, "I have fought a good fight, I keep the faith, I finished the course; henceforth there is a crown of righteousness laid up for me (2 Timothy)

We must be vigilant and stand firm.

July – Day 1

Text: Psalm 66:3, 5 KJV

"Say to God, How awesome are Your works!' Come and see the works of God; He is awesome in His doing toward the sons of men."

Thought: "Our Awesome God!"

The word "awesome" is tossed around a lot these days. When you talk about cars, chicks, cute guys, certain foods, celebrities, changes or current music; someone will say, "That's awesome!"

But if we call stuff on earth awesome and then call God awesome, we diminish how truly awesome He is. Maybe it would be best for us to reserve the word *awesome* for our reference to spiritual things or God Himself.

Trivializing God is no trivial matter. He is far more than a companion who will fit into our "buddy system" or a divine ATM responding to our impulses. Until we are shocked by the awesomeness of God, we will be way too impressed with ourselves and lose the joy of the privilege of belonging to an awesome God.

A look at the Psalms puts it all in perspective. Our text emphasizes the point very well. He is awesome in all His dealings and devotion to humanity.

For what could be more awesome than the love that compelled Jesus to go to the cross for us?

Talk With God:

"O Lord, as we begin this day, we give you the praise that is justly due your Name and we desire to walk in honor of You throughout this day each step of the way. Help us to reserve our awesome consideration for You only and to demonstrate and display our reverence and respect for your Word and your works. Amen!"

July – Day 2

Text: Luke 15: 20 KJV

"And he arose, and came to his father, But when he was a great way off, his father saw him, and had compassion "

Thought: "God is always ahead and will give Directions!"

A man who hated his wife's cat decided to get rid of it. He drove 20 blocks from home and let the cat go. But when he returned home, the cat was sitting in the driveway. The next day the man decided to drop the cat 40 blocks from home. But the exact same thing happened again. The cat was waiting for him. The 3rd day he drove 10 miles away, turned left, went past a bridge, made 2 rights, 3 lefts, crossed some railroad tracks, and made another right before he stopped and scooted the cat out of the car.

Hours later, the man called his wife. "Honey, do you see the cat?" "Yes, why?" "Put that cat on the phone," he said in frustration. "I need directions back home."

A silly little story that has a serious message for us. So many times, we attempt to rid our lives of God's presence. Yes, we do. We possess ill feelings and blame it on something other than our own attitude and inner condition. However, the more we push God away the more He loves us and desires to commune and continue with us.

We may even go out of the way to discourage God from dealing with us; yet in His great and gracious love He stays one step ahead of us and is ever ready when we reach the point of acceptance to direct our lives.

God will never resist our efforts to push aside but will keep coming back to challenge our heart for acceptances.

The prodigal son demanded his goods, departed from home, delighted in doing his own thing, became deserted and downcast, dreamed of making things right and was drawn back home. Back home, he received divine forgiveness, dressed anew and directions for a fresh start.

As we confront our situation in life, God is waiting and willing to assist with directions.

Talk With God:

Lord, I know sometimes I have internal feelings that should make me feel shameful and guilty. And I should acknowledge them and accept your guidance for my life. Forgive me and form within me a clean heart and an upright spirit. I long for your presence to be rich and real. Amen!

July – Day 3

Text: 2 Timothy 4:10 NKJV

"for Demas has forsaken me, having loved this present world"

Thought: "Unwilling To Pay The Price!"

Adam was walking around the Garden of Eden feeling lonely, so God asked, "What is wrong with you?"

Adam said he didn't have anyone to talk to.

God said he would give him a woman for a companion. She would be a good cook. She would always agree with Adam's decisions. She would bear his children. She would not nag and would always admit she was wrong after a disagreement. She would never have a headache and would freely give love and compassion.

"Wow! What would a woman like this cost me?" Adam asked.

God said, "An arm and a leg."

Adam said, "What can I get for a rib?"

A bit off line in accurate scripture interpretation, but an acceptable thought for a great message, "Unwilling to pay the price."

Many have been unwilling to pay the price for the freedom of our democracy. They desire their rights to speak up but deny their opportunity to defend on the battle fields. I salute those who have taken a stand and been a soldier for our great country and kept alive our freedom.

I also salute those who have been willing to surrender their lives to the Savior and paid the price of cutting the strings that kept them attached to the things of this world, contrary to the will of God. We see in our text, that Demas, a co-worker with Paul, was unwilling to pay the price of following the plans Christ had for his life.

Our freedom, both nationally and spiritually is free; but it cost everyone an allegiance.

Talk With God:

Lord, thank you for providing our redemption. However, challenge me to make the choice to maintain that freedom by separating myself from anything that would harm or hinder my relationship with you. Keep our nation free and challenge me to do my part in standing for heavenly righteousness and human rights. Amen!

July – Day 4

Text: Matthew 5:14-16 KJV

"Ye are the light of the world…Let your light so shine before men, that they may see your good works, and glorify your Father which is in heaven."

Thought: "To God Be The Glory!"

I like a story that I read once. It was about an attitude and an action made by a small lad at a Fourth of July picnic.

The annual Fourth of July picnic and fireworks sponsored by a local church was a major highlight of the community. Last year's pyrotechnic show will not be forgotten by all those standing around a young fellow named Donnie, who was sitting high on his father's shoulders. When the last ball of fire streaked across the sky and the audience was cheering, little Donnie kept looking up into the sky and saying, "Thank you, God."

It is one thing to be grateful and gloriously celebrate Independence Day. However, I wonder if our celebration demonstrates an expression of praise to a personal and powerful God Who provided such independence. Do we light up the atmosphere of our life with gratitude and glory to God Who has given us reason to celebrate? Do we light up the lives of those around us with assurance and anticipation of daily communion and celebration?

Let us never forget the prayers and pledges men and women have made during years of country's existence. Let our thoughts, our talk and our task demonstrate an appreciation and an allegiance to God for the privilege and pleasure of enjoying this great nation America.

Talk With God:

"Heavenly Father thank you for the foundation of which our great nation was founded. We celebrate our freedom and we desire to focus our attention and allegiance to you in order to praise you and pierce the hearts of others with a message of hope and happiness. Amen!"

July – Day 5

Text: 1 Peter 5:8-9 NIV

"Be self-controlled and alert. Your enemy the devil prowls around like a roaring lion looking for someone to devour. Resist him, standing firm in the faith"

Thought: "A Breach In The Wall!"

"The 4,000-mile-long Great Wall of China was built to keep out invaders from the north. The first wall was constructed by Shi Huangdi, the first emperor of China, who lived between 259 and 210 B.C. But in AD 1644, the Manchus broke through the Great Wall and overran China. They did this by bribing a general of the Ming dynasty to open the gates.

During the reconstruction of ancient Jerusalem, Nehemiah understood the acute danger posed by those who opposed the rebuilding of the city's ruined walls. So he commanded constant vigilance. Half of the workers were to stand watch while half rebuilt the walls (Nehemiah 4:13-18).

As believers, we must be vigilant that nothing breaches our spiritual defense. We must stand guard in our heart, in our head (what we think) and in what our hands do. We must not allow our secular and spiritual adversaries to scale over, slice through or slid under our defenses (Ephesians, chapter 6 and Galatians, chapter 5).

The apostle John warns us of enemies from three directions: the lust of the flesh, the lust of the eyes and the pride of life (1 John 2:16). These enemies have a way of luring us away from God and His Word and leaving a gap for the enemy to sneak in.

Let us be alert to what entices us today. Let us give our total allegiance to the Lord and His way of life.

We are in a warfare yet our weapons are not physical nor psychological; but "mighty in the pulling down of strong holds" (2 Corinthians 10:4).

As we walk the path of life today in our social setting (job, school, shopping or recreation), let not the enemy catch us off guard by an attitude or an action that would be detrimental to our spiritual well being. Let Him guide us and let Him guard us.

Talk With God:

Lord, I desire to walk and work for you. In doing so, I must learn to watch – guard against the influence and influx of the temptations of the enemy. Support me, strengthen me and secure me in your mercy and magnificent Word. Amen!

July – Day 6

Text: Romans 8:37, 39 KJV

"We are more than conquerors through Him who loved us…(and nothing shall) separate us from the love of God which is in Christ Jesus"

Thought: "Defensive and Determined"

Gettysburg, Pennsylvania was the site of a battle that turned the tide of America's Civil War. One of the focal points of the conflict was a rocky knoll called Little Round Top where Colonel Joshua Lawrence Chamberlain and the men of the 20th Maine Infantry stood their ground. Had the Confederate troops gotten past Chamberlain's men, some historians believe the Union army would have been surrounded – possibly leading to the loss of the war. The "20th Maine" was the last line of defense.

As believers, we are engaged in a vital and very visible war. As we battle the temptations, tricks and tactics of the devil (Ephesians, chapter 6); we are called to wear the armor of God and to be willing stand firm in the conflict.

And like the Gettysburg soldiers, we have a "last line of defense." For us, though, this defense is greater than any hair-brain idea, heavy artillery, and half-tested maneuver. It is greater than any human force.

Paul says in our text, that our ultimate confidence is in the undying love of Christ. It is concrete, continual and completely reliable.

When the enemy seems overwhelming and over confident, we have an unbearable last line of defense. Our faith will not be deflated, our hope will not be dissolved, nor our love defeated. We will "be more than conquerors through Him who loved us."

Talk With God:

"Father, we are but children sometimes. Our faith and hope grows dim, but our love for you is strong and your love for us is sensed. Therefore, today, help us to clearly see that defeat is not on the agenda. Your love for us is strong enough, sweet enough and stable enough to guarantee us the victory. Amen!"

July – Day 7

Text: James 1:22 KJV

"But be ye doers of the word, and not hearers only, deceiving your own selves."

Thought: "Talk It – Walk It!"

Thomas Jefferson once said, "It is our lives, and not in our words, that our religious belief must be read."

Another great saying is: "You may be the only Bible some person may read."

What about this often quoted remark: "Action speaks louder than words?"

Let us mention another phrase that would fit in this message: "A picture is worth a thousand words."

And I am sure you have heard this statement – "If we talk the talk, let us walk the walk."

All five of these remarks deal with our daily walk -- not just our daily words we speak or the divine Word we read. For it is easy to speak words when necessary but fail to live them out in our walk. It is easy to know the Word of Truth yet fail in manifesting it in our steps. To back up our talk and God's thoughts with our walk takes effort.

Let us be consistent in declaring words and demonstrating those words. In doing so, we are able to communicate a message of truth that others will recognize and receive. Our life will be one of faithfulness and fruitfulness.

Talk With God:

"Each step of each day, O Lord, let my speech be seasoned with your Word that I may walk in the appointed and approved way you would have me go. Amen!"

July – Day 8

Text: Galatians 5:1 NIV

"It is for freedom that Christ has set us free. Stand firm then, and do not let yourselves be burdened again by a yoke of slavery."

Thought: "Liberty!"

A young couple went on a cruise for their honeymoon. When they got back, the bride called her mother. "How was the honeymoon?" asked the mom.

"The honeymoon was fine," she replied. "But as soon as we returned to the apartment, he began using horrible language. Things I'd never heard before. Terrible 4-letter words. I want to come home!"

Alarmed, the mother asked, "What 4-letter words?"

"Dust, iron, wash, cook!" the daughter replied.

The honeymoon is not the totality of the marriage –there is work to be done. The same is true with out spiritual and social liberty.

Liberty – a value packed word to most Americans. A word of whose blessing we enjoy yet have paid dearly to possess, and will pay again in the future to maintain. Perhaps that is why we in this country are vulnerable to such expressions as "Do your own thing;" or "I'll do it my way;" or "No strings attached." These expressions seem to offer items and interest and involvement without a price. However, you can rest assured you will pay in the long run.

The real idea of liberty is not freedom from all restraint but a privilege to partake and participate in the quality of life that is uplifting to you and those you come in contact with. Liberty is an enjoyment of a quality of life that has been won by paying the greatest price – our blood.

And the greatest liberty is being set free from sin and the second death; and to be enriched and enjoy the quality of life found in the relationship with Jesus Christ.

Don't just do your own thing today, but accept the real thing and do the right thing – walk in appreciation and allegiance to the One Who made it possible, Jesus Christ.

Talk With God:

"Thank you Lord for a day in which you have made and manifested your glorious liberty to all who will yield to your will and be yoked to your way of life. Help me to live in appreciation to all who made this country free and live in allegiance to you who made this life free. I love you and desire to love others through you. Amen!"

July – Day 9

Text: I Corinthians 15:58 NIV

"Let nothing move you. Always give yourselves fully to the work of the Lord"

Thought: "Conditions Of Victory!"

A man was driving down a road. A woman is driving down the same road from the opposite direction. As they pass each other, the woman leans out the window and yells, "Pig!"

The man immediately leans out his window and yells, "Dummy."

They each continue on their way. When the man rounds the next curve, he crashes into a huge pig in the middle of the road and just misses getting killed.

Remember: If mankind would only listen instead of identifying their own character, things would be different.

Battles may be won or lost depending on how well a soldier guards against the infiltration of the enemy. A few lax moments could mean the difference between victory and defeat.

Which would you rather have – victory or defeat? I don't think I really need to know the answer; for we all desire to win and enjoy the sweet smell of success – leaping into the air, high-fiving, and rejoicing.

However, it is up to YOU - - -

The condition of your physical body, the alertness of your mind, and the devotion of your spirit will determine the outcome. These things kept strong will resist in the influence of external circumstances – worry, weariness, willful neglect or wrongful indulgences.

The battle is not easy but you are promised the victory if you have Jesus Christ on your side. For the Bible says, "the victory is our faith in Christ" (1 John 5:4).

He enables us to resist the enemy, rely on Him and run the course.

Talk With God:

"Lord, I know you have chosen me to be your son, your servant, your soldier; however, I find myself so weak at times. I need you to keep me in remembrance of the need to condition myself for your service and as your soldier. I begin this day with a word from You and a word with you; therefore, enrich my life to live accordingly. Amen!"

July – Day 10

Text: James 1:22 NIV (*italics denotes personal comments*)

"Do not merely listen to the word, and so deceive yourselves. Do what it says (*and in doing so develop character*)."

Thought: "Glorious Destiny!"

A nation's destiny is not in its learning or the amount of information it acquires – it is in its character. The heart of the culture is the culture of the heart. The only way to form character is through a belief of the heart.

If we believe in the things of temporal nature, that of this world; then our destiny will be of temporal, tangible and trial-and-error matter. If we believe in the things of God; then we will develop a character that is holy, honorable, and honest.

What are the things of God – His gracious fruit, His glorious gifts, or His grand promises? As we yield to His instruction and His inspiration, we will develop a wholesome and wonderful character that emulates Him and ensures our destination.

A relationship with God will assure us of a glorious destiny. There is no other way to build character that will stand the test of time and the trial of a lifetime. There is no other condition of heart that will be rewarded as strong, sure and steadfast at the end of the journey

We can read, research and richly build up a knowledge of God's word and God's world; but if we fail to apply the principles of a godly life in developing character, we will not be privileged to pride ourself in the gifts of goodness and godliness.

Talk With God:

"It's me again Lord, I face another day and I desire you to walk with me. I want to have a heart that will praise you, please you and promote peace among those I exist with (and sometimes that is not easy including living with myself). Guide me this day I pray. Amen!"

July – Day 11

Text: Matthew 6:9-13 NIV

"Our Father in heaven, hallowed bye your Name, your kingdom come, your will be done on earth as it is in heaven. Give us today our daily bread. Forgive us our debts, as we also have forgiven our debtors. And lead us not into temptation, but deliver us from the evil one."

Thought: "Foxholes Produces Faulty Faith!"

During a time of war we have often heard the expression, "There are no atheists in foxholes." And that is true. I served in the military during the Vietnam conflict and you look to a higher power when you are confronted by the enemy.

This proves that deep within man's heart is an awareness of God's existence. Sometimes it's camouflaged by shallow reasoning, stubbornness, or a selfish refusal to bow to the Lord's plans and purposes. It may even be covered and concealed, but it is there just the same.

Often it will take a crisis or some imminent danger to remove the mask of infidelity.

How much better it would be to acknowledge the Lord when the sun is shining and all is well than to wait for an emergency. He wants to be your God in every circumstance of life. And He will be if you "believe that He is." Don't let your faith be built on foxhole experiences. Believe that you can petition Him in every crises you face; and that you can also praise Him in each step of life.

To believe in the existence of God is to include Him in your daily plans of life. He will grant you the peace, the power and the provisions for an enriching and enjoyable day.

Turn to Him, tune Him in and trust Him with every situation – the preparation for the day, the performance of the day, and the petitions during the day and the praise at the close of the day. This is what the Lord's Prayer is all about.

Talk With God:

"Lord, I don't need a crisis to make me aware of your awesome existence and your abiding presence. I acknowledge you and ask you to equip me for this day; that I may enjoy it and be enriched by all that happens. Amen!"

July – Day 12

Text: Malachi 3:6 NIV

"I the Lord do not change. So you, O descendants of Jacob, are not destroyed."

Thought: "Guidance In Change!"

I was amazed as I watched the change of the guard at the tomb of the Unknown Soldier at Arlington Cemetery in Washington D.C. It was astonishing to watch an officer of the United States Marine Corp bark out orders to the soldiers at the change of the guards. The officer spoke precisely, personally and with power and authority. Without losing a step, the soldiers change their positions and the new guards take over the lonely vigil.

Life is filled with changes, yet one of the most fearful experiences of life is learning how to deal with those changes. Whether it is life or death, joining or separation, leading or following, all of these can be part of the constant change of daily life. But God, who never changes, can help us to accept the changes in our personal lives.

He is the supreme commander and is sensitive to our every change. He is in control and is capable in giving advice and granting His anointing to comfort us. He is willing to build our courage and boost our confidence. Yet, we must reach out to Him and receive from Him. We need not loose a step in accomplishing the task of life as we obediently and orderly follow His dictates.

He will guide you through this day and will give you the strength to endure any change that may come your way.

God spoke through the prophet Malachi words of encouragement. He declared that He never changes and He would always stand ready to restore and refresh His people as they face change (from a sinful nature or social changes caused by death, division, disease).

Talk With God:

"Heavenly Father, I am grateful that I can depend on you to steady me and strengthen me in the changes that come into my life. Whether it is simple or serious, I lean on you. Amen!"

July – Day 13

Text: 1 Thessalonians 5:15 NIV *(italics denotes personal comment)*

"Make sure that nobody pays back wrong for wrong, but always try to be kind *(and helpful)* to each other."

Thought: "Different Is Good!"

The story is told of Will, who lived in a neighborhood for several months; yet was still considered an outsider by many of the neighbors. He wore clothes that were a bit out-of-date and did not socialize much.

However, one day the house across the street from Will's residence caught fire. A small child was still inside. Many of the neighbors watched the burning house but were afraid to venture inside. But Will dashed across the street, into the house and appeared back outside, blackened by smoke and somewhat singed, with the small child in his arms.

Will none too soon save the child from the fire; for as soon as he appeared on the front lawn with the child, the roof caved in.

After this incident, he didn't become friends with all, but he did become a friend to the family across the street as they rebuilt their home.

Friend, as we live in the neighborhood called the world, let us be a little different due to Christ-like-character and let us not be afraid to be singed by the ridicule and rejection of the world. Let us be willing to rescue the trapped (in sin) children from a burning hell.

We may not make a difference in the lives of everyone, but someone will be grateful down the road and welcome us into their circle of fellowship. Until then, be faithful, be fruitful and focus on living for Jesus.

Talk With God:

"Good morning Lord, I begin a new day that may bring an opportunity for me to share a gracious word, a gentle touch, a gritty deed or just enjoy a grand day. However, whatever may come my way, I will be an example of your love and your life. I love you. Amen!"

July – Day 14

Text: John 1:41 NIV

"The first thing Andrew did was to find his brother Simon and tell him, We have found the Messiah (that is, the Christ). And he brought him to Jesus"

Thought: "A Recommendation Worth Checking Out!"

Friends, think for a moment and make a true evaluation whether or not the following statements apply in your life:

Failure will hurt but not hinder!

Disillusion will create pain but not dishearten!

Sorrow will shake me but not break me!

Hope will set the music ringing and quicken my lagging pace!

Can these four circumstances prevail and still find you moving ahead at a steady pace?

If not maybe your need a friend, someone to counsel, comfort or built your confidence.

I do not favor you checking out the web dating service. I do not request that you drive the streets looking for a companion to soothe and satisfy you. I do not suggest that you let your fingers do the walking through the yellow pages attempting to find legal advice listing. However, I **DO** recommend that you turn to the Word of God and read the promises available to you and realize the true relationship that you need to bring stability and satisfaction to your life.

Jesus is a friend that sticks closer than any family member and shares His love and liberty with you as you fellowship with Him. He is our help, our hope and our happiness.

In our text, we see that many anticipated the appearing of the Messiah and when Andrew received the revelation that Jesus was the One, he desired to recommend Him to his brother. Do you recommend Jesus via your lifestyle or lip service?

Talk With God:

"Lord, I really don't know how I would react to discouraging and devastating news. I know the world is in rough shape and many are experiencing such news. Therefore, I place my trust in you and know you will provide whatever I need whenever I need it. Thank you. Amen!"

July – Day 15

Text: Joshua 1:9 NIV

"Have I not commanded you? Be strong and courageous. Do not be terrified; do not be discouraged, for the Lord your God will be with you wherever you go."

Thought: "Listen to God and Let Him Make A Way!"

There is an old legend of a general who found his troops disheartened. He believed it was owing to the fact that they did not realize how close they were to the other divisions of the same army. A dense growth of small trees and shrubbery blocked their awareness of the close proximity of their neighboring group.

Orders were given to burn the underbrush. It was done and they saw that they were not isolated, as they had supposed. They were part of one great army. The result was their courage revived and they went forward in triumph.

A similar situation may exist in your life. Many times problems, perplexing crises, personal difficulties and pain of fear build up in our lives to such a degree that we can't see any help or hope. We feel isolated and insecure.

Yet, if we will trust in the unseen hand of God; He will "burn the underbrush" and enable us to focus on the presences, the power and the promises of God. With a renewed heart, we are able to move forward and fight the battle reinforced with assurances and allegiances.

God is aware of our every move, He is available to come to our aid and He is able to accomplish what ever needs to be done.

Talk With God:

"Lord, I know I have faced seemly uncertain situations in the past and received the secure undergirding signal from the pages of your Word and from the Person of the Holy Spirit. Therefore, as I move forward, I look to you to make clear my surroundings and confirm my support as I press on. Amen!"

July – Day 16

Text: John 3:16 NIV
"Whosoever believes in Him shall not perish but have everlasting life."

Thought: "A Spiritual Treaty!"

We are told that William Penn stood in the center of a company of Indian chieftains and said, "My friends, we have met on the broad pathway of good faith. We are all one flesh and blood. Being brethren, no advantage shall be taken on either side. Between us there shall be nothing but openness and love."

Jumping to their feet these Indian chiefs replied, "While the rivers run and the sun shines, we shall live in peace with the children of William Penn."

Although no record of this treaty was made on parchment, yet the war whoop of the Indian was not heard again in Pennsylvania for more than seventy years.

It is this bond of faith in God that brings peace within our relationships of life. Not for seventy years, but forever.

Have you accepted the terms of faith and faithfulness that Jesus Christ has made available to all humanity? It will produce a greater peace that any man made lip or legal treaty agreed on.

Consider this day as a day of renewal in your relationship with Jesus. Simply believe in the words and works of Christ. In doing so, you will find that peace will prevail within your soul.

Talk With God:

"Lord, I have made a decision today to renew my commitment to you. I desire to live at peace with my own heart and know your peace. I desire to be at peace with my fellow man. Forgive me of my shortcomings and forge new strength into my relationships with man. Amen!"

July– Day 17

Text   1 Corinthians 15:55 NIV

"Death has been swallowed up in victory. Where, O death, is your victory? Where, O death, is your sting?"

Thought: "Life's Greatest Enemy!"

Four elderly gentlemen were out golfing one day.

"These hills are getting steeper as the years go by," one complained.

"These fairways seem to be getting longer, too," said another.

"The sand traps seem to be bigger than I remember them," said the 3rd senior.

"Hearing enough complaints form his senior buddies, the oldest and the wisest of the foursome piped up: Just be thankful we're still on the right side of the grass!"

Death is man's greatest enemy. It comes to one and all – the wealthy, the wretched, the wandering, and the well-known. It snatches away the early infants and creeps upon the elderly. Death is a separator! Death is sorrow! Death is suffering! Death is something no one desires to talk about or think about. However, it is an inevitable reality. Many have died defending our great country and many will die doing so in the future.

No human alive knows when and where death may come; but we can be prepared for it. We can make plans that will benefit our family on earth and benefit us in eternity.

It is important that we believe in the resurrection and the life that Jesus makes possible for us. It is important that we live a life that will justify our claim of a belief in Christ as Savior. It is important that we live looking for that blessed assurances that Jesus will come again. If we live with these three keys locked in our thinking, we will not fret nor fear the enemy of death.

Talk With God:

"Lord, I am thankful for those who have given their life for our liberty, both the soldier and the Savior! I desire to live in a way that death will be a conquered foe when the end of my time on earth comes. Keep me and guide each day is my prayer. Amen!"

July – Day 18

Text: 2 Chronicles 7:14 NIV

"If my people, who are called by my name, will humble themselves and pray and seek my face and turn from their wicked ways, then will I hear form heaven and will forgive their sin and will heal their land."

Thought: "The Other Side Of the Picture!"

I read a beautiful story recently. It was a story of what it takes to put our country back to together – from a child's point of view.

A father wanted to read a magazine but was being bothered by his little girl. She wanted to know what the United States looked like. Finally, he tore a sheet out of his new magazine on which was printed the map of the country. Tearing it into small pieces, he gave it to her and said, "Go into the other room and see if you can put this together. This will show you our whole country today."

After a few minutes, she returned and handed him the map, correctly fitted and taped together. The father was surprised and asked how she had finished so quickly.

"Oh," she said, "on the other side of the paper is a picture of Jesus. When I got all of Jesus back where He belonged, then our country just came together."

Soooo. . . when we get Jesus back where he belongs – our country will come together!

It is so astonishing that we think the answer to our country's restoration has to be so complicated. When you have tried many avenues in the attempt to correct the problems and fail; why can't we simply look on the other side of the puzzle? If we did, we would find a child like solution – a complete commitment to Jesus Christ.

To seek God's forgiveness, to separate our self from sin and stand in the Word of God will provide the restoration we need.

Talk With God:

Lord, help us to quit being so political correct and learn to lean on you for our daily guidance and grace to success. For it is in you that we have the answer and the avenue to restoration. This is my personal prayer for my heart, my home, my homeland and all humanity. Amen!

July – Day 19

Text: Psalm 31:3 NIV

"Since you are my rock and my fortress, for the sake of your Name lead me and guide me."

Thought: "I Go To The Rock!"

The Rock of Gibraltar towers 1, 396 feet above the Mediterranean Sea. In the shelter of its caves, along the inaccessible sides of the rock, people have found safety during war. Men from all ages have trusted in this rocky stronghold. It is known as the most impregnable and unshakeable fortress in the world.

On many occasions you, as well as I, have felt the need for a stronger power to take up our defense. We long to flee to a rock so strong that nothing can shake or move it. We need a fortress so high and holy that nothing can reach us as we rest and know His assurance of victory.

Well, friend, Christ is that Rock.

He is the place of hiding. He is the place of help. He is the place of hope. Only as we make our habitat in the cleft of the rock will we experience the true shelter of safety.

Not only is He our rock and fortress in time of storm, He is our daily habitat for fellowship and feasting for spiritual renewal.

Talk With God:

"Lord, I am glad to know I have a hiding place in you. You are my fortification and in you I shall fight my battles of life. Therefore, lead me this day in standing firm in the freedom you have granted. Amen!"

July – Day 20

Text: Matthew 7:24 NIV

"Therefore everyone who hears these words of mine and puts them into practice is like a wise man who built his house on the rock."

Thought: "Obedience to Law is Liberty!"

An appropriate inscription over the massive entrance of a courthouse in Cleveland, Tennessee, reads, "Obedience to Law is Liberty."

How true! There is not solid and sure liberty in any other source. Just doing what you please, and following impulse, is not freedom. Obeying a sudden impulse to follow the primrose path usually starts or strengthens some bad habits which forges shackles on our character and fades the true picture of freedom.

A lawless person is never free.

Neither are you if you are disobedient to the laws of God. He says, "do justly, love mercy, walk humbly with God...live soberly, righteously, godly in this present world...love God with all your heart, mind, soul and strength and your neighbor as thyself."

Are you a lawless person but one who seeks freedom? Invite Christ into your life and seek His grace, guidance and gladness. In doing so, you will find the desire and the determination to live in the guidelines of God's holy law.

Obedience to the will and word of God is like a foundation of rock that will withstand the winds and waves of adversity that come to rob us of the liberty and life we enjoy in Christ.

Talk With God:

"Lord, it is me again. I start my daily journey looking to you and leaning on you for your love, liberty and laughter. I want to honor you this day and help someone along the way. Fill me, focus me and flow through me. Amen!"

July – Day 21

Text: Romans 3:23 NKJV

"For all have sinned and fall short of the glory of God."

Thought: "Let Your Aim be a Priority!"

A salesman was driving down a country road when he sees a young kid in front of a barn. On the barn are painted 5 targets with arrows in the bull's-eyes of each target. Screeching to a halt, he runs over to the kid.

"Son," he says, "how did you hit all those bull's eyes?"

"Well, I took each arrow, licked my fingers, and straightened the feathers like this," the boy demonstrated. "Then I aimed with my hand against my cheek, let it go and wherever the arrow landed, I drew a bull's-eye."

Independence is not won by shooting aimlessly, but taking aim at the target first.

The Apostle Paul (in our text) told the Romans that every person has "missed the mark" in attempting to please God and fulfill God's plan for humanity. Each person has taken shots where they pleased and attempted to cover up their wild shooting by using excuse targets.

However, it will not succeed. We must come to grips that God has clearly painted a target for every life to take aim and learn how to achieve a bull's-eye. Yes, we may shoot wildly in attempting to fulfill the goal, but our efforts are now in line.

As the Apostle Paul stated to the church at Philippi, "press toward – shoot at the target." The writer of Hebrews stated, "run the race looking unto Jesus Christ – shoot the arrow looking at the target."

Talk With God:

How foolish man is sometimes O Lord. We live as if we have no goal or aim in life; thus resulting in discontentment and disappointment. Teach us how to direct and where to direct our steps each day in order to successfully walk the path of acceptance and accomplishment that has eternal value. Amen!

July – Day 22

Text: 1 Kings 19:11-12 KJV

"The Lord passed by, and a great and strong wind rent the mountains, and brake in pieces the rocks before the Lord; but the Lord was not in the wind; and after the wind an earthquake; but the Lord was not in the earthquake; And after the earthquake a fire; but the Lord was not in the fire; and after the fire a still small voice."

Thought: "Whisper Me The Truth!"

It has been said, "People will believe anything that you tell them, if you whisper it."

The reasoning is that people feel that you are letting them in on a great secret that only you and they will know. They feel special that you have included them in your great thought.

If this is true, may I whisper to you a secret? Listen closely!

"Did you know that Jesus Christ gave His life for you?" Yes sir! Yes Madam! If there were no one else, Jesus would still have offered His life in order that **YOU** may have everlasting life.

And would you like to know something else?

If you have not begun to live this life Jesus has to offer, you may do so today – this very moment. That's right! This very moment can be the beginning of a new day, a new life for you.

Christ is willing to come into your heart, cleanse you of self and sin, and claim you as His very own. He will forgive you, free you, fortify you and prepare your future.

Neither I nor God will attempt to get your attention with an enormous wind force, nor an earthquake, nor an enlightening ball of fire; but in a small, sober, still voice of truth. The first three power displays by God may have awakened Elijah to a sobering reality that God was real but it was the small still voice that confronted Him with comfort and courage for the day.

Let God comfort and challenge your life to come to grips with the reality of who God is and what God desires to do for and with you.

Talk With God:

"Lord, I am grateful that I have heard your voice speak softly in my heart and convince me that I need you. Now create within a clean heart and renew a right spirit within me that I may share softly and sweetly and straightforwardly the message of hope. Amen!"

July – Day 23

Text: Job 22:21 KJV

"Acquaint now thyself with him, and be at peace: whereby good shall come unto thee."

Thought: "Surrender and Know Peace!"

The story is told of a French ship that was seen fleeing from an English warship after the Battle of Waterloo. The British cruiser pursued the fugitive and after a hard chase, overtook her. The French commander hauled up the white flag and surrendered. The English captain laughed and asked him what he meant by surrendering. "Don't you know the war is over, and peace has been made for months?"

"Why, no," said the French commander, "I thought we were still at war. I tried to escape. When I could not, the only thing left to do was to surrender."

These two captains shook hands and sat down. The English captain said, "There is peace because there is peace at headquarters."

Peace has been made at headquarters for every man who will accept it. The Commander of Grace, Jesus Christ, has made it possible by His death on Calvary.

It is up to each person engaged in life, to learn the truth. The victory has been won. Accept it by faith and live in peace.

Surrender your life to Christ who pursues you with words of welcome not words of war.

Talk With God:

"Lord, I know we must endure battles in life because the enemy will not surrender; but you have assured us that victory has been won. I accept that victory. Amen!"

July – Day 24

Text: Proverbs 14:34 KJV

"Righteousness exalteth a nation; but sin is a reproach to any people."

Thought: "God is our Source of Strength & Success!"

Just prior to the beginning of the 1800's, fifty-five men gathered in Philadelphia to write a constitution for an infant republic. On the desk the only book to which these gentlemen of superior intellect referred in their deliberations was the Bible.

I know many deny this truth and have contradicted the principle that America is a nation built on the principles of God's Word. However, the evidence is overwhelming that the very purpose and plan of this nation is to be nation under God.

Benjamin Franklin said, "If it be true that a sparrow cannot fall to the ground without His notice, surely a nation cannot rise without His aid."

Why not take time to reflect on the belief of our great forefathers and put your trust daily in the one true omnipotent God?

Aren't you worth as much as a sparrow?

God thinks so, therefore, turn to Him, trust him and take Him at His Word.

We are the crowning creation of God; therefore, it is His design and His desire to establish us and enrich us. Let us lift our cup of devotion to Him and ask Him to fill it full of His glory and His grace.

Talk With God:

"Lord, I firmly and faithfully believe that you are our reason for being. Therefore, give us courage to declare and the confidence to demonstrate that our nation, the Untied States of America, is a nation birthed by Godly principles. Amen!"

July – Day 25

Text: Proverbs 3:21-22 KJV

"Keep sound wisdom and discretion: so shall they be life unto thy soul, and grace to thy neck."

Thought: "Grace Will Solve The Problems of Guilt & Greed!"

Psychiatrists tell us two of the major problems in our country today are the problem of guilt and greed.

Thousands have suffered the agony of nervous breakdowns and mental collapses because they have not been able to deal with the guilt and satisfy the greed in their lives. Millions of dollars are spent every year in research and for rehabilitation centers to treat the guilt ridden and greed driven of our society.

But I share a beautiful message for you my friend. If you are struggling under a heavy load of condemnation and consumed with living an affluent lifestyle beyond your means, there is hope and help.

I know pharmaceutical aid is available and physiotherapy is a worthy treatment; but Jesus Christ is the personal physician who has already intervened in your behalf and is willing to intercede in your behalf today and provide a complete cleansing for your life.

True forgiveness and true freedom is available. True contentment (happiness and satisfaction) is found in the work and the word of Christ. All things are possible to those who believe.

Turn it over to Christ, trust Him to deal with it and stayed tuned into His Word on a daily basis.

Talk With God:

"Lord, I struggle with guilt and/or greed. Forgive me, free me and focus me on your way of living. Help me to understand your Word that I may grow stronger and more stable each day.

I love you and know you love me. In your name I pray, Amen!"

July – Day 26

Text: Proverbs 3:5-6 KJV

"Trust in the Lord with all thine heart; and lean not unto thine own understanding. In all thy ways acknowledge him, and he shall direct thy paths."

Thought: "In God We Trust!"

Three years after the pilgrims landed at Plymouth, a disastrous drought destroyed every hope for food, and none could be secured from England. For nine continuous hours the hardy little band of pilgrims were on it knees in a plea for survival. Before evening, it rained.

Many may say it was a coincide, yet because of such moves by the people of our early beginning millions of United States coins change hands daily imprinted with the declaration "In God We Trust."

A move has been made to remove the phrase from our coins. May it never succeed?

As a nation our trust must be in God, individually and collectively.

We as citizens of this great nation must never succumbed to the demands of the ungodly, to deny, or delete the proclamation that our nation is a nation under God and a nation who must renew their trust in God or fall.

It is amazing that we have endured victoriously (droughts, depression, declared war and disease) and experienced prosperity over two hundred years trusting in God. Yet in the forty years of attempting to remove God from our nation (schools, legislatures, courts, pledge and currency) we have failed (in military conflict; in reducing crime; in combating drugs, divorce and disease). Do we not see what a difference trusting God makes?

Talk With God:

"Lord, I am thankful for our democracy. I am thankful for the divine guidance you have given to our leaders that would listen and learn. I am thankful that I have the opportunity to challenge myself and others to return to a daily soul searching and seek a renewal and revival of our nature and our nation. Amen!"

July – Day 27

Text: Joshua 1:5-6 KJV

I will be with thee: I will not fail thee, nor forsake thee. Be strong and of a good courage: for unto this people shalt thou divide for an inheritance the land, which I sware unto their fathers to give them."

Thought: "Democracy and Divine Guidance Go Hand-In-Hand!"

The ideal of freedom and liberty as our forefathers visualized it was borne out of a strong faith in God. Human rights, as our Constitution and Bill of Rights refer to, are the by-product of men's sincere belief in the Holy Bible. The Four Freedoms which came about as a result of WWII and the guaranteeing of civil rights to the underdog are the offspring of Christian faith and a vital belief in the Old and New Testament doctrine of God and man.

If we desert the Bible and renounce our Christian heritage, can this democracy survive? If we forsake Christian ideas and a religious interpretation of life, can human rights survive? Can a nation of free people continue where faith in God is forsaken?

The answer to all three questions in the preceding paragraph is No. We must maintain a constant dedication and determination of devotion to God, His Word, His Work and His Way.

We must be convinced that when our forefathers sought religious freedom and was directed to "the land of the free and the home of the brave," it was no mistake. God ordained it and ordered it so. Let us not forget. As they sought God, let us continue seeking God to grant to us His divine freedom and give us our democratic freedom of life.

Talk With God:

"Lord, Once again in this celebrated month of democratic freedom, I say thank you for our liberty. I also desire to blaze the trail of devotion to you in my daily life. Amen!"

July – Day 28

Text: Psalm 105:8 KJV

"He hath remembered his covenant for ever, the word which he commanded to a thousand generations."

Thought: "God Never Forgets!"

An elderly gent was invited to dinner at the home of an old friend. Throughout the conversation, the guest was impressed by the way his friend preceded every request to his wife with endearing terms – Honey, My Love, Darling, Sweetheart, Pumpkin, etc. The couple had been married almost 70 years and, clearly, they were still very much in love.

While the wife was in the kitchen, the guest leaned over and said to his host, "I think it's wonderful that, after all these years, you still call your wife loving nicknames."

To which the husband replied with a sheepish smile, "The truth is, I forgot her name about 10 years ago."

Man is truly forgetful. Many forget those who have served our country with dignity, determination and devotion. Many forget the Savior Who lived in ridicule all His life and lay down His life willingly for the redemption of all humanity. Many forget their personal duty to continue in the path of devotion to country and to Christ.

The Psalmist declared that the Lord would remember His covenant for a thousand generations. He is not about to forget nor forsake those who trust Him.

Talk With God:

Lord, thank you for those who have shed their blood for the freedom of our country. Thank you for shedding your blood for my freedom from sin. Help me to never forget to perform my duty and prove my devotion to my country and to my God. Amen!

July – Day 29

Text: Job 23:10 KJV

"But He knoweth the way that I take"

Thought: "He Knows and That's All That Matters"

A minister was visiting a 95-year-old church member at the nursing home.

"How are you feeling?" the pastor asked.

"I'm just worried sick!" the woman replied.

"What are you worried about, dear?" the clergyman asked. "You're getting good care, aren't you?"

"Yes, they are taking very good care of me."

"Just a little arthritis."

"So what's the matter?" her pastor asked.

The lady leaned forward in her rocking chair. "Every close friend I ever had has already died and gone to heaven. I'm afraid they're all wondering where I went."

Of course we know that no one in heaven is thinking earthly thoughts that would cause distress. However, we see a great message found in this bit of humor.

Today, we need to continue the faithful fight of faith and continue running the course of life with determination if we are to finish triumphant.

This is true as citizens of earth and citizens of heaven. We can not allow anything to hinder our fight nor finishing the race. We must stay true in our thoughts, our talk and our trail of life. In the church, in the community, in the country—we must be faithful and fruitful in our allegiance.

God knows our faithfulness and is ready to welcome us when our race is complete on this earth.

Talk With God:

Today, Lord, I do not want the faithful soldiers of our country or the faithful pioneers of our faith to ever be forgotten or forsaken. I desire to remain faithful and fruitful in carry the banner victoriously to the end. Amen!"

July – Day 30

Text: Daniel 11:32 KJV

"The people that do know their God shall be strong, and do exploits."

Thought: "Empowered For Great Exploits!"

Visualize with me a giant Titan missile standing on the launching pad at Cape Kennedy, Florida. The shiny projectile represents millions of dollars and hundreds of thousands of hours of dedicated labor. Designed to explore new recesses of space that would bring mankind one step closer to outer space planet exploration.

In the control room all was in readiness. Buttons were pushed, and tons of metal began to lift. Suddenly, somewhere in that maze of wires and components, something went wrong. There was a spark; the dangerous fuel exploded. The fireworks lit up the southern sky. The fall of a Titan! What a waste!

Did you realize that every human being has the potential of being like the Titan missile? We are built to carry a precious payload that will advance the plans of God for greater relationships with Him. We can soar into life controlled by the Master designer. Yet, sin can bring us crashing down, ending all dreams of great exploits for God.

However, if we allow our Chief Engineer, the Holy Spirit, to monitor our systems (personality, conscience and interpersonal relationships) we will avoid crucial mistakes that will spark a devastating consequence.

Keep a fresh awareness of God through His Word and through personal prayer. It will enable us to posses the power of a Titan and do great exploits for His Kingdom.

If we did this as an individual, a family and a nation; what a differences it would make.

Talk With God:

It is my desire O Lord to live for you. I am not always faithful or fruitful for you; yet work with me and help to deepen my relationship with you through my understanding of the Word and my undergirding of the Holy Spirit in my daily life. Amen!

July – Day 31

Text: Ephesians 5:1-2 KJV

"Be ye therefore followers of God, as dear children; and walk in love, as Christ also hath loved us, and hath given himself for us."

Thought: "If at First You Don't Succeed, Try Again and Again and Again!"

History is full of great men who would not have succeeded if they had given up the first time there were defeated. Even in our present day we observe successful men who made it because they would not quit.

How about you? Would you classify yourself as a determined individual? Or when you try to make a friend and don't seem to get to first base – do you give up?

How about the desire to overcome a potential harmful habit? Once, twice, maybe three times you try, and then just give up.

What about your desire to live a good moral life? You do pretty good until you run into some old buddies who begin rubbing you the wrong way.

Mistakes and failures will happen. We are only human. But we must learn to give it all to Jesus and then grow in the knowledge of His Word and His amazing grace. Godly character cannot be bought at the local store or give over the counter at the pharmacy. It is developed by daily interest and inspiration found in the Bible and the belief in God.

Keep trucking on the path of righteousness (for it is not your path but His path and He is undergirding you) and keep trusting in His Word (for it is not your word but His Word and it is truth without error and will not lead you astray.)

Talk With God:

Lord, I make a lot of mistakes. I am weak. Our nation is weak. However, we know that you are strong and in our weakness we are made strong through you. Thank you for that promise. Keep us devoted and determined in our efforts to walk the path that you lead us in. Amen!

Step 8 – August
"Back To School"

Well, summer is coming to a close and the ringing of school bells is approaching rapidly. The moment has arrived to purchase school supplies, prepare for bed earlier and personally shopping for new school clothes. The time to hit the books, having the opportunity to make new friends, and happily learning new and more advanced things is quickly arriving.

It is also a great opportunity to get back into daily devotions with family members. It is time to teach our children to pray -- thanking God for His keeping presences and to ask Him to guide them in their studies. It is time to emphasize the importance of applying oneself to study in order to make the grade – not only in secular knowledge but also in Biblical knowledge. It is the prime time to get back into Sunday school after a summer absences. We must teach ourselves and our children the necessity of physical growth, mental growth and spiritual growth. At the beginning of the school year is the golden opportunity for such training.

It is also a great occasion to invite unsaved and unchurched class friends and families to God's House for worship each Sunday. By this action we spread the importance and inspiration of our relationship with Jesus Christ – the Forgiver of sin, the Friend at all times and the Future for every life.

Enjoy these daily devotions that give comfort and courage for daily living and learning. Experience the challenge of each devotion to grow in your relationships with Heavenly Father and humanity. Gain the insight and inspiration that the Word of God gives.

August – Day 1

Text: Micah 6:8 NIV

"He has showed you, O man, what is good, and what does the lord require of you? To act justly and to love mercy and to walk humbly with your God."

Thought: Application Of Learning"

The poet T. S. Eliot once said, "The greatest proof of Christianity for others, is not how far a man can logically analyze his reasons for believing, but how far in practice he will stake his life on his belief."

Let me ask you, How far will you go to proof your devotion and dedication for Jesus Christ?

Did you know that our attitudes and actions each day demonstrate the depth of our devotion to Christ? The tone and tactic in which we response or react determines the true nature of our spiritual dedication. Our interest and involvements in life depict our obedience to the duty that God's Word calls for us to follow.

Now, God knows we cannot live in perfection in the human life. The curse of sin hinders that from existing. The natural state of man rebels against God. However, once we have submitted our life to Christ, surrendered our total being to His control and strive to obey; we will walk in a manner that is pleasing to God and prove to man that we are dedicated to serving the Lord above everything else in life.

We must do unto others as we desire of them. We must desire kindness and deliver kindness in our words, our walk and our work. We must walk in humility, honesty and holiness. We must possess a reverence and respect for God; and a resistance against those things that are ungodly. This is the requirement of man in living out his devotion to God.

Remember: it is not what we learn but how we apply the learning to our lives.

Talk With God:

"I know that true devotion requires much of me O Lord. And I want to please you and present you to others by the way that I perform my devotion in daily living. I shall live in obedience to your Word and as I overcome, I will use every opportunity to witness for you. This I pray. Amen!"

August – Day 2

Text: II Corinthians 3:2 Amplified Bible

"[No, you] yourselves are our letter of recommendation (out credentials), written in our hearts, to be (perceived, recognized,) known and read by everybody."

Thought: "An Open Book"

It took me a while to author my first book although I had written for a number of years and continue to add to my manuscripts information that I would think of or run across in reading other material. But when I decided to enrich my life personally, to encourage others and to edify God and publish my manuscripts; I came upon a grand discovery. We are all writing a book of our life every day.

We are daily writing a chapter upon the tables of the conscience of others, in God's chronicles in heaven and in the demonstration of our own conduct and conversation. We are displaying our devotion to the Savior or to self. We are making an impression on the lives of those about us. Each person, every day, influence others either beneficially or badly.

Therefore, our attitude and action are important. Our thoughts conveyed in our words and walk count. Our dialogue and demonstrations of life form character that is duplicated by others.

We must be cautious for character determines our destiny. What we are shows where we are going. The fruitfulness and faithfulness of our life depicts our devotion and direction of our life.

So, I ask: What reward or results will our behavior on earth bring in the end? What on earth are we doing for Heaven's sake? You are an open book—let us produce some good reading by following the steps of Jesus.

Talk With God:

"I am glad that I have Your letter to read, Your life to review, Your love to receive. For without it I could not write a living message that would benefit me nor man. Thank you for lifting me up and giving me the opportunity to lift the spirits of others. Amen."

August – Day 3

Text: I Corinthians 15:10 KJV

"But by the grace of God I am what I am: and his grace which was bestowed upon me was not in vain; but I labored more abundantly."

Thought: "You Are An Exception!"

Many people become tied up in their own image of themselves. They do so in two ways. They may have an exaggerated view of themselves or they have an exceeding low esteem. Both views are dangerous and deadly. They will rob an individual of any potential a day may bring.

First, ego is always a problem. It allows self to get in the way of success and satisfaction (Proverbs 16:18 & 29:23). If we humble our self before a caring, compassionate and concerned God; we can be empted and exalted at the same time (Psalms 51:10-13) and become an exception to the rule. Sin and self-centeredness will destroy any man; but submission to God will exempt you from destruction and cause you to become a delight and perform a duty unto God.

Secondly, man shackles himself with excuses, exemptions and executions in facing daily life. What in the world do I mean by such jargon? How many times have we made excuses for failing to live a life filled with the love, light and liberty of God? How many times have we denied ourselves the opportunity for growth by exempting ourself from being happy and hopeful because we declare that our circumstances and conditions can not or will not change? How often have we condemned ourselves for failure? Why in the world do we want to deny and destroy the opportunity to be an exception to the rule? God has made us and respectfully formed us. He favors us. He desires to fashion our daily lives in a way that will help us, give hope to others and honor Him.

Let us become willing to accept His inspiration, His instruction, His integrity, in order to portray His image. In doing so, we become engrafted into His family, enriched in His Word, enabled by His Spirit, enlighten for His Work and elected to enter His Kingdom.

Talk With God:

"Thank you Lord for making me an exception. For in you, I become strengthened, stable and will survive any encounter of this day. I will shine in your love. I will honorably represent you in my meditations and my manifestations of daily life. Amen!"

August – Day 4

Text: Hebrews 3:14 KJV

"For we are made partakers of Christ, if we hold the beginning of our confidence stedfast unto the end."

Thought: "Consistency is the Key!"

Each day that we exist and each step we take must be consistent regardless of who we encounter or what we have to endure.

We cannot straddle the fence or become a fence sitter, hoping to please everyone and hoping every situation will be a pleasant one. It is literally impossible. Plus the fact you will eventually fall off – possibly on the wrong side.

The battle lines are sharply drawn between good and evil. The call has to be clear as to whom we will serve daily and devotedly, and seek counsel in times of difficulty.

When we choose to surrender our life to Christ and walk in fellowship with Him, we have made a decision that will grant to us both earthly and eternal benefits and blessings.

Faithfulness to this choice will not create a bed of roses for us, but will give us strength to escape the temptations, endure the trials and enjoy the time God grants us in this life.

Just remember, it is not foolish to give up what we cannot keep in order to gain something that we cannot lose. Earthly things will decay, die and dissolve with time; yet the eternal relationship with Christ will be a constant as long as we desire, do and delight in His will for our life.

Talk With God:

"Lord, I know that decisions are made every day. Many of these decisions are self-centered, sinful and simply made to fit into the social circle of life. However, give me the grace and the gall to make the right choices in life. I want to be a consecrated, consistent and confident follower of you. Amen!"

August – Day 5

Text: Luke 12: 23 KJV

"The life is more than meat, and the body is more than raiment."

Thought: "Success Is More than What We May Think"

Let me ask you a question? What is your concept of success?

Is it a four-bedroom brick house with all the modern conveniences? Is it a porche or some other fabulous automobile? Is it a well-paying job with perks during employment and great retirement package at the end? Is it vacations in some exciting and elaborate location? Is it having a family that is well thought of and children who are "making it" scholastically and socially?

All the things mentioned have become a reality for some and simply dreams for others. And what person would not desire to enjoy such pleasure and privileges. However, there is more to success that material things, monetary gains and moments of great pleasure.

Somehow, we have to shut out the voices of the secular world calling, conniving and commanding us to dream, drive and divulge in all these things. We have to shut out the clamor of "keeping up with the Joneses' lifestyle." We have to turn down the advice of this world, tune in to the heavenly channel and train our thoughts to count the cost and consider the options of true success.

True success is living a life that is more than meat and material. It is having a relationship with the King of Kings and considering the purpose of promoting His Kingdom.

Once we consider the steps of true success, we will realize it begins with "seeking first the Kingdom of God and His righteousness."

Talk With God:

"Lord, I do enjoy many of the physical blessings we have been privileged to partake of and possess. However, I pray that nothing will ever take priority over my relationship with you. For to me this is real life and real success. Hold me tight and help me to remain true in fulfillingl your will which will be success to me. Amen!"

August – Day 6

Text: Galatians 6:14 KJV

"But God forbid that I should glory, save in the cross of our Lord Jesus Christ, by whom the world is crucified unto me and I unto the world."

Thought: "God's Plus Sign!"

A story is told of a group of university students who were coming home after a night of partying following a victorious football game. Their drunken leader noticed a cross on the steeple of a church. Jesting, he shouted, "Ye mathematicians look at God's plus sign."

Before that night was over, one of the students made a dynamic decision. Convicted by the Holy Spirit, he committed his life to the One Who hung on that "plus sign." He became a believer by accepting the fact "that Christ crossed out his sins on that plus sign."

The cross of Christ is not a minus. His gospel is not negative. Faith is always positive. Faith either removes mountains or tunnels through them. When we identify with the power of God's plus sign, we can know the faith that will cultivate our soul's soil and plant a new life that will produce fruit unto righteousness and not rebellion.

Our days are numbered in heartbeats. Is your life adding up? If not, perhaps you should take another look at God's plus sign. It definitely will make a difference in your life.

The Apostle Paul declared the importance of the cross by stating that it enabled him to live a life separated from the world of sin. And friend, that is a definite plus.

Talk With God:

"Lord, I am grateful that you have an additive that will change our entire makeup. I am glad that we can believe in the work of the cross and be changed into a new creation loved, lead and given true liberty in life. Amen!"

August – Day 7

Text: Hebrews 6:12 KJV

"Through faith and patience inherit the promise."

Thought: "Lean Your Whole Weight On!"

The story is told of a great missionary's search for a word to use for faith. He was attempting to translate the scripture into the native's own language. The search seem futile, there was apparently no word for "faith." Then one day a native came into the study of the great missionary and flung himself down on a chair, rested his feet on another chair, and lay back full length, saying how good it was to lean his whole weight on those chairs.

Wham! Instantly, the missionary had found his word for faith. He stated that faith meant "to lean your whole weight on." He used it in his translation and marveled at the results as the natives read the passages of Acts 16, "What must I do to be saved?...lean thy whole weight on the Lord Jesus Christ, and thou shalt be saved."

Have you leaned your whole weight on Jesus? Today is the day! Now is the time!

You can trust Him will any and all your situations of life. He cares for you and through His Word is willing to counsel you regarding each condition.

He is already aware of the circumstances; so why not trust Him with them. Why don't we simply lean our whole weight on Him Who loves us and will lift us up?

Throughout this day, put your whole weight on Him. He is big enough to carry you victoriously from the rising of the sun to the setting of the same.

Talk With God:

"Thank you Lord for being aware of our situations and accepting our acknowledgement of them to you. I have no one else to lean on; therefore, I lean on you Lord. Amen!"

August – Day 8

Text: Luke 18:17 KJV

"Whosoever shall not receive the kingdom of God as a little child shall in no wise enter therein."

Thought: "Be Like A Child!"

Did you ever watch a little child take a lesson in model drawing? Never two strokes of the pencil are taken without a glance at the model. Sometimes after glancing at the model, the child may erase a line or make the line a little different. He looks at the model, and then draws again. Looks at the model and erases. Looks at the model and draws again. Over and over the process continues until the pattern is finished.

In the Bible, we are challenged to become like little children. Not in the matter of throwing a temper tantrum but in the spirit of humility, honesty and happiness in being led or in learning how to accomplish things in life. Most children learn best by imitation of a true model (a parent or their peers).

Therefore, do we have a real desire to imitate our maker, Jesus Christ? If we do, then we are going to be giving constant glances at the model – His Words, His Walk, and His Work.

Problems, pressures, and pitfalls of life will be easier to deal with if we see how Christ experienced, endured and escaped.

Talk With God:

"I am so glad that I have a Friend like you Lord. I am glad I can yield myself to you and become yoked with you as "we" face conditions, circumstances and crises together and triumphantly. Amen!"

August – Day 9

Text: Psalm 119:11 KJV

"Thy Word have I hid in my heart that I might not sin against thee"

Thought: "Prevention and Provision!"

It has been said, "An ounce of prevention is better than a pound of cure."

How true such a statement is! However, it is impossible in some instances to prevent the headaches, hardships and heartaches that we have to content with.

Yet, let us not fret; for in the midst of such stress and distress, we can find comfort and courage.

No one is exempt from troubles and trials; but friend; you can be exempt from hopeless despair and helpless fear that may accompany the storms of life.

How? You say.

It is through Jesus Christ, our anchor and assurance, in every storm and situation of life.

There are times that He offers security against the storms, but He always offer security amidst the storm. To every one who trusts Him, He provides a safe landing, when the winds cease to roam and the waves cease to roll.

So, when storm clouds hover over you physically, psychologically or spiritually; He will be the calm in the midst.

He will provide the peace, power and the promise of preventing and provision.

Talk With God:

Lord, the world is so corrupt and many times the circumstances of life seem so overwhelming. Yet, I know in the midst of it all you are only a heartbeat away. I am so thankful I have your peace and your promise to undergird me as I face situations. You are always present to give me counsel, comfort and courage. Thanks for your deliverance and your direction in life. Amen!

August – Day 10

Text: 2 Corinthians 4:8-9 KJV

"We are troubled on every side, yet not distressed; we are perplexed, but not in despair; persecuted, but not forsaken; cast down, but not destroyed."

Thought: "Positive Verses Negative"

After a very rainy and unpleasant summer weekend, Jim reported for work as usual on Monday morning. Shortly after his arrival, the office telephone rang. Jim's boss called to inform him he would be several hours late for work due to a minor automobile accident.

Soaked to the skin and very much upset, Jim's boss arrived at the office about eleven o'clock that morning.

"Good morning," Jim said as usual.

The boss snapped back, "What's good about it."

Jim replied, "Well, in some ways, it may not appear pleasant, but you could have been seriously injured and in the hospital or possibly dead."

The boss agreed.

Folks, the unexpected does happen. The unpleasant events do occur. The unexplainably does disrupt our plans and purposes. However, God never changes. He is always the same and is willing to undergird us with His constant love, consideration and care.

With a friend like Jesus, we have someone that lifts us up in our failures, frailty and frustrations.

Or we may need to be a friend, which has Jesus abiding within, ready to lift others up when the life seems topsy turvey.

Talk With God:

Life is sometimes crazy, confusing, and complicated. Yet, O Lord, you are steady and sure. I am grateful for the assurance found in a relationship with you. Help us to stand fast in such a blessing and to share such a delight to others as we encounter moments of perplexity.

August – Day 11

Text: Acts 26:22 KJV

"I continue until this day"

Thought: "Repetition Can Be Beneficial!"

All of us are bound to repeat ourselves. All of us are bound to repeat ourselves. (Told you so). In fact, it seems most of our days are repetitious – we get up, get dressed, eat, go to work, come home, eat, rest, sleep and start over the next day. We sweep the floor, vacuum the carpet, clean the dishes, wash the clothes, fuel the cars, fix the meals, go shopping, etc. We do it again and again; then again and again. Sometimes the routine seems endless and we ask ourselves, what's the point of it all?

Yet, it is a part of life. It makes life continue. It provides life with essential cleanliness and conditions for positive progression.

However, the manner in which we view such repetitious obligations depend on our relationships in life. How much desire, devotion and duty we want to maintain with family, friends and the Heavenly Father. We either respond to our daily circumstances just to get it over with or we look at life and our activities as an opportunity to be enriched and to enjoy.

It is through repetition that character is formed, Christian faith is made stronger, confidence is increased and courage is developed.

Therefore, if life seems to be a grind, use it to sharpen your character.

The Apostle Paul, enroute to Rome, declared that he would continue to be a witness to both small and great as long as he was allowed and able to repeat the message of hope. Let us be challenged to repeat again and again the praises of God in our daily lifestyle.

Talk With God:

Thank you Lord for your faithfulness in your passionate walk to Calvary. Thank you for your continued faithfulness this day. Guide me and give me grace to smile, share and show your love every step of this day. Amen!

August – Day 12

Text: Ephesians 5:16 KJV

"Redeeming the time"

Thought: "Time is Valuable!"

I remember when I was a kid, we use to tell little moron jokes. One in particular was the one that asked why little moron threw the clock out the window. The answer was, because he wanted to see time fly.

The older I get the quicker time passes (or so it seems—it may be that I don't get as far along in the time as I use to). However, time is very important. We should use it beneficial. Every thing we do should be an enjoyable or enriching experience.

The New Testament disciples were not losing time when they sat down beside their Master, and held quiet conversation with Him under the olives of Bethany or by the shores of Galilee. Those were their school hours; those were their feeding times.

The healthiest person, the one who is best fitted for Godly living and Godly labors, is he who feeds most on Christ – His Words, His Walk and His Works.

To feed on Christ we must invite Him into our hearts and indulge in moments of personal Bible Study and personal prayer time. In these moments, we learn from Him and lean on Him. It is our opportunity to grow in the grace and knowledge of Jesus Christ and develop character that portrays Him to those we come in contact with.

Time with the Word of the Master is not wasted time – it makes time more worthwhile. Therefore, spend some time with Jesus.

Talk With God:

Oh how we humans waste time. Help us O Lord to redeem the time by making time for you (in prayer) and your Word (in study). Help us to take time to attend your house in order to worship You. Equip us and encourage us to use the opportunities to witness personally for you. Amen!

August – Day 13

Text: 1 Corinthians 9:27 KJV

"But I keep under my body, and bring it into subjection; lest that by any means, when I have preached to others, I myself should be a castaway."

Thought: "Discipline!"

A wise old workman shared some good advice to a young worker one day. He said, "If you can't give orders to yourself, then you will have to accept orders from someone else."

Blessed is the man who has learned this lesson, and who has determined to discipline himself – the one who has set a goal for himself and is relentless in his demands upon himself. He will find that life rewards him with inner satisfactions and outward sanctifications.

There is little hope of any great satisfaction in the life that is lived without discipline. And friend, discipline must find its way into all areas of our life: mental, moral, and material. For as we discipline our lives for use by the Master, we are able to master our lives for usefulness.

The Apostle Paul knew the importance of preaching discipline. He also knew the necessity of practicing discipline personally. No one can be a disciple of the Lord without entertaining and exercising discipline. Discipline of mind, body and soul is very important to being a follower of Jesus Christ.

Talk With God:

My, how, we fail when it comes to disciplining our lives in service for you. We live and learn by each step we take. Be patient as we learn to live and live to love like you O Lord. Strengthen us! Stabilize us! Amen!

August – Day 14

Text: Matthew 11:29 KJV

"Take my yoke upon you, and learn of me; for I am meek and lowly in heart; and ye shall find rest unto your souls."

Thought: "Learning as we Live!"

Experience is a great teacher.

I have often heard that individuals who do not have much book learning but have learned from the hard knocks of life make the better worker. The reason being that they have ground out the methods of getting the best job done and deleted the methods that didn't seem to aid in accomplishing the task.

We really learn the most from what affects us personally – that which attracts us, aids us or accomplishes our goal. Whether it is a mountain-top experience or a valley crisis; we are able to learn and grow if we allow it to be a personal desire and drive.

However, in our efforts to endure experiences, we sometimes become disappointed and discouraged. In these times we need comfort, courage and confidence undergirding us. Jesus is a friend who provides these things to reassure us.

The Bible declares that He is the lily of the valley, the beautiful rose of Sharon, the bright and morning star and the fairest of ten thousand.

So, as you trod life's road, living, loving and learning from your personal experiences, always include Christ in your every experience. He will be your reinforcement and reassurances.

Talk With God:

Lord, we walk a rough road at times and the path is trying; however, we lean on you for your words of wisdom. In your words we find rest and reassurance and we grow in our relationship with you. Your humility, honesty and holiness convinces us to learn as we live. Amen!

August – Day 15

Text: Song of Solomon 2:15 KJV
"The little foxes, that spoil the vines."

Thought: "Spiritual Termites!"

According to a UPI report several years ago, a number of pamphlets entitled "The Control of Termites" were stored in the mailing room of a western university. Believe it or not, termites gobbled their way through the little booklets, and no one noticed until the damaged was done. Those hungry little pests destroyed the information that could have prevented this from happening. All the facts contained in the leaflets didn't do a bit of good. Why? Because knowledge was not applied!

This story reminds me of some individuals today. They go to church every Sunday, singing songs of praise and soaking up Biblical teachings; listen to religious radio and television programs of gospel songs and sermons; yet fail to put any of the praise and principles into daily practice. These individuals become preoccupied with earthly things that they allow the spiritual input to be stored away until it is destroyed by neglect and negative thoughts of life.

Are there spiritual termites in your life that need to be exterminated? Do we allow little things to draw our thoughts away from the truth –God's teachings? Do we become so pre-occupied with daily activities that we leave out a moment with God? Do we push thoughts of praise and petitions of concern to the back of the mind instead of letting them occupy the forefront of our thought life? Do we fail to see opportunities of witnessing and working for God in our relationships with others each day?

Remember: Truth stored in the head should be used to stir the heart and strengthen the hand. When the opportunity arrives, let us absorb the truths of God's revelation and relationship. Let us record it within so we can reflect it outwardly.

Talk With God:

Lord, give us the determination to listen, learn and live your inspiration. Help us to hear and heed your instruction. Make your life our delight in order that our delight may demonstrate your life. Amen!

August – Day 16

Text: Philippians 4:11 KJV

"For I have learned, in whatsoever state I am, therewith to be content."

Thought: "Bittersweet!"

I read an article once that displayed a great truth. It read like this: While examining a clover blossom, a little boy was stung on the hand by a bee. He ran screaming to his mother and shouted, "I hate them bees! I hate them bees!"

She did what she could to ease his pain and then gave him some bread and honey. As he eagerly devoured it, she said, "You really like that, don't you?"

"Yeah, I love it," he gulped.

Then she explained that the same kind of bee that had stung him produces the delicious honey he was eating."

The lesson is clear: Along with the sweets of life we can also expect to feel its stings.

You will be able, like the Apostle Paul, to let your response to adverse and trying circumstance give evidence that you have learned to be content in whatever state you find yourself – when you live in the confidence of God's Word.

Life is bittersweet. We enjoy the treats and triumphs we experience, yet sometimes; we have to endure the bitter moments of distress, disease and disappointments.

We know not what today may bring, but we can know that Jesus will stand with us regardless of the conditions.

What a joy in knowing that in the valleys and in the victories of life, we have a companion that will love us and lead us.

Talk With God:

Thank you Lord for giving us grace to experience the healthy and happy moments of life; as well, as the hurts and hardships of life. Through it all, we can see victory in you. Amen

August – Day 17

Text: 2 Corinthians 12:10 NIV

"When I am weak, then am I strong."

Thought: "Change Can't to Can!"

So often I'm reminded of the story told by Norman Vincent Peale about his fifth grade class and their school teacher. It was said that each and every morning as class began, the teacher would write in large, bold letters the word **C A N ' T** on the chalkboard. He would ask the class what it spelled. They would answer with a loud shout, "can't" Then he, in one big swipe of the eraser, would remove the ' and the **T.** He would repeat his question, what does it now spell? The students would yell "can."

This he did to prepare their minds for the day's learning activities. He attempted to discover and develop a positive view in each student about their school work and eventually in their life's work.

It was a simple physical task with a smart positive thought.

We can erase the negative ('t) from the difficult task of life if we allow God to be our help, hope and honor. Just as the kids were not capable of eradicating the large written ('t) with a single stroke of the eraser; we are unable to remove the negative habits, hurts and hang-ups in our lives in a single effort. However, God is able to do all things and He will enable us to do so with His help.

Christ is the Master Teacher and he desires to aid us in beginning each day with a pure, positive and progressive note. Look to Him, listen to Him and learn from Him as you begin this day.

Talk With God:

Lord, I love that old hymn, "Just a closer walk with thee." For in it, I find the reassurance and reinforcing words, "I am weak but thou art strong; Jesus keep me from all wrong." Jesus, you are my strength, my song and my salvation. I rejoice in you. Amen!

August – Day 18

Text: 1 Samuel 25: 29 KJV

"But the soul of my lord (David) shall be bound in the bundle of life with the Lord thy God."

Thought: "Happy Birthday To Me!"

Today is a special day – it is my birthday. Happy Birthday John!

I don't mind getting older. Two reasons: I have been blessed with another year of opportunity and I have more reasons to express appreciation to God.

But in getting older, I am prone to be forgetful.

I remember hearing a cute little joke about a very absent-minded person. Any time someone would ask her how old she was, she would begin to sing, "Happy Birthday to Me!" In doing so, she would remember her birthday and how old she was.

I am sure each of us is forgetful at times. No matter how hard we try to remember an item we are suppose to pick up at the store or a particular chore we were going to do today; we manage to forget something. Or perhaps you are like me in attempting to recall a person's name. I sometimes catch myself going down the alphabet attempting to recall what the name begins with. However, many times I fail to recall; then when I am not attempting to remember, it pops up in my mind as clear as day.

However, friends, let me remind you that God is never so preoccupied or personally forgetful that He does not recall His love for you and has not forgotten what you share with Him. He is listening, leading and loving us in every circumstance and condition we are confronted with. We do not have to wonder or recall specific words to say or the proper way to address Him – We just need to fellowship with Him and fervently share our hurts and hungers with Him.

Just as God bound up his servant David's life and kept it safe, so has he keep all who trust in Him.

Talk With God:

God you have been so good to me. You have blessed me with another year. You have given me a wonderful family and a host of friends. I love you and long to live for you and never forget the blessings and benefits you have placed in my life. Continue to grant the comfort, courage and confidence needed to stay in tune with you and to share the timeless blessings with others. Amen!

August – Day 19

Text: 1 Samuel 16:7 NIV

"For man looks at the outward appearance, but the Lord looks at the heart."

Thought: "The Internal Condition Gives Life!"

Recently a huge tree in Colorado fell to the ground with a resounding crash after having stood majestically on a hill for more than 400 years. It was a mere sapling when Columbus landed in San Salvador. Over the centuries it had been struck by lightning fourteen times, braved great windstorms and even defied an earthquake. In the end, however, it was killed by some little beetles. Boring under the bark, they chewed away it's mightily fiber; until one day that lordly king of the forest came thundering down.

So, too, apparently insignificant sins often make substantial inroads into our spiritual lives, and if left unchecked may cause our downfall.

Remember, a little bit of neglect of communion with God in personal prayer and the precious study of His Word will add to your trouble, subtract from your energy and multiply your difficulties.

Keep a constant vigil on your internal condition of life – maintain a right perspective toward life and right relationship with God. These two principles will prevent an infestation of our spiritual life and spare us the decline and death of a happy and spiritual healthy life.

God knows that the internal condition of man is what is essential for life; that is why the prophet of the Lord declared and dejected King Saul. His heart had become dominated by self rather than by God. His life and leadership had turned from being spiritual-directed to self-directed and this condition contaminated the attitude and action of King Saul.

Talk With God:

Lord, keep my heart filled with your love and your light that I may see the path of righteousness clearly. I want my heart and head to be spiritually controlled and not self-dominated. Amen!

August – Day 20

Text: Matthew 14:31 KJV

"And immediately Jesus stretched forth his hand, and caught him, and said unto him, O thou of little faith, wherefore didst thou doubt?"

Thought: "Stay Afloat!"

While walking along the shores of the Dead Sea one day, a man lost his balance and fell into the water at a point where it was rather deep. Never having learned to swim, he was panic stricken. In desperation he began to thrash about with his arms and legs, fearing he would sink and drown. At last completely exhausted, he felt he could do no more. Crying out to God for help, he prepared for the worst. What a surprise awaited him; for as soon as he relaxed, the water bore him up. He had forgotten the Dead Sea is so full of salt and other minerals that if a person lies still, he can easily float upon its surface.

This story has a profound lesson for us. When we cease our fretting, completely rest in God's loving arms, and confidently trust in His promise; we will find serenity and security.

In our text, Jesus had come unto the disciples walking on the water. Peter requested that he be permitted to come to Him. Jesus obliged him. But Peter saw the waves and felt the wind, and became afraid and began to sink. He cried to Jesus and (of course) Jesus rescued him but also challenged him – why did you doubt?

Jesus has never let His people sink when He granted permission to do a particular thing (even walking on the sea). We must take Him at His Word.

Talk With God:

Thank you Lord for allowing us the opportunity to trust you to keep us afloat. Help us to hear and heed your Word. Walk with us and work with us as we walk the stormy seas of life. Amen!

August – Day 21

Text: Malachi 3:8 KJV

"For I am the lord, I change not."

Thought: "A Changeless Christ!"

In 1928, two brothers picked up a stone in their yard. They kept this unusual rock around for fifteen years before discovering it was a diamond. During those years, that rock didn't change. It was the same precious diamond in 1943 that is was in 1928. The difference was in the knowledge the two brothers possessed regarding the diamond.

Like the two brothers, we must know the true value of what we possess as believers, if we are to benefit from it. Christ is the Rock of our Salvation. He is the chief cornerstone of our faith.

The diamond never changed, neither does Christ. He is always the same. Yet, our concept of Christ must always increase.

We must learn who Christ is and how much He really loves us. We come to the revelation that His promises are made to enrich and enable us to succeed in life.

We must come to the conclusion that the more we value Him and learn of Him, the greater His value becomes to us.

We live in an ever-changing society. Thank God for a genuine leader and living example that never changes – Jesus Christ. He is the same yesterday, today and forever. Amen! And Amen!

He is a contemporary God with an old-fashion message that still brings victory.

Talk With God:

Lord, thanks you for being ever the same. Thank you for still providing the avenue to walk, the answer to seek and the anchor to hold. Amen!

August – Day 22

Text: John 3:18 KJV

"He that believeth on him is not condemned; but he that believeth not is condemned already, because he hath not believed in the name of the only begotten Son of God."

Thought: "You Must Follow The Directions!"

In the 1960's, the Kingston Trio released a song called "Desert Pete." The ballad tells of a thirsty cowboy who is crossing the desert and finds a hand pump. Next to it, Desert Pete has left a note urging the reader not to drink from the jar hidden there but to use its contents to prime the pump.

The cowboy resists the temptation to drink and uses the water as the note instructs. In reward for his obedience, he receives an abundance of cold, satisfying water. Had he not acted in faith, he would have had only a jar of unsatisfying, warm water to drink.

Sometimes life can be like an arid desert. We become overwhelmed with difficulties and disappointments and desire only a drink that will refresh, renew and restore our faith and focus.

And what a blessing when God takes a simple experience or single incident and produces an overflow of thirst-quenching water that satisfies and supplies our every need.

However, when we fail to accept the instruction and follow the directions of which God has provided, we rob ourselves of the essential ingredient and inspiration necessary for an abundant life.

Lord, how many times have we launched into the day without receiving instructions and inspiration from you and your Word? Cause us to pause and pursue a moment of reflection in your Word and a moment of renewal in our relationship with you.

Talk With God:

Lord, I want to be obedient to your will and your words. I desire to quench my thirst each day for spiritual renewal and leave influence and inspiration in order that others will follow suit. Oh how our world needs to drink from the well of living water. Amen!

August – Day 23

Text: Romans 5:21 KJV

"That as sin hath reigned unto death, even so might grace reign through righteousness unto eternal life by Jesus Christ our Lord."

Thought: "Sin Puts The Bottle On The Street, Bt Grace Picks It Up!"

I read a beautiful lesson about a coke bottle one day. Allow me to share it with you.

A man was waiting at the traffic light, when he noticed the driver in front of him drinking a bottle of Coke. When he finished the drink, he opened his door and set the glass bottle on the street and drove away.

"That was wrong!" the observing individual said to himself. He thought, "Such an act of selfishness could cause someone to have a flat tire or even an accident." He decided to pick the bottle up as he drove by.

Later that same day, the man was listening to a message regarding the grace of God and how it intervenes in a life of sin. As he listened, the thought came to him, "Sin puts the bottle on the street, but grace picks it up."

Wow! What truth to remember!

Selfishness we lead a life to break the law, endanger others and never give a second thought about it. Yet the deep concern for life and the law causes grace to act. Not only in picking up the bottle but cleansing the heart of the transgressor.

Talk With God:

How true the fact, sin causes man to break the law; yet how wonderful to know that your grace comes along and removes the sin. Thank you for your amazing grace that picked up the sinner and removed the stain of sin from his life. Amen!

August – Day 24

Text: Psalm 139 3 KJV

"Thou compassest my path and my lying down, and art acquainted with all my ways."

Thought: "You Can't Hide From God!"

Once I learned how to operate the computer with some success, I found myself using it more and more. It is a fascinating machine. The games and graphics are unbelievable. I do not play many games on the computer for fear of becoming hooked and wasting my time. However, I read recently that a number of computer games come with a special feature called a 'boss key." If you're playing a game when you're supposed to be working, and someone (like the boss) walks into your office, you quickly strike the boss key. Your computer screen changes immediately, hiding what you've been doing.

However, attempting to hide from others when you are doing something wrong is not new and did not come into being with the invention of the computer or computer games. People have been hiding wrong doing since the beginning of time to avoid admitting responsibility and feeling guilty.

But as the saying goes, you may fool some of the people some of the time; but you can't fool all the people all the time.

If we attempt to hide our sins (wrong doings) from others, you may succeed. But you will never be able to hide them from God. He sees you and will sentence you if you continue playing the game. However, God would rather teach you discipline and discipleship.

I am glad that I know that He knows. In this knowledge, I am challenged to confess my wrong and confess my need of Him to live in a manner that would glorify God.

Talk With God:

Yes, guilty would be the verdict if I had to ever answer to making an attempt of hiding my attitude and action from God. I have failed by either placing the blame elsewhere or simply saying what or who does it hurt. You know this already Lord; but I need to seek of you to search me again and renew a right spirit within me. Amen!

August – Day 25

Text: Genesis 1:27 KJV

"So God created man in his own image"

Thought: "Appreciated Allegiances to God"

Today is the birthday of our youngest daughter, Melissa. She was the smallest of our three children when she was born. She was allergic to everything the first six months of her life. But soon she outgrew her allergies and began to develop into a healthy individual. Today is she the tallest of the three children and appears to be the healthiest. For this special blessing of a touch to her physical life, I deeply appreciate the Lord.

She is named after my wife, Elaine. However, everyone says she has the character of her father – Me. Now that can be heartache and a headache. Not really – I hope. God has blessed her with musical talent and she can sing beautifully. I pray her allegiances to God will be a life long dedication.

Just as Melissa has been named after her mom and has an almost identical character of her dad; each of us should desire and devote our self to Christ to the point that we are known as "Christians" and portray a character that emulates the traits of the Lord.

Regardless of whom we confront or what the condition that develops, we must possess an appreciate for God and an allegiance to God. He will care for us and carry us through every circumstance triumphantly.

Talk With God:

Thank you Lord of creating us with a living soul that will last forever. Thank you for giving us an example that we may develop that soul to take on your character and quality of life. Thank you for desiring your design to be like you and to dwell with you forever more. Amen!

August – Day 26

Text: Deuteronomy 4:23 KJV

"Take heed unto yourselves, lest ye forget the covenant of the Lord your God"

Thought: "Remind Me Dear Lord!"

In reading a Far Side cartoon recently, the caption read, "Superman in his later years." It shows the elderly Man of Steel perched on a window ledge, ready to leap, as he looks back and says, "Now where was I going?"

The older I get, the more forgetful I become. Yet, I pray each day that I will never forget the promises and precepts of God. I desire to always remember to praise Him for His multifold blessings.

Yet, as I see church growth decline and demoralization increase; it is apparent that man is forgetting God.

Man has become increased in goods, interested in entertainment, involved in pleasure, idolized by self (what's in it for me—have it your way—you deserve a break today). There is no room or reason for God.

God help us. We need you more today than we ever have.

Remind us of the importance and the influence of our relationship with you. Let us never forget how much you love us. For in our relationship with you we have a foundation that will not fail; we have fruit that will provide for our well-being; we have a fortitude against the enemy, natural and supernatural; we have a fellowship that can not be broken and a future that is guaranteed.

In our scripture text, God issued exhortation to obedience. He challenged the children of Israel through Moses. He still challenges His creation through His Word and His witnesses.

Talk With God:

"Lord, you have proven yourself faithful through the generations. Thank you for care. Remind me each day to remember and renew my covenant with you. Guide me this day. Amen!"

August – Day 27

Text: 1 Samuel 15:17 KJV

"When thou wast little in thine own sight, wast thou not made the head of the tribes of Israel, and the Lord anointed thee."

Thought: "Big & Broken"

Today is my big son-in-law's birthday. The reason I say big, is because Clayton is over six feet tall and weighs in the neighborhood of 300 pounds. He is retired from the Navy. He is big and strong for he is constantly involved in physical activities. He built his own house – literally cutting the trees down and made lumber for his two story hillside house. He enjoys doing things with his hands. He is devoted to the church and his conviction of Christ. He has a big heart and a big body. He is a good son-in-law.

Saul of the Old Testament was such a man. He was head and shoulders above everyone else. He was of kingly stature and mighty in strength as a soldier of war. Yet, Saul let his personal attributes and physical stature robs him of the humble spirit needed to be God's man.

Jesus was acquainted with physical ability. He grew up under the tutor of carpentry – pure physical labor. I believe He was a man of muscle as well, as a man of miracles. His compassion reached every arena of life. He endured the physical hardships and the spiritual heartaches of life. Yet, Jesus was big enough to handle every situation. The reason was His willing to yield to the will of the Father.

When we possess a heart of compassion, we can do greater things for God. And when we allow God to couple our physical talents and toughness with His spiritual character, we can do greater things for His glory.

Humble yourself to God and yield your abilities to the work of the Lord.

Talk With God:

Thank you Lord for every muscle, every mental concept and every moral fiber you have graced us with and gifted to us. I desire to be useful in your hands. Mold me into a vessel meet for the Master's use. Amen!

August – Day 28

Text: Deuteronomy 6:7 NIV

"Impress them on your children. Talk about them when you sit at home and when you walk along the road, when you lie down and when you get up"

Thought: "Words Of Truth!"

Have you ever glanced at the cover of magazines as you waited in the grocery store checkout lanes? It seems that sex and social approval tops the list of headlines. Close behind these two are finances, fitness and fraud. None of these magazines offers any positive and pure thoughts for life. No soul food whatsoever. Just slander, separation and scandals.

No wonder the thoughts of man are so corrupt and the tempers of man flare out of control. The wrong reading material is promoted and participated in.

We must learn to read the pages of God's Word and find true satisfaction for which our soul is craving.

The word "Bible" simply means "book." Therefore, let us "search the scripture" . . ."let us study to show ourselves approved unto God". . . "Hear and keep the commandments of the Lord."

The Word of God does more than inform, it inspires and initiates truth within our heart.

Our scripture text explores the importance of searching, sharing and seeking a knowledge the Word of God

Talk With God:

"Lord, we need a revival of the knowledge of God's Word both in our head and in our heart. Challenge us to read and apply the Word of God to our hearts, our heads and our homes. In doing so, help us to scatter the seed of the Word wherever we go and in whatever we say. Amen!"

August – Day 29

Text: II Corinthians 7:10 NIV
"Godly sorrow brings repentance that leads to salvation and leaves no regret."

Thought: "A Simple Reality!"

Two and two makes four – that is mathematics; hydrogen and oxygen forms water – that is chemistry; Christ crucified is the power of God unto salvation – that is revelation. But how do you know?

Put two and two together and you have four, count and see. Put hydrogen and oxygen and you have water – frozen, liquid or in gas form. Test and you prove it. Believe in the Lord Jesus Christ and you shall be saved; try it and prove it.

Our forefathers had to experiment, yet we have the facts before us. If we reject the discovered truths of life, we will not receive the benefits.

We live in a time where knowledge has grown to such degree, only a selected few have the ability to comprehend and continue the advancements in the high-tech world. We all enjoy and are enriched by the modern conveniences, yet we do not understand the make up of such.

I do know that if I follow a certain guideline or program, I will succeed at performing the task. I am glad that I have learned to acknowledge and accept the gift of salvation by confessing my sins and committing my life to Him. I know He will work with me to walk worthy of Him?

The writer of our scripture text challenges us to behold the plan of salvation and believe it. That is a simple reality that each individual is faced with.

Talk With God:

"Lord, I thank you for loving me. Thank you for making it possible to be rescued from sin and receive forgiveness. Guide me and give me understanding to perform my daily walk with you. Amen!"

August – Day 30

Text: Acts 20:24 KJV

"None of these things move me, neither count I my life dear unto myself, so that I might finish my course with joy"

Thought: "Learning From Adversity!"

A notable quote of anonymous source says, "If we can accept each adversity of life as a kick in the pants instead of a slap in the face, adversity then becomes a step up the ladder of success."

Another quote I heard when like these, "when you find yourself in hot water, go ahead and take a bath; it will put things in the past and clean you up for the future."

Still another quote that goes along with these two was: "When you are knocked to your knees, go ahead and seek God in prayer – you will become taller than trees."

Lessons can be learned from these simple and silly little quotes. They pack a serious note of endurances and escape in the experiences of life.

Therefore, when we are faced with situations that may kick our feet from under us or knock us a loop like hitting a brick wall -- shake yourself and clear the birds whistling over our head -- Then pick yourself up and learn from the encounter or experience.

Many will not take this view of adversity. Humanity always wants to seek the cause and view the damage of adversity instead of focusing on the lesson we can learn.

Jesus Christ is our wonderful Counselor. Under his guidance we can see clearly and think soberly regarding the experiences in life.

Whatever we have to experience, we can endure.

Talk With God:

We may not understand Lord why some things happen; however, enable us to learn from every experience we go through. Whatever the day may hold for us, give us grace and strength to endure. Amen.

August – Day 31

Text: 1 Thessalonians 5:22 KJV

"Abstain from all appearance of evil."

Thought: "We Can't Blame God for Yielding To Temptation"

An overweight fellow decided it was time to shed some excess pounds. He took his new diet seriously, even changing his driving route to avoid his favorite bakery. One morning, however, he arrived at work carrying a gigantic coffee cake. Everyone scolded him, but he had an explanation.

"This is a very special coffee cake," he said. "There was a detour so I had to drive by the bakery this morning. I felt this was no accident, so I prayed, "Lord, if you want me to enjoy a delicious coffee cake with my co-workers, open up a parking place in front of the bakery."

"Sure enough," he said, "the 8th time around the block, there it was!"

Don't think "shame on that man." You and I have been guilty of doing things very similar. It amounts to blaming God for our weakness. Which is wrong within itself?

God doesn't lead us into temptation. He is ever presence to deliver us from the traps and temptation that would hinder and hurt our relationship with Him.

We must avoid areas of our life that would cause us to be drawn into partaking of those things or neglecting those things that are harmful to us – physically, mentally and spiritually.

God could shut down every place and shut up every person that stirs up negative and evil controversy in this life; yet God had rather we lean on Him to direct our lives.

We must make an effort to shun the very appearance of evil and keep a focus on the glory of our Lord.

Talk With God:

Lord, I do need your anointing and your amazing grace to face, fight and fling aside the temptations and tactics of the enemy of my soul. Go with me each step of every day. Amen!

Step 9 – September
"Back – To - Basics"

The only way to win over temptations is to rely on the good old-fashion gospel of Jesus Christ. We must get back to the basics of life.

What are the basic's of life? Some would say the 3R's: Reading, 'riting and 'rithmetic. Some would say, God, country and family. I would say both.

We have a society that has more college graduates than ever before, yet we have a society that does not know how to read, write nor do simple math. The electronic age has made dummies of us in respect of the 3R's.

The same is true of our moral obligations to God, our country and our families. We have more problems that deal with moral issues than ever before; yet we still ask why? The reason is three fold: we have eliminated our personal and daily devotion to God, we have eroded our country's core values and we have eradicated the harmony and happiness of the home and the family.

Come on folks; let us get back to the basic principles and philosophy that made our nation – the education program, the moral standard, the family values and the democratic state of being. We must find time to re-evaluate and restore respect and reverences in the places, positions and people that need it.

As a small boy told his dad one dad in response to the question, "Son, do you know what the Bible is?" His response was "yes, dad, it is basic instruction before leaving earth."

How true. Let us never forget the importance of getting back to the basics in our heart, in our homes and in our homeland.

September – Day 1

Text: Galatians 6:8 NIV

"The one who sows to please his sinful nature from that nature will reap destruction."

Thought: "Sin Is Dangerous & Deadly!"

Bob found a tiny snake in his backyard. It was just a little thing, so he brought it into his home. He thought it would make a good pet. As he listened to the local news that night, he learned that a baby boa constrictor was missing from the city zoo. Bob knew he should return the snake. He knew how dangerous an adult boa was. But it was such an unusual pet he kept it, fed it, and played with it. He intended to get rid of it before it became an adult. However, Bob waited to long. One day the snake wound itself around Bob and began to squeeze. Bob was crushed to death.

Friends, Satan tries to make self-centeredness and sin habits look harmless. His temptations are always appealing. Individuals fed and playfully fondle harmful habits and hurtful attitudes the same way Bob played with the boa. Thinking, it's not hurting anyone and it makes me happy. However, just as Bob thought he was in control of the situation; people think they can manage their attitude and actions.

Yet, if caution is not taken, there will come a day when the effects of being self-centered and entertaining sinful habits will become so strong it will crush you to a spiritual death.

Let us be cautious regarding the thoughts we think, the talk we engage in, and the things we do in life. Don't let them grow to the degree that they dominate you and rob you of the blessings of genuine liberty of life.

Yes, the pleasure of sin appeals to the carnal nature of man and we think that we can control it. However, as we become attracted, attached and affected by its influence, it is too late. Without warning, it will sap the very life of anything good from us and leave us with nothing but a destiny of destruction and death.

Talk With God:

Lord, help us to be aware of the dangers of turning our attention to things that will harm our relationship with you. Keep our minds fresh with your Word and feet planted firmly on the path of righteousness in order that we may not be deceived and detoured from the path of life. Walk with us this day. Amen!

September – Day 2

Text: Psalm 61:3 Amplified Bible
"For you have been a shelter and a refuge for me."

Thought: "We need a Shelter in Time of Stress & Storm"

I remember hearing a story told by a very faithful church member several years ago. He said when he would get upset or did not understand why something occurred or when he faced a situation of which required deep consideration and definite direction; he would steal away to an old tree stump in an open grassy area in a small clump of woods. There he would talk with God and take a moment to listen as the Holy Spirit would speak to his heart and fill his mind with pure, positive and peaceful thoughts regarding his dilemma.

Every man must have someone or something in which he hopes, on which he leans, to which he retreats and retires, with which he fills up his thoughts in facing experiences of life. A place or person he confides in when he is pressed with troubles, trials and temptations. A spot or a specific person to which he takes himself in sorrow and in struggles to draw comfort and courage.

Many individuals think a good place of refuge is found at the local pub and with the bottle. Some turn to the recliner and a good novel. Others explode and cause abuse at home and on the job. However, a quiet place with the Wonderful Counselor is the greatest place of refuge, release and research.

It is reassuring and reinforcing to know there is someone to call on or cry to when the waves are high and the winds are harsh.

Jesus would steal away to the garden and gain strength from the Heavenly Father.

We too can pause morning, noon or night and speak with the Lord Jesus Christ. He is always available. He is sufficient and able to supply and strengthen. Trust in Him.

I love a song our youngest daughter sings, "I Go To The Rock." There we can find calm, comfort and courage.

Talk With God:

Lord, how often I have to pause, during the day and in the darkness of night, and whisper the words, "It's me again Lord; I got a problem I can't solve, I've got a prayer that needs an answer." It is so wonderful to sense your presences and hear your voice of encouragement. Thank you Lord for being that Person and that place I turn to. Amen!

September – Day 3

Text: Psalm 23:5 NIV

"You anoint my head with oil, by cup overflows."

Thought: "Fill My Cup to Overflowing"

One night in ancient times, three horsemen were riding across a desert. As they crossed the dry bed of a river, out of the darkness a voice called, "Halt."

They obeyed. The voice then told them to dismount, pick up a handful of pebbles, put the pebbles in their pockets and remount.

The voice then said, "you have done as I commanded. Tomorrow at sun-up you will be both glad and sorry." Mystified, the horsemen rode on.

When the sun rose, they reached into their pockets and found that a miracle had happened. The pebbles had been transformed into diamonds, rubies, and precious stones. They remembered the warning. They were both glad and sorry – glad they had taken some, and sorry they had not taken more.

Don't let this day be a day in which you are both glad and sad.

As believers, during our devotional time, we are so guilty of pausing just long enough to feel good about our self then we continue on the journey. However, if we would take a little longer – not only to look into the Word of God but to listen to the voice of God – we would be stronger longer and more satisfied down the stretch.

God has great treasures for you in His Word, therefore, allow the Holy Spirit to enrich your live daily and overflow your spirit with abundant life.

Talk With God:

"Lord, we are thankful for each moment we pause to fellowship with you and be filled with your grace and guiding presence. Fill our life to overflowing that we may squeak with your delight as we walk our daily path. Amen!"

September – Day 4

Text: Psalm 27:13 NIV

"I will see the goodness of the lord in the land of the living."

Thought: "I Saw A Bit Of God Today!"

I read an article the other day entitled, "I Saw A Bit of God Today!" Permit me to share it with you.

"As I went about my chores today, I knew that God was present. . .

When the man at the wallpaper store said, "Take the whole roll home and see if it matches." It reminded me, God is helpful.

When my niece suggested, "If I fold the clothes, you won't have that job to do." It reminded me that God is thoughtful.

When a shopper motioned, "Go ahead of me, you have just a few items." It reminded me God is considerate.

When I saw a boy cradling a hurt kitten in his arms; It reminded me that God is compassionate.

When I heard a man say to his wife, "Don't hurry, I'll wait for you." It reminded me that God is patient."

Let me challenge you to look for God wherever and in whatever you do today. Let me encourage you to show God to others in your own conduct, conversation and countenance.

God is present in every circumstance. He is helpful, thoughtful, considerate, and patient. We need only to focus and see His abiding presences.

Talk With God:

Lord, teach me to look for you as I travel each step of each day. Enable me to see your blessings as you reveal yourself in the smallest occurrence. Enrich me with the privilege of knowing you are before me, beside me, beneath me and behind me as I walk the path of life. Amen!

September – Day 5

Text: Psalm 37:23 NIV

"If the Lord delights in a man's way, he makes his steps firm; though he stumble, he will not fall, for the Lord upholds him with his hand."

Thought: "Only One Day at a Time!"

A lady met with a serious accident, which necessitated a painful surgical procedures, and many months of confinement in bed. When the physician had finished his work and was taking his leave, the patient asked, "Doctor, how long shall I have to lie here helpless?"

"Oh, only one day at a time," was the cheerful answer. And the poor sufferer was only comforted for the moment, but many times during the succeeding weary weeks the thought, "only one day at a time," came back with a soothing influence.

You know Christ is the Great Physician of the body and soul. He speaks the same words to each of us regardless of what we encounter or have to endure – "Only one day at a time." When trials and troubles come our way, let us allow our Creator, caretaker and comforter – Jesus Christ – to perform a spiritual procedure and then step by step encourage us as we walk the road of recovery, restoration and renewal.

As we take this day, let us walk by faith and believe that God is with us to enrich us and encourage us. Regardless of how we feel at this moment or what we may encounter in the moments ahead, we shall take it in stride and succeed by the gracious empowering of the Master's strong hand.

Talk With God:

Lord, enable us to be convinced that each step we take every day is ordered by you and nothing shall confront us which we shall not be able to endure or escape. Amen!

September – Day 6

Text: Psalm 34:8 Amplified Bible

"O taste and see that the Lord [our God] is good! Blessed—happy, fortunate [to be envied] – is the man who trusts and takes refuge in Him."

Thought: "Goodness!"

When someone asks me how I am doing, I have on numerous occasions replied, "I am doing good. Mother never had to pay me to be good, she always said I was good for nothing."

Although I have stated this, the contents are not true. I had a good and godly mother.

Charles Kingsley once spoke of goodness by saying, "it was not merely a beautiful thing, but by far the most beautiful thing in the whole world. So that nothing is to be compared for value with goodness; that riches, honor, power, pleasure, learning, the whole world and all in it, are not worth having in comparison with being good; and utterly the best thing for man is to be good."

But to be good according to the Word of God is to have Jesus Christ. For the Bible says, "The fruit of the Spirit is . . . goodness." It also bears out that there is none good except one – Jesus Christ.

You may have thought all along that you were pretty good. For man usually bases his personal evaluation against others; therefore, in comparison to someone else's character and conduct you may be morally or materially or monetarily above them; however, it wrong for us to justify our worth by comparing our lifestyle with another.

We must compare our life with He who is life – Jesus Christ. When we do this, no one is considered good. However, we become good and godly when we accept the will and way of Jesus Christ, who is the essence of goodness.

Talk With God:

Lord, without you we are good for nothing. But with you, it is a whole new ballgame. We become your child of whom you are well pleased. Thank you for taking my filthy rags of sin and shame and giving me garments of salvation and a robe of righteousness. Let me walk before you this day in the goodness of your character. Amen!

September – Day 7

Text: James 3:5 Amplified Bible

"Even so the tongue is a little member, and it can boost of great things. See how much wood or how great a forest a tiny spark can set ablaze!"

Thought: "Small Can Be Sufficient!"

A tree can produce a million match sticks, yet a single match can destroy a million trees.

How true the preceding statement is! A single tree is capable of being trimmed and cut in a manner that a million or more matchsticks can be produced; yet a single matchstick tipped with a combustible head can ignite and eliminate a million or more trees.

Did you know that your tongue can produce a million words of allegiance and appreciation yet a single word spoken by the same tongue can destroy all the praise you offered?

God designed the tongue to be a tool for speaking. Yet the tongue can only speak what the mind directs it to. If the mind is filled with filth and foul language, then out the mouth words of negative and nonsense. If the mind is filled with the attributes of the Spirit (Galatians 5:22-23), then words of positive thought, pure intent and praise will flow.

Let our conversations be as the truth of the Gospel.

As I have said and heard others say, "If you can't say something good don't talk." We should speak words toward others that we would enjoy hearing ourself.

Words can bring cheer to the sad, comfort to the broken, courage to the defeated, and confidence to the weak. Let us be challenged to speak words that will bring delight not words that are damaging, disappointing or detrimental.

Talk With God:

Lord, today and every day, I wish to speak words that will be unique in bringing health, harmony, happiness and hope. Enrich me and enable me to be constructive with my thoughts that are translated into talk. Let the words of my mouth be acceptable in your sight. Amen!

September – Day 8

Text: Isaiah 17:10 KJV

"Because thou hast forgotten the God thy salvation, and hast not been mindful of the rock of thy strength."

Thought: "Keep In Mind!"

Permit me to share with you the word of St. Francis de Sales. "Every morning compose your soul for a tranquil day, and all through it be careful often to recall your resolution, and bring yourself back to it, so to say. If something discomposes you, do not be upset, or troubled; but having discovered the fact, humble yourself gently before God, and try to bring your mind into a quiet attitude. Say to yourself, Well, I have made a false step; but now I must go more carefully and watchfully. This do each time, and you shall not become discouraged but encouraged and depend on the true guide, the Lord Jesus Christ."

A search of His wonderful Word each morning produces a solid and sure principle to recall each step throughout the day. The moment by moment recall of His promises and presence will provide thanksgiving for your relationships and thoughts of peace knowing He cares and will carry you through whatever you encounter.

In our scripture text, Israel is threatened for their unwillingness to keep in mind the power, presence and promises of God. They fail to recall the precious memories and powerful moments of a true and triumph God.

Talk With God:

Lord, enable us to keep you in mind as we travel throughout each day. Help us to start with a moment of renewing and refreshing our relationship with you; then continue to maintain a close, courageous and confident reminder of that relationship.

September – Day 9

Text: Psalm 23:2-3 NIV

"He makes me lie down in green pastures, he leads me beside quiet waters, he restores my soul. He guides me in paths of righteousness for his name sake."

Thought: "Pause, Yet Press On!"

Robert Frost in his famous poem, "Stopping by woods on a snowy evening," tells about a man whom some picture as an old country doctor making a house call far out in the country after a full day's work.

Driving along the edge of the woods that cold snowy night, he stopped for a moment and became absorbed in the beauty and blessed quietness he found there. As he paused, a wave of weariness swept over him, and he pondered how wonderful it would be if he could stay there and rest. Yet, something inside made him continue on his way.

There is not a person alive that doesn't desire to pause and ponder the idea of relaxing and resting from the hustle and bustle of everyday living. Yet, somehow we must keep on keeping on in this life's journey. We must make the necessary provisions of living and keep the promises made.

However, you can be refreshed and reassured that there is a genuine friend who has an unseen arm of courage and anchor of confidence that will strengthen you and keep you each and every step of each and every day.

Our scripture text reminds us that God is a Great Shepherd and we are His sheep. He will lead us not into temptation but will renew the inner man day by day with clear, cleansing water and a fresh, flowing breeze of heaven that will restore and ready us for the journey of righteous living.

Talk With God:

Thank you Lord for your abiding presence that will gird me with renewed strength, guide me in refreshing paths and grant me the realism of living for your glory. Amen!

September – Day 10

Text: John 4:13-14 NIV

"Jesus answered, everyone who drinks this water will be thirsty again, but whoever drinks the water I give him will never thirst. Indeed, the water, I give will become in him a spring of water welling up to eternal life."

Thought: "Connected!"

A United Press release in a Midwestern city told of a hospital where official discovered that the firefighting equipment had never been connected. For thirty-five years it had been relied upon for the safety of the patients in case of emergency. But it had never been attached to the city's water main. The pipe that led from the building extended four feet underground and there it stopped. The medical staff and the patients had felt complete confidence in the system throughout the years. However, they had a false security. The system lacked the most important thing – water.

This illustrates the condition of many people in our society today, especially in the matter of spiritual salvation. They have never been connected to Jesus Christ – the source of living water. Although you may have moral principles and material possessions, you lack the righteousness which is of God by faith. You have never allowed the flow of living water to cleanse away your sins and cause an overflow of peace, power and personal fellowship with Jesus Christ.

Be sure you are hooked up to the source of life and it more abundant. You will need the refreshing relief when fires of adversity flame up.

What a delight it is to know that the Lord is our source of relief and reassurance when we are thirsty, when we are troubled and when we are torched by the fiery darts of Satan.

Talk With God:

Thank you Lord, for the opportunity to have a relationship with you. Thank you for being sure the work is complete and we are connected to the source of living water. What a joy it is to know we have complete assurance that we are connected. Amen!

September – Day 11

Text: Ezekiel 18:31 KJV

"Make you a new heart and a new spirit."

Thought: "The Heart Procedure!"

Today is a day of remembrance. First, no one alive at the turn of the century will ever forget the events that took place in 2002. Terrorist attacks on US soil that took the lives of hundreds and destroyed millions of dollars in property. The events changed the lives of thousands across the land and around the world.

Secondly, our youngest grandson, Dawson, was born one year later. He was born with a heart malfunction – SVTs. Many times his little heart would speed up and beat over two hundred times a minute turning him into a limp and almost lifeless form. We spend many a moment in prayer, performing exercises on him during the attacks and speeding up the highway to the Children's Hospital. For six long years, he battled the malfunction of his heart, braved the hospital ER visits and bore the burden of constant doses of medicine. Then one day the heart specialist told us they were ready to do the procedure of hoping to correct the problem.

They performed a heart procedure that corrected the problem, eliminated the medicine and attacks, and gave him a new lease on life. He is full of energy, smart and realizes God's hand was and is on his life.

Every person must experience a heart procedure in order to gain a new lease on life. Just as our scripture text states, we must allow the Lord to correct the problem – which is transgressions in our heart – and consecrate our spirit.

As we commit our lives to God each day, we are literally giving Him charge to cleanse us from any wrong, correct our focus and create within the right spirit. When we do this, our relationship with life is improved.

Talk With God:

Today and each day, O Lord, correct the erratic thoughts and things of my heart that may not be in line with your divine will. Create within me a renewed spirit that honors you and gives happiness, health and hope to my life. Amen!

September – Day 12

Text: Acts 17:28 KJV

"For in Him we live, and move and have our being"

Thought: "Accomplishments!"

Have you ever said, "Oh, I could never do that? I'm just not creative."

It seems we all think "the other guy" is the one who is creative, gifted, and talented.

You may think you're not creative because you see creativity as limited to things like writing poetry or music, or painting pictures, or the performing arts or personally inventing something fantastic. Yet, in reality, creativity is ever so much more common that that.

Creativity is calling into being anything that did not exist before. Creativity is calling into being harmony where there has been a troubled relationship or order where there has been chaos. Creativity is causing the fruit of the Spirit (Galatians 5:22-23) to blossom and bring beauty and fragrance to life. Creativity is just part of our potential as creatures of God.

We must wake up our creativity by realizing our relationship with the Creator of the universe. God did not create us to be nothing. He gave us the opportunity, we must take the initiative.

I love that song, "Jesus Use Me!" In this song, I find that when I make myself available to the abiding presence and abounding power of God, I can be creative with my life. I can accomplish! I can fulfill! For my life is in His hands to discipline, design and develop for my good and His glory.

Talk With God:

Jesus, I am glad that I know you are my Creator, my Confidence and my Creativity. Remind me each day that I am what I allow you to make me and where you are permitted to use me. Amen!

September – Day 13

Text: James 1:22 NIV

"You see that his faith and his actions were working together, and his faith was made complete by what he did."

Thought: "Available and Applied"

I read a story recently concerning a confrontation that the great English theologian, John Wesley, experienced. It told of a time when he was preaching that the town bully began heckling him. The bully was a large, unkempt man and he shouted at Wesley, "We've had Christianity for over 1700 years now. What's it ever done? We're in just as big a mess now as we've ever been in."

Wesley looked at him for a moment. Then he said, "my good man, don't you know that we have had water for much longer than that, but you're still got a dirty face. You're got to use something before it works."

Faith is like that. For it to be effective in saving, stabilizing and strengthening a life, it must be accepted and applied – beheld and believed.

The promises of God have been available to man ever since his creation, yet repeatedly man has refused to apply (believe, use, accept) the principles of God.

Today is a new day. It is the first day of the rest of your life. Begin afresh with a firm conviction that God's presence, God's power, God's peace and God's principles are going to be applied to your life. When done, it will enhance you, encourage others and exalt God.

Talk With God:

Thank you Lord for making available to me the riches of your word, your works and your way. Thank you for convincing me to apply your law, your liberty and your love to my life. It has made a difference in me. Guide me in steps I take this day. Amen!

September – Day 14

Text: Psalm 139:23-24 KJV *(personal comments in italic)*

"Search me, O God, and know my heart: try me, and know my thoughts: And see if there be any wicked way in me, and lead *(discipline, direct, develop)* me"

Thought: "Is It I?"

Somewhere I read about the wretched violinist who began a concert complaining about the poor quality of the instrument he was using. Another instrument was obtained and music grew worse. Still a third instrument was presented to him and he was so embarrassed by the sour notes that he crashed the instrument into splinters.

A subdued voice from the audience was heard to say, "The violin is blamed for the poor quality of music. Perhaps the musician should look at himself."

Individuals are bent on murmuring and complaining about the sour notes of life, yet the Word of God reminds us that, "and He beheld all that He had made, and it was good."

Maybe, instead of being critical and complaining or blaming, we need to begin evaluating our dedication and determination of being committed to doing our part. It may take a change of attitude and action to accomplish the task. However, let us be willing to look at ourself and consider the possibility.

The Psalmist desire was to be in the will of God. He knew God was aware of his past circumstances, present conditions and personal pursuits. Therefore, he sought for God to search his life, knowing that God would take care of providing the external instruments of use once he was yielded to inventory and inspiration.

Let God search us daily, and then direct us in making heavenly and harmonious music of life throughout the day.

Talk With God:

Lord, I am grateful for the opportunity to play in your orchestra on earth. Empower me and enrich me to put forth my best in producing music of praise. Amen!

September – Day 15

Text: Psalm 118:24 KJV

"This is the day that God hath made; we will rejoice and be glad in it."

Thought: "This Is God's Day!"

If someone gave us a million dollars, we would not hide it in a box and do nothing with it. We would not wake each morning worrying about an essential item we needed. We would not wonder what we would spend it on tomorrow. We simply would enjoy the opportunity of having received such a marvelous monetary gift. It would become a daily enjoyment to experience.

It is not likely that you would be one who receives a million bucks, but you are given a new day every 24-hours.

If we fill our hours with regrets over the failures of yesterday, and with worries over the problems of tomorrow, we have no today in which to be thankful, thoughtful and truly happy.

How true this statement is! And how sad it is that many people live with such a downhearted attitude.

However, if we awake to a new day (and it is oblivious we did for we are reading this devotion); let us focus on this day and not let yesterday nor tomorrow ruin it for us. There will be enough troubles, trials and triumphs to face today without even considering those things behind us and those things before us.

Keep in mind, that today may be the last day of your life – make it your best day. It will be the first day of the rest of your life – therefore, we have an opportunity to begin afresh.

Take each step as if we are walking the path of life hand-in-hand with the King of Kings. Speak each thought with the guidance and grace of God. This is His day – the Lord has made it and He will work all things together for good if we will love Him, live for Him and let Him lead us.

Talk With God:

Today, Lord, is a gift from you to each of us. Teach us to enjoy it and be enriched by every encounter we experience. Help us to rejoice and render praise regardless of our circumstance or condition, remembering that you are walking by our side and on our side. Amen!

September – Day 16

Text: 1 John 2:16-17 NIV

"For everything in the world – the cravings of sinful man, the lust of his eyes, and the boasting of what he has and does – comes not from the Father but from the world. The world and its desires pass away, but the man who does the will of God lives forever."

Thought: "Avoid & Avail!"

Carbonic acid gas, commonly known as choke-damp, is usually found in pits or the bottom of old wells. It is so called because it has often suffocated those who came into contact with it.

Life is filled with polluted, poisonous and potentially deadly temptations, traps and tricks. In the pit of iniquity and in the old wells of worldliness this soul-choking damp still abounds. If you wish your spiritual life choked, just go down into the darkness of prayerlessness, into the drained and empty well of neglectfulness of God's Word, and comb the pits of the world's pleasures. Heed not the warnings of the Holy Spirit and you will find there is enough poison gas there and will take your heavenly breath away.

Avoid the above by maintaining a consistent prayer life, a committed study of God's Word and a consecrated life style. Allow God to keep a fresh flow of heavenly oxygen into your spirit to give you the attitude, action and allegiance for a holy, honorable and happy life.

As we walk in the boldness and breathe of God, we are able to avoid and avail in this sinful and sinking world. We shall stand and shout His praises for the victory over the wrong, wicked and the wretched plans of the enemy.

Positioned in Christ puts us in a heavenly atmosphere where we can avoid the poison and pollution of this world.

Talk With God:

Because these sin-pits exist everywhere in today's society; Lord, warn us of the dangers, wrap us in your power and walk with us that we be not led astray. We need your spirit, your signal and your safety. Amen!

September – Day 17

Text: Job 1:21 NIV

"The Lord gave and the lord has taken away, may the name of the Lord be praised."

Thought: "The Lord allocates, allows and anoints!"

I read an article once that told of a family in northern Michigan who lost all they had in a killer tornado that ripped through their home. However, the family was spared and as they climbed up from the storm cellar and viewed the damage, the man of the house paused and said, God has a hand in everything that happens to us for we are his.

But you may ask how the fierce winds of adversity can create worship in the heart! The answer is clear: by anchoring our faith in the love and leadership of God, and by saying through our tears, "The Lord gave, and the Lord hath taken away; blessed be the name of the Lord."

Remember: when you are swept off your feet, slip down on your knees and give praise to God.

As you walk through the trials and troubles of daily life, keep your focus and fix your hope in Christ. The things of this world will pass away one day any way, therefore, don't attach yourself to earthly treasures that may dissipate or be destroyed at any time.

The Lord does bless us with many treasures, talents and things; but he also allows those things to decay, be destroyed and die. Yet take heart for He will anoint us with his keeping power and presence. He will grace us with those things which will not die, diminish nor be destroyed.

The patriarch of the Old Testament, Job had been blessed extraordinary – he had homes and health, family and friends, property and plenty of cattle, wealth and a wonderful relationship with God. Yet Job loss everything, except his wife and his relationship with God. In it all, he declared it was temporary – here today, gone tomorrow – and it was not the real treasure anyway. His relationship with God was what mattered most.

Begin this day, brave the events of this day and behold this day at its closing as an opportunity to bless the name of the Lord regardless of what may happen.

Talk With God:

Thank you Lord for the promise that you will give me the internal faith and fortitude to trust you regardless of what comes. I lean on you and love you. Amen!

September – Day 18

Text: 1 Thessalonians 5:17 NIV
"Pray continually"

Thought: "A.S.A.P.!"

We live in a society where messages are put in abbreviated form, which is, using letters to form messages or to identify organizations. In personal phone texting, I saw one the other day that said OMG which meant "oh, my goodness!" In the abbreviations of department titles, we have seen the letters FBI, which stands for "Federal Bureau of Investigation." In the business world, we see companies like ABC or NBC that shortens their name from "American Broadcasting Company," and "National Broadcasting Company." Even in religious circles we see PTL which stands for "Praise The Lord" or "People That Love."

I like using the letters ASAP. It normally stands for "As Soon As Possible." I am a "Type A" personality. I am always in a hurry and most of the time I want a response from others in a hurry. God has helped me greatly with being less anxious and more patience.

And the way He has helped me is by giving me another meaning for this abbreviation. No, it is not my idea, but one day I came across it and the Holy Spirit placed neon lights flashing around it –not really. However, it became a blessing to me and very beneficial. ASAP should mean "Always Say A Prayer!"

If we would learn to prayer more, we would be able to enjoy life better and be able to express God's love and liberty greater.

Just remember: In regard to prayer, we need both to pray and be remembered in prayer. It will make your day better. It will benefit those you encounter and assist you in your daily experiences.

Talk With God:

I ask you Lord to bless my family, my friends and my foes. I ask you to direct my steps and develop within me a spirit of prayerfulness. Help me to be conscious of your abiding presence and anointing power. Amen!

September – Day 19

Text:　Luke 9:62 KJV

"And Jesus said unto him, No man, having put his hand to the plough and looking back is fit for the kingdom of God."

Thought:　"Be Determined!"

From history we find that people laughed at Christopher Columbus, but he went on to discover America, the greatest nation on the face of the globe today. They said Alexander Graham Bell was a madman, but he went on to invent the telephone and began the journey that evolved into the high-tech society of which we can't live without. Many people said the Wright Brothers were fools, but hey built an airplane that would fly and set the stage for modern aircraft.

Friend, if we look at our circumstances and listen to the opposition in attempting to live for Christ we may become dishearten, doubtful and defeated. But if we focus our eyes on God, feed on His Word and faithfully follow Him; we shall be encouraged, enriched and energized for His service and our spiritual success.

Heaven is worth making an effort no matter who says what. You can be on the winning side.

In our text, we see Jesus responding to the excuses given by three who were asked to follow Him. Friends, when Jesus speaks to our heart to be his disciple, we must be willing to decide, devote, discipline and become determined to put forth our all in following Him. Not a one of those mentioned above achieved their goals by allowing distractions, detours and delays to hinder their push forward. Neither should we.

Therefore, today, be determined to stand tall, smile and seek to fulfill His will in pursuing the goals He has challenged you with.

Talk With God:

Lord, I may never amount to much in this life nor achieve great success according to this world; but I am determined to please you, promote your kingdom and be presented the prize of eternal life. Amen!

September – Day 20

Text: Ephesians 1:4 Philips NT in Modern English

"For consider what he has done – before the foundation of the world he chose us . . . in Christ to become. . . his holy and blameless children living within his constant care."

Thought: "No Accident, It Was Planned!"

Have you ever heard anyone comment, "That was no accident; it was planned?"

I am sure most of us have heard it said or maybe even spoken it ourselves. And it is true on occasions. Such an occasion was the death of Jesus Christ on the cross.

For you see, mankind needed a Redeemer – humanity needed someone or something to perform the necessary act that would deliver all from the snares of sins. Jesus Christ, the Son of God, was willing to become the sacrificial Lamb. He was willing to be robed in flesh and shed His precious life's blood. It didn't just happen on the spur of the moment. It was planned in the beginning by the supreme, supernatural and sovereign God.

And it is no accident that you feel guilty at times when you do wrong. It is no accident that you feel lonely at times. It is no accident that you feel discontent and desire something to feel the vacancy in your inner being. God created man with a soul. And that soul – spirit – desires a relationship with a sinless God. Therefore, the Holy Spirit brings guilt of wrong, gnawing for right and groaning for the relationship that satisfies.

It is not accidental that you are in this life. You were created to become acquainted with and walk in accord with the Master of Life – God. You may buck the plan but happiness, hope and harmony will never be yours without a relationship with God. God has made it possible through Jesus Christ for us to become holy and blameless children of God.

The plan is prepared. The participation is up to you. So, is this day! It wasn't created overnight. It was planned. You can walk worthy of its blessing by beginning it with a fresh taste of His Word and a fresh touch of His Spirit.

Talk With God:

Lord thank you for knowing the order of the day. I don't, but I will follow your instruction, inspiration and inhabitation of my life. Love me and lead me. Amen!

September – Day 21

Text: Hebrews 6:11 KJV

"And we desire that every one of you do shew the same diligence to the full assurance of hope unto the end"

Thought: "Insurance or Assurance?"

I would like to ask you an important question, in fact, it is really several questions?

Do you have adequate insurance coverage? Is your home adequately covered if something catastrophic were to occur? Will the coverage be enough to rebuild and refurnish your home? Do you have complete coverage – collision and liability – on your automobile? Is your health insurance adequate for the procedures and period of stay in the hospital, the physician's care of you and your prescriptions? Do you have supplement medical coverage for dental and eye care? Do you have burial or life insurance that will aid your family?

No, I am not taking a survey nor do I sell insurances. However, I do believe that insurance coverage is very important for you and your family.

Although you may have adequate insurance coverage that will provide satisfactory care, comfort and construction (replacement); but it can't provide internal strength and stability.

The plan of salvation and the promised benefits offered by the Son of God, Jesus Christ, will provide that internal inspiration and instruction for times of crises and in the course of daily living. It is available free of charge. It is the only plan in which benefits will not change from state to state or from age to age.

Claim the benefits today and walk with assurance that your agent, Jesus Christ, has you in His hands.

Talk With God:

I am glad and grateful for the blessed assurance that I have in you Lord. I am thankful for the knowledge of your Word and the keen awareness of your Spirit that is available to me and abides with me. Today, I shall walk in that assurances and attempt to witness that blessed hope to others in what I say and do. Amen!

September – Day 22

Text: Hebrews 3:14 KJV

For we are made partakers of Christ, if we hold the beginning of our confidence steadfast unto the end."

Thought: "Consistency!"

Did you know the cheetah, a hunting leopard, can travel seventy miles an hour? The cheetah is one of the swiftest of all the animals, but he does have one physical problem – he tires quickly. He can run at top speed only a few hundred yards and then he can quickly be outdistanced by other animals. He lacks the strength and endurance for a long race.

Spurts of enthusiasm won't do!

We must be consistent in our life style.

And speaking of life styles – do you have a profitable life style? -- One which offers satisfaction today and tomorrow. A life devoted to and directed by Jesus Christ.

In Jesus we can be both faithful and fruitful regardless of the circumstances and conditions. He cares for us and will carry us through life.

Our relationship with Christ is based on a decision we made to surrender our all to Christ at the point of conviction and conversion. It is kept fresh and flowing as we live daily in a consistent devotion to His Word, His Will and His Way.

Life may go up and down at times. It may go round and round. But let us keep our focus and faith on Him. He will take us up the hill and down the hill. He will enable us to make the full circle when we get spun around by circumstances in life. Just stay true and stay tuned to God's voice.

Talk With God:

Lord, you are always consistent. You waver not! You wander not! You waste not! Therefore, enrich me and enable me to be faithful in my relationship with you and with others. Amen!

September – Day 23

Text: Matthew 6:6 NKJV

"But when you pray, enter into thy closet, and when you have shut the door, pray to the Father in secret; and the Father which sees in secret shall reward you openly."

Thought: "The Prayer Closet"

In the 1980's I read a story of a very famous individual. I will not mention his name, but a certain celebrity enjoyed being the center of attention. Because he was a witty conversationalist he usually did become the focal point of any gathering.

But one evening while attending a dinner things didn't go his way. Nobody seemed interested in what he had to say. Those who did listen disagreed with his opinions. Finally, he jumped up from where he was sitting and left the room, slamming the door behind him.

In the silence which followed, one of the guests said, "Well, he's gone." But the hostess replied, "No, he isn't. He went into the closet."

Friends, it is important to possess the right attitude toward one another. If we don't we may wish we had a closet to hid in.

The best attitude can be developed from the closet – the prayer closet, that is. In communing with Christ, we can become like him -- possessing a pure attitude and performing the proper action.

Remember: Prayer is not a one-way street. It is not a time to always present your petitions to God. It is not a time to complain. It is a time of relationship. It is a time to praise Him for what He has already granted and gives to you. It is time to devote yourself afresh to His will for your life. It is a time to thank Him for His promises yet to be received. Steal away and commune with Him on a daily basis.

A prayer closet can be anywhere you pause and shut out the noise of life, then commune with the Lord.

Talk With God:

Lord, I am glad that I can commune with you anywhere, anytime. Do not let me come to you to grip, but to give you my heart to renew and my mind to refresh. I need the best you have for me to confront and combat the circumstances of daily life. Therefore, equip me with your Spirit. Amen!

September – Day 24

Text: Psalm 5:3 NIV

"In the morning, O Lord, you hear my voice; in the morning I lay my requests before you and wait in expectation."

Thought: "The Beginning of Each Day!"

I have trouble with my back being stiff first thing in the morning. A friend, with medical knowledge, told me to do a few simple exercises with my legs prior to getting out of bed would ease the discomfort. I tried it and it helped.

I have always felt that a few moments spent talking sincerely and simple with Christ before getting out of bed in the morning would make a big difference in the way I felt personally and reacted toward others. If I were to survey the days gone by, I would have to admit that the mornings I spent a moment with God produced a better day than the mornings I rushed into the day's activities without spending a moment of prayer and Bible reading.

Therefore, I am convinced that the waking moments of each day will be the sum total of a person's thinking processes. Our attitudes and actions will reflect our beginning moments.

If we meditate on God's Word, our thoughts will be to become engaged in wholesome and wonderful relationships throughout the day. If our thoughts are built on disappointment, dreariness, and dread; we probably will carry such attitudes throughout the day.

Let us be challenged to reflect on God's keeping power, our keen awareness that we need Him for the journey ahead and our knowledge of God's gracious and glorious promises. It will make a difference.

We have nothing to lose and everything to gain by beginning our day with a moment with Christ.

Talk With God:

Lord, today, I begin with a moment of spiritual exercise. I desire to be faithful and fruitful today for your glory. Use me to touch a life and make a difference. Amen!

September – Day 25

Text: Matthew 5:13 NIV

"You are the salt of the earth!"

Thought: "S.A.L.T.!"

Acronyms are words that are abbreviations for certain messages. The word "salt" has been used as a message of challenge to witness for Jesus Christ. Although in our scripture text, the literal use of the word is implied. However, let me use the word in acronym form to simply expound the meaning of our text.

S.A.L.T. means "Sharing Agape Love Today!"

It is the privilege and potential of every born again believer to share the total self giving love of Jesus each and every day. We must strive to exemplify a lifestyle that portrays the love of God.

The reason this thought is so real to me as I write this evening is due to the fact that I have just experienced such agape love extended to my family. Our home was hit with a mirco-burst wind (unformed tornado) that did almost $30,000 damage. We were unhurt, yet we had a lot of cleaning up and fixing up to do. I had an important meeting the afternoon following the storm in a city an hour and a half away, yet I needed to get some things done in our damaged condition. My retired neighbor, George, came to the rescue -- Aged but agile and aggressive in tackling the problem at hand. What a blessing! Kevin, Dana and Emily from the church came without invitation and picked up where George and I left off. They did a magnificent job even in my absence. Helping them was another church couple – Kelly and Linda. These folk demonstrated a love without reservation and restraint. To them all I am grateful.

I wish to challenge each reader to realize that Jesus gave His all for us. The least we can do as believers is to give our all to Him and in service to others prove our obedience to be the salt of the earth. As we obey God's directive and love others unselfishly, we are the salt (seasoning) of which Jesus spoke. Therefore, on the job, at home, in the school; let us sprinkle the love of Jesus.

Talk With God:

Lord, I am grateful that you indwell lives and inspire lives to walk and work in genuine love. I am thankful that I can be one of those individuals. Help me to be willing to demonstrate Christ likeness and genuine love in my everyday lifestyle. Amen!

September – Day 26

Text: Song of Solomon 2:14 Amplified Bible

"In the seclusion of the clefts in the solid rock, in the sheltered and secret place of the cliff"

Thought: "Rock of Ages!"

A young English writer went for a walk one day. He became so engrossed in the beauty of the country side that he fails to notice the storm clouds rolling in. As it became dark he realized the conditions. He headed home, however, the rain came so quickly and hard, he was forced to seek shelter. As he stood in the shelter beneath the cleft of a great limestone rock he penned these words, "Rock of Ages, cleft for me, let me hide myself in thee."

In the times in which we live, we can see the storms gathering – environmentally, economically, emotionally -- everywhere and fear begins to grip our hearts. We, like Augustus Toplady, begin to look for shelter from the storms. There is a shelter for those who know Christ, the Rock of Ages.

Have you placed your hope and help in the Rock of Ages? He is stable, sure and solid. He will be a companion to you, a cover for you and a comfort to you.

In our scripture text, Solomon echoes the desire of the Great Shepherd to see the beauty and know the protection of His sheep. Just as God, the Bridegroom desires to behold the peace and pleasantness of His bride. He leads us to safety and shelter.

Talk With God:

I am glad that I am your child Lord. I can rest in the knowledge that you care for me and will carry me to safety, shelter and satisfaction regardless of the circumstances I encounter. Lead me this day and enable me to share the provisions, promises and protection you offer your children. Amen!

September – Day 27

Text: Isaiah 61:3 NIV

"To bestow on them a crown of beauty instead of ashes, the oil of gladness instead of mourning, and a garment of praise instead of a spirit of despair."

Thought: "The Spiritual Touch-Up!"

Once there was a grand photograph that had brilliant color, beautiful composition, lots of contrast and interest, everything you could want in a picture. But something had gotten on the camera lens when the picture was taken, and a heavy dark line ran across it, ruining the whole effect.

The developer of the film noticed it and thought, too bad; yet his co-worker took a closer look and with a smile begin to touch it up – now it looked as brilliant as it was suppose to.

One black mark – one big mistake, one bad fault – can ruin a person's life, but it doesn't have to. God has a way of touching up our lives and making them useful.

The Master designer and developer of life are available to whoever calls on Him.

The precious blood that Jesus spilled on Calvary is able to touch a life and transform it into the beauty and boldness that it was intended to be. Faith in that act will cover every black mark of sin and selfishness and cause a newness to be portrayed.

Seek him out and let him develop your life into something beautiful

Talk With God:

"Lord, it is a delight to know that your life's blood can eradicate the marks of sin in our life and that your love can touch us on a daily basis. Help us maintain a portrait of you that others may see, seek, surrender and serve you. Amen!"

September – Day 28

Text: Job 23:11-12 NIV

"My feet have closely followed his steps, I have kept to his way without turning aside. I have not departed form the commands of his lips, I have treasured the words of his mouth more than my daily bread."

Thought: "Protect & Project His Image!"

I read on several occasions where someone entered a museum or art display and damaged a portrait or sculpture. The deliberate act of defacing or destroying a work that took months or even years can be done in seconds. It takes great genius to produce a work of art, yet it takes only a careless or thoughtless hand to destroy it. Even the smallest child can drop a priceless vase and shatter it beyond repair.

I do not believe that I will ever break into a building to destroy or even damage something of value nor do I think the majority of the world's population will. Yet, I do believe that we are guilty of damaging and potentially destroying something more precious than a work of art.

Now to damage or destroy something of little value is no big deal, yet to deliberately damage and destroy the most precious item in existence – our soul – is of serious consequence.

Each of us is guilty of damaging our spiritual image before God and man. We fail to use caution in what we say, where we go, and what we do; until it is done. A careless word, a corrupt thought, a critical attitude or a condemning deed will mar the precious creation of God – our personal being.

Is it our desire and delight to mar beauty or maintain beauty? It is a choice we make every day. We must maintain our spiritual image. We can protect and project the beauty of the Lord through prayerfulness and pondering His word on a daily basis.

Talk With God:

Lord, I am grateful for granting me the opportunity to be created with a soul that will exist eternally. I am glad I have the opportunity to allow you to reign in my soul and make me righteous. Therefore, please help me to maintain a lifestyle that will portray your beauty and cause others to see your glory and honor and desire you. This is my prayer today. Amen!

September – Day 29

Text: Psalm 35:17 KJV
"Lord... rescue my soul!"
Thought: "Spiritual CPR!"

I carry the Red Cross certification for life saving technique training.. I also carry a "Spiritual CPR" card in my wallet. Both of these are important certifications for life saving.

The training in CPR enables me attempt to revive a person who has quit breathing or whose heart has quit beating. I was taught to follow four basis steps – Check for breathing and heart beating; tilt head and clear airway; compress chest in designated location in a designated manner, breathe into mouth while pinching off nose. The other card is a witnessing tool that reminds me that as a born-again believer I am to share my spiritual CPR – Critical Path to Redemption (plan) with others.

God has graciously rescued me and received me with His plan of salvation. There are four basis steps in this procedure also. Acknowledge that you need a Savior to give you the gift of eternal life; Believe that God loves you and will redeem you; confess your sins; then declare Him as the Lord of your life.

Did you know that you can perform spiritual CPR on your self? You may not be breathing spiritual life nor have the heartbeat of God; but you can be restored to the life that God has intended for you. Simply follow the A-B-C-D steps mentioned above. When this is done seek out a Bible-believing church and learn to spend time daily with God in prayer and His precious Word.

I am glad that I have been trained and attempt to maintain my knowledge of CPR, both in the physical sense and the spiritual sense. I only pray that I will be able to apply it when necessary to save a life.

Talk With God:
What a delight to know that we can make a difference. What a joy it is to know you have made a difference in my life and given me the desire to make a difference in the life of others who need rescuing. Amen!

September – Day 30

Text: John 14:6 Amplified Bible

"Jesus said to Him, I am the Way, and the Truth and the Life; no man comes to the Fther except by (through) Me."

Thought: "Taste!"

I am sure you are familiar with the taste test that several companies use to compare their product with other products of like substance – the pizza and soft drink taste test are two common ones viewed on television.

Well, I would like to offer a real taste test. Let us use the word "TASTE" as an acronym for the phrase "The All Sufficient Truth Endures!"

Life is full of advertisements and alluring promotions that attempt to convince man to try their products – refreshing beverages, restaurants, recreation items, read the list – it goes on and on. Yet such fads come and go.

In the area of religion, we find it is no different. It seems the diversity of beliefs and the "divine' competition grows by the year. Yet, there is only one truth and that truth will provide substance and prevail in any situation of life. That truth is Jesus Christ! When you explore the Bible and experience a relationship with Christ, you will find that He is "the all sufficient truth that endures."

We must not be deceived by every wind of doctrine, but believe in He who endured the cross (the price of victory) and prepare a place for us in eternity.

Let us walk the path before us this day convinced that Jesus Christ loves you and will lead you with His keeping power.

Talk With God:

Lord, I am well aware of the false hopes promoted in today's world, but I am also aware of the peace, power and promise of your presence to govern and guide me through life. Thank you for allowing me to taste and testify of "the all sufficient truth that endures."

Step 10 – October
"Bearing Fruit "

Summer has ended and winter is on the horizon. Yet sandwiched between the two seasons is the Fall Season. As I fall back to the memories of yesteryears, I find October to have been a time of year that produced a variety of views.

For some, it meant harvesting crops – which provided income for both the laborers and the land owner. For kids in my neighbor, it provided an opportunity to tease the squirrels as they gathered acorns for winter food. For politicians it was a rush to finalizing their campaign for office. For store owners, it was time to put out the costumes, candy and countless decorations for Halloween. For the youth, church and community hayrides were common. For the nature-minded individual, a drive through the country side and view the changing scenes of color.

A very special event was the Fall Revival at church. The evangelist would challenge the congregation to not let the lazy days of summer nor the lingering chill of winter cause a lapse in the believers' commitment to the Great Commission of the Scriptures – Faithfulness and fruitfulness.

It is very important that the Church collectively and the Christian individually remain rooted in God and render fruit of righteousness each step of each day. In the castle of our own home, in the church worship services, and in the community; we must bear fruit that will promote the principles of God's Word – that is, the Person of Jesus Christ and the Plan of salvation.

As you go through the month in reading these daily devotions, I pray you find humor, help, happiness, hope and an honest challenge to bear fruit that will enrich lives and enlarge the Kingdom of God.

October – Day 1

Text: Romans 12:9 Amplified Bible

"[Let your] love be sincere – a real thing."

Thought: "Repaint and Thin No More!"

Hoping to help his small struggling church save money, Pastor Jones decided to paint the church exterior himself, but all he had on hand was one bucket of paint. So he collected a bunch of empty buckets and some water, which he used to thin the paint enough to cover the building. Then he spent the whole day painting.

That night it rained and washed off all the paint. The pastor was so discouraged and asked God, "Why . . . why Lord, did you let it rain and wash away all my hard work?" To which God replied, "Repaint and thin no more!"

If this were a true story, I do believe that the minister was sincere in what he did. However, I do find a wonderful challenge for each of us within it's message.

Too often our efforts are watered-down and we lack a total commitment in our duty to man and God. We strive to do the work yet fail to prepare properly.

In doing God's work and in daily walking with God, we need to equip ourself with prayer, praise and the promises of God. These ingredients will bring getting stability. Without them, it is as if we simple added water to sustain us.

Talk With God:

"Lord, we desire to be sincere and successful in our efforts in walking with you and be a witness for you. Therefore, remind us to allow your Spirit to fill our life as we begin each day and as we take each step. Amen!"

October – Day 2

Text: Psalms 19:14 KJV

"Let the words of my mouth, and the meditation of my heart, be acceptable in thy sight, O Lord, my strength, and my redeemer."

Thought: "Coffee Break!'

I read a cute little story recently that provided a powerful revelation of how we look at each other.

Every Sunday morning at the same point in the service, the pastor left the platform for a brief time to talk to the kids in children's church. One new member didn't understand what was going on, so following the service one Sunday he headed straight to the pastor and made this remark, "Preacher, you are the first pastor I ever saw who takes a coffee break during the service."

No, the pastor was not taking a coffee break; however, the lady assumed a motive without knowledge of the facts.

You and I both are guilty sometimes of wondering why people do certain things or react certain ways. In fact, we may become indifferent toward them: ignore their actions or isolate ouself from them.

However, our relationships are built on caring. Therefore, we should never talk about someone behind their back or be critical of their habits and hang-ups nor should we ignore their hurts or hunger to overcome. We should always bear fruit of compassionate feeling and friendship.

Talk With God

"Lord, I desire that my talk and my thought life be approved of you and adaptable to building hope and a bridge of help to others. Grant me your touch and guide my life throughout this day. Amen!"

October – Day 3

Text: Luke 15: 4, 8 NIV

"Suppose one of you has a hundred sheep and loses one of them. Does he not leave the ninety-nine in the open country and go after the lost sheep until he finds it? Or suppose a woman has ten silver coins and loses one. Does she not light a lamp, sweep the house and search carefully until she finds it?

Thought: "It is not What We Lost, But What We Have Left That Matters!"

Have you ever lost anything? I am sure you have. In fact, we all have at one time or another.

And did you grieve over that which you lost? Again we agree, we probably did, especially if it was something of value or a sentimental keepsake.

But did you know it is not what we lose that matters, but it is what we have left.

When we loose our material possession, our much-loved ones, or our mobility and health; it is gone . . . we can't do much about it. But on the other hand we can rejoice that we still have a personal family member or friend left, some possession or personal property worth hanging onto, a little physical strength and health left.

Likewise with your life span. Have you wasted most of your life away by living without the Master and music of life, Jesus Christ? Many have a religious view but do not have the peace, perpetual joy and promises that Jesus fills a life with. Yet, today, you have time to ask Jesus to touch your life and transform your attitude and aspirations. He will do so.

Consider the chapter of Luke that I listed as our daily reading today. It contains three stories about individuals who had lost something or was lost themselves. However, when each found what they had lost, they commenced to rejoice and celebrate.

Today is a day of celebration regardless of what you may face or fail in. Trust in the one who loves you and will lift you up.

Talk With God:

"Lord, I do not know what I will face today nor do I know where I may fail; but I seek your wisdom and your word to give me reason to celebrate. If I lose my self-control or my sense of direction or my sincere desire to touch a life, reach out and pull me back in line. Amen!"

October – Day 4

Text: I Corinthians 15:58 NIV

"Therefore, my dear brothers, stand firm. Let nothing move you. Always give yourselves fully to the work of the Lord."

Thought: "Hang On!"

I have heard the quote, "when you get to the end of your rope, tie a knot in it and hang on," repeated many a time. It is a constant reminder of the importance of never giving up.

I know I have meditated on this quote before and I am sure you have felt disappointed and discouraged – at the end of your rope. But what is even more devastating is being at the end of your rope and not having the strength to tie a knot. Have you been there and felt like that?

If so, some have seen the intervening hand of a family member, a friend, a fraternity or organization; yet others have experienced the ever extended hand of the Heavenly Father.

If we stay committed to the task of bearing the fruit of the Spirit (Galatians 5:22-23), we will be able to recognize our steps if they grow slow or stop. For you see, even in times of laboring for God, sickness, sadness, sorrow and sin will attack and even attach itself to us. It is in these times that we can call upon the Lord and receive the undergirding help of God's hand. God will also encourage others to reach out and encourage us.

We must keep in mind that sometimes, we encounter others who are attempting to tie a knot and hang on. It is then our privilege and pleasure to reach out to them and assist in their restoration.

Whether it is us or someone else, hang on should echo from our heart. For this is what God's Word comforts us and challenges us with.

Talk With God:

"Lord, it is me again. I need your daily guidance. I want you to touch me in order that I can touch others. Amen!"

October – Day 5

Text: Matthew 25:21 Amplified Bible

"His master said to him, Well done, you upright (honorable, admirable) and faithful servant! You have faithful and trustworthy…"

Thought: "I Serve!"

The crest of the Prince of Wales bears the simple watchword, "I serve." What a wonderful and worthy motto.

We can not determine whether our faces shall be uniquely beautiful or ugly, our bodies graceful or grossly deformed. But the shaping of our personality is in our hands. It is up to each of us individually whether our dispositions are sweet or sour, noble or nasty, harmonious or hateful.

The motto, "I serve" always denotes real power and perpetual authority. For when we are willing to serve, we become masters -- masters over our response to situations and reactions to circumstances.

Service to Christ grants us power, prestige and position. Service to man opens friendships, fairways and futures. So bear the motto, I serve.

Talk With God:

"Lord, I am willing to serve. I may be limited in my abilities, but I stand ready to share, shine and stand for you. I give my all in order that I may gain all that you have for me – duty, delight and destination. Amen!"

October – Day 6

Text: Luke 11:4 KJV

"And lead us not into temptation, but deliver us from evil."

Thought: "Deliver Us Some E-mail!"

Children, in saying their nightly prayers can make some unique request and unmatched revelations. One particularly I remember reading was by a three-year-old.

Each evening before bedtime, for several weeks, a mother taught her three-year-old daughter the Lord's Prayer. She would repeat it line for line as her mother would recite it to her. One night the young toddler told her mother she was ready to try it on her own. Mother glowed with pride and listened to each word right up to the end. "And lead us not into temptation," she prayed, "but deliver us some E-mail. Amen."

I believe God has a sense of humor, or I would have been put out to pasture instead of pastoring.

The simple illustration is both comical and challenging. However, we must be careful not to allow the world's terminology to replace the essential messages of God's Word.

Man is guilty of ignoring portions of God's Word and identifying principles of God's Word as traditions customs and spiritual applications of Biblical times only.. While this is true in particular settings, the central message remains. The principles, prophecies and precepts are not limited to times or traditions but true for all ages.

God doesn't send "email" but He does receive "knee-mail." And the more we communion with Him the greatest potential exist that we will be delivered from evil. He will lead us "in paths of righteousness." He will laden us with power to overcome. He will love 24/7. He will lift us up when we are down. As we grasp the Word and keep a firm grip on it; He will give us victory over every temptation.

Talk With God

"Lord, you are Truth and I faithfully cleave to You. I will fix my focus on You and ford the streams I have to cross with your guiding hand. Amen!"

October – Day 7

Text: I Corinthians 9:22 Amplified Bible

"I have [in short] become all things to all men, that I might by all means – at all costs and in any and every way –save some [by winning them to faith in Jesus Christ]."

Thought: "Influence Is Contagious!"

It has been said, "No man can wrap his cloak about himself and say that he will stand alone, that his life shall not influence nor be influenced by other lives."

Why, even the mountain that lifts its snowcapped summit to the clouds is enclosed around with influences that constantly change its characteristics. The sun melts its ice-bound top, and the showers plows furrows in its gigantic sides. The loggers cut its timber landscape and lodges are built for littering and leisure populations.

You will personally influenced your surrounding by your attitude and action. You will make an impression on someone positively or poorly. You will influence others by the way you maintain and use your possessions. The way you treat your family and friends, pets and property will have an impact on others. The priorities and pleasures of your life will influence others.

You will be influences by your surroundings. The actions and reactions of others will have an impact on your thoughts. It is important to pick cautiously the surrounding we place ourselves in and let us meditate, move and mingle in a way that we only allow pure and positive influence to come from our life and into our life.

In our text, the Apostle Paul desired to bear fruit that would convict, change and commit others to serve to Jesus Christ. Stephen influenced Paul (Saul of Tarsus) and Paul influenced the world through his works and writings of the importance of knowing Jesus Christ.

Let us not be influenced by a world of sin but let us bear fruit that would influence the world of the saving love of God.

Talk With God:

"Thank you Lord, for allowing others to influence me. Thank you for the inspiration of the Word. Allow me to influence others with my attitude and actions. Amen!"

October – Day 8

Text: Galatians 2:20 KJV
"...the life that I now live in the flesh, I live by the faith of the Son of God..."

Thought: "Life!"

You know, time stands still for no one. Humanity moves quickly from infancy to childhood to adolescence. Once the teen years arrive, young adulthood advances rapidly upon the frame work of youth. Soon, the mid-adult stage is reached and almost instantly we find ourselves senior citizens. The shadow of life's sundown is soon viewed and the exit from the stage of life approaches. However, life is a wonderful experience.

We see life created, celebrated, enjoyed and experienced. We must learn to appreciate the opportunity of life and live in a manner that is looked back on with no regrets and looked forward with greater anticipation than ever before.

However, such manner of life is experienced only if we have had a relationship with Jesus Christ and allowed it to overflow in our relationships of daily life.

A life of an indwelling Christ will keep a person happy, hopeful and filled with healthy thoughts. It will provide a peace, a power and a promise for every step of each day.

To experience a life with Christ, enriches our journey in life and enables us to enjoy a foretaste of life eternal.

Talk With God:

"Lord, thank you for this day. It is a day you have given me to live to the fullest by being faithful and fruitful in my relationship with you as my Heavenly Father and my fellow man. Show me the way, share with me your love and strengthen me to do your will. Amen!"

October – Day 9

Text: John 10:4-5 KJV

"...the sheep follow him: for they know his voice. And a stranger will they not follow..."

Thought: "The Call Is Certain!"

A story is told of a little dog that strayed from its master onto the field before the beginning of an athletic event. From the grandstand of one side of the field, one person whistled. Suddenly many were whistling, waving and welcoming the dog to come to them. In the middle of the field, the little dog, filled with confusion and fright, crouched to the ground. Then, a boy at the end of the field put two fingers into his mouth and whistled shrilly and loudly. The little dog, recognizing his master's call amidst the others, leaped to his feet. With ears erect, the dog ran swiftly to its young master.

There are many things that cause frustrations and fear, yet be still and listen to the call of the Creator, comforter and caretaker of life, Jesus Christ.

He knows when we need His presence and He is keenly aware of our every situation. His call is clear; His cause is sure. He will not lead us into temptation, troubles or tremors. Listen for His voice and look for His outstretched arms.

Just as the frightened dog resisted the call of many, he responded to the call of his master. Even so, each believer can trust the call of His Lord. In times of fear, we can know the saving and secure sound of the voice of our Lord.

Talk With God:

"Lord, I am grateful that you know where we are in our journey of life and regardless of the conditions, you speak with words of comfort, courage and confidence. Keep me in tune to your voice that I hear and heed your call. Amen!"

October – Day 10

Text: I Corinthians 16:9 KJV

"For a great door and effectual is opened unto me."

Thought: "OpportunityAwaits!"

A story is told of a deeply religious man who was perched on his roof loudly praying while floodwaters licked at his feet. His pastor came by in a boat and said, "Get in!" The religious man replied, "No, I'm up here praying, and I know God will grant me a miracle."

Later the water was up to his waist, and another boat floated by and that rescuer yelled for him to get in. The pray-er responded that God would answer his prayers and give him a miracle.

With the water chin high, a helicopter threw down a rope ladder and told him to climb to safety. He again turned down the offer. "My prayers will be answered."

Finally he gulped his last breath and found himself at the gates of heaven. With broken faith he cried to St. Peter, "I thought God would grant me a miracle. He let me down."

"I don't know why you're complaining." St. Peter chuckled. "We sent you two boats and a helicopter."

Silly and sad, yet sometimes a truth. Individuals have a tendency to overlook every day miracles that God provides. And with that every day provision, God has given us an opportunity to be blessed and be a blessing to others.

Talk With God:

"Thank you Lord for making provisions for my life. Help me to possess the wisdom and the knowledge to be responsible in accepting your assistance. Help me to portray good common sense that I may build relationships with others as I labor in your Kingdom. Amen!"

October – Day 11

Text: Proverbs 27:1 NIV

"You do not know what a day may bring forth."

Thought: "Change Is A Challenge!"

There is a widespread saying, "if you don't like the weather, just wait a minute, it will change."

Life is a constant changing picture. We move through both good times and times of groaning. We experience satisfactory health and sickness. We taste moments of prosperity and poverty. Sometimes we are afflicted and hurt, while at other times we are happy. But in all situations God's Word shows us how we are to respond.

The Word of God is available to us – on the very top of the mountain and in the valley below. The Word of God expresses that God wants to share in our steps regardless if they are steps through floods, the fire or the fight of battle.

I am reminded of the words of a beautiful song that provides me comfort and courage. Ira Stamphill wrote this song back in 1930, yet today it stills echoes reassurance. Verse three of "I Know Who Holds Tomorrow" says, "I don't know about tomorrow, It may bring me poverty; But the one who feeds the sparrow; Is the one who stands by me. And the path that be my portion, May be through the flame or flood, But His presence goes before me, And I'm covered with His blood. Many things about tomorrow, I don't seem to understand; But I know who holds tomorrow, and I know who holds my hand."

Yes, I realize the environment changes from day to day. I have to come to grip with the changing economy. I know the education system grows more complex from year to year. I see styles change from generation to generation. I see my life and its appearance and abilities change as I grow older. Yet, I know that God is always the same and will abide with me in every change

Talk With God:

Yes, Lord, change is a challenge. It can be delightful, yet it can be difficult. Therefore, Lord, help me to remain steadfast in my commitment to you through each change. Let me be filled with your love and your light that others may be enriched in my experience with change. Amen!"

October – Day 12

Text: Ephesians 2:8-9 KJV

"For by grace are ye saved, though faith; and not of yourselves; it is the gift of God: not of works, lest any man should boast."

Thought: "Strings Attached!"

Important Notice! You are a Winner! Congratulations, you have been chosen! You may be the lucky winner of $50,000 or a brand new BMW. If your number or key matches the one in the square, you will be able to take your choice of a new home, a yacht, or a world cruise!

We have seen these headlines across our computer screens and read them on flyers sent through the mail.

Usually each announcement has a string attached. You must enroll in our exciting new club today. You must test drive this vehicle. You must attend a 30-minute presentation.

Strings! Companies offer what seem to be a fantastic giveaways or great bargain. They claim to be uninterested in your money. Yet most Americans have learned that "free" prizes are not always free.

However, Jesus offers salvation and eternal life absolutely free! You can't buy it, barter for it nor borrow it. It is given to you in exchange of your wasted and worthless life. His offer has no strings attached, and its worth far more than anything this world could offer.

Jesus' offer is not only free but it is open to everyone regardless of age, race, gender, vocation or nationality.

You have everything to lose if you refuse it, and everything to gain if you accept it (Matthew 15:26 KJV).

His treasure of salvation is more valuable than any purchase, prize or privilege you can obtain in this life. And it has no strings attached, although you will have a heart-motivated desire to serve the Lord.

Talk With God:

"Lord, I am aware that salvation is a gift from you. It cannot be obtained by wages, works nor words; but by simple and sincere belief in You. Help me to be enriched by it and to enjoy it each step of every day.

October – Day 13

Text: Psalm 119:11 KJV

"Thy word have I hid in mine heart, that I might not sin again thee

Thought: "Trash Baskets!"

I recall a story of a daddy listening to his four-year-old daughter say her prayers. She was repeating the Lord's Prayer. When she got to the part about forgiveness, she stated seriously, "And forgive us our trash baskets as we forgive those who put trash in our baskets."

Wow! What a message!

Are we ever filling our baskets (mind and heart) with trash? It is almost impossible to listen to conversations in life without hearing trash. Lyrics of songs and the language of movies are filled with trash talk. Programs on television and periodicals are interlaced with words of vile and vulgar language. We must use caution to not dwell on the lyrics, language or even look at certain magazines and movies.

We must daily seek the Lord to cleanse us and clear us of any trash that has been thrown into our life.

The Psalmist David stated in our scripture text, that filling our heart with the Word of God would give us guidance and help guard against the influence and infiltration of such useless and unrighteous trash.

Talk With God:

"My how language has changed. Everyday language is filled with criticism, condemnation and cursing. Therefore, O Lord, challenges me to fill my mind with your Word that I may allow my speech to be seasoned with grace and allow my mind to guard against the verbal attacks of the enemy. Amen!"

October – Day 14

Text: Hebrews 4:12 The Message

"God means what he says. What he says goes. His powerful Word is sharp as a surgeon's scalpel, cutting through everything, whether doubt or defense, laying us open to listen and obey. Nothing and no one is impervious to God's Word. We can't get away from it—no matter what."

Thought: "Spiritual Scalpel!"

A story is told of surgeons bending intently over the disease ridden body of a middle-aged man. Bright lights overhead illuminate the scene as razor-sharp scalpels and probes search for the cause of disease. Hours pass. At last a surgeon's knife exposes the dreaded malignancy. A deadly tumor is removed, and a life is spared.

Friend, we must let the powerful, penetrating, precious Word of God search our spirit and soul. Everything is laid open by the piercing, two-edged sword and revealing light of the Word. And if sin is found, just as the surgeon's knife clipped the physical malignancy, the Word believed can cause an eradication of the spiritual malignancy and deliverance from spiritual death.

Allow the deep penetrating, discerning power of God's Word to reveal and to rid us of deadly sins in order that we may have happiness and hope experienced and expressed in our life.

Talk With God:

"Lord, I know there are times when our lives develop spiritual malignancies and need to be removed. Therefore, examine me and eradicate anything that would hinder, hamper or hurt my relationship with you. Amen!"

October – Day 15

Text: Psalm 23:2-4 KJV

"He maketh me to lie down in green pastures: he leadeth me beside the still waters. He restoreth my soul: he leadeth me in the paths of righteousness for His name's sake. . .Yea, though I walk through the valley of the shadow of death, I will fear no evil: for thou art with me: thy rod and thy staff, they comfort me."

Thought: "So Far Today!'

One fellow shared one day a prayer he prayed. It went like this: "So far today, God, I've done all right. I haven't gossiped, haven't lost my temper, and haven't been selfish, grumpy, nasty, or overindulgent. I'm really glad about that.

"But in a few minutes, God, I'm going to get out of bed, and from then on I'm probably going to need a lot more help.

"Thank you, In Jesus' name, Amen!"

I am sure that each of us could pray this prayer every morning. Before we face the reality of a day, we do pretty well in disciplining ourself and devoting our life to God. However, once we take on the world, once we begin trotting the path of life, we are definitely in need of extra help – supernatural help. We will encounter situations that destroy us. Therefore, we need the comfort, courage and confidence found in His Word and His Wonderful presence.

The Psalmist knew God would quench his thirst, quiet his troubled mind and quicken his weary being. He knew that God would settle his quaking spirit when circumstances arose that was beyond his ability to handle.

Talk With God:

"I am grateful that I can awake in the morning with the realization that you are with me and that I can begin the day restful, refreshed and renewed. I am glad that I know you will walk with me and whatever I encounter, you will be my strength, song and my shield. Amen!"

October – Day 16

Text: Philippians 2:15 KJV

"That ye may be blameless and harmless, the sons of God, without rebuke, in the midst of a crooked and perverse nation, among whom ye shine as lights in the world."

Thought: "It Will Come Up Again!"

A story is told of a family who lived in sunny Arizona during the winter months and in Wisconsin during the summer months. Well, they had a custom of burying their perishable garbage under the lemon tree both for fertilizer and to improve the soil.

However, on a return trip to Arizona they had found the lemon tree full of lemons; and around the tree luscious honeydew melons.

They advanced to thank their neighbors for planting the melons. They only replied, "We didn't do it; they grew from the garbage.

Life is like that. Words and works which we toss out take root and grow in the lives of others. But the question is, what are we planting?

Remember: the hope for tomorrow lies in the seeds we plant today. Therefore, let us plant seeds that lighten the load of others, lift up the spirit of others and light up the life of Jesus for others to see.

Talk With God:

"Lord, let me be constantly aware that what the words I speak, the walk I take, the work I perform will influence others. Help me to live in a way that others will consider the results in my life and connect with it in their life. Amen!"

October – Day 17

Text: 3 John 1:2 KJV

Beloved, I wish above all things that thou mayest prosper and be in health, even as thy soul prospereth."

Thought: "Fertilize Your Life!"

A story is told of an old Vermont farmer who gave advice to a young neighbor. The young man was complaining because a certain weed, called the devil's paintbrush, was ruining his hay crop. The old farmer replied, "Fertilize your land, my boy, fertilize your land."

This is good advice to people in general. When weeds are allowed to grow in our life, they choke and crowd out the harvest crop. But let's take the advice and fertilize our being.

Fertilize our mind with good thoughts, fertilize our body with nutritious food and right exercise and then fertilize our soul with the fruits of the spirit (Galatians 5:22-23). It will kill the weeds every time.

If we have been given divine power to be born again in the newness of life, we should add to our "faith virtue; and to virtue knowledge; and to knowledge temperance; and to temperance patience; and to patience godliness; and to godliness brotherly kindness; and to brotherly kindness charity" (2 Peter 1:4-7 KJV). Doing such is an act of fertilizing our life.

Check out the words a little chorus of praise states, "Thank you Lord for saving my soul; thank you Lord for making me whole; thank you Lord for giving to me; your great salvation so rich and free." And if we are thankful, then we will fertilize our life with goodness and mercy all the days of our life.

Talk With God:

"Dear Lord, I am thankful for your wonderful gift of salvation. And I desire to devote my life in service to you. Therefore, help to cultivate my life with right enrichments that will make for a wonderful harvest and personal happiness. Amen!".

October – Day 18

Text: Philippians 4:13 KJV

"I can do all things through Christ which strengtheneth me."

Thought: "From An Alcorn To A Giant Oak Tree!"

Lyman Abbott says I pluck an acorn and hold it to my ear, and this is what it says to me: "By and by the birds will come and nest in me, By and by I will furnish shade for the cattle. By and by I will furnish warmth for the cattle. By and by I will be shelter from the storm to those who have gone under the roof. By and by I will be the strong ribs of a great vessel, and the tempest will beat against me in vain, while I carry men across the Atlantic."

"O foolish little acorn, will thou be all this?" I asked.

And the acorn answered, "Yes, God and I."

And how true the story is. God will develop the oak and man will design its use.

God has designed humanity to develop and become devoted to the task of worthiness. It is up to each of us to grow and develop. We must conquer and become confident that God will give us the purpose, the protection and the provision to become what He had designed us to be. And we have the promise of God's Word that we can become the person we should be by devoting our self to Him, depending on His strength and developing one day at a time. Just as an alcorn will not become a giant oak tree overnight; neither will we become complete in a day. We must trust Him and allow Him to train us, try us and temper us.

Talk With God:

"Lord, I appreciate every natural ability you have given me; but help me to realize that complete maturity comes only when we allow you to work through us. I yield myself to you. I will be yoked with you. I will yearn to be what you want me to be. And I will be YOUR person when this life comes to a close. Amen!"

October – Day 19

Text: Ephesians 6:13-14 KJV

". . .and having done all to stand. Stand therefore. . ."

Thought: "Stand!"

Our emotional make up is a strange creature. We are capable of expressing anger, anxiety, allegiance, anticipation, alienation, adoration, acceptance, astonishment, arrogance and affection. Each is a part of our God-given nature. However, they must be controlled.

And the degree of our discipline of these expressions determines our maturity. The perfect example of emotional maturity is that of Christ. Even though he was doubted, denied, despised, deserted, disfigured and put to death; He proved his love for all humanity and paved the way for eternal life. His life's purpose and prayer was to do the will of the Father (Luke 22) and forgive what all others did to him for they knew not what they were doing (Luke 23).

We will face situations in our daily walk that will cause a reaction or face circumstances that will demand a response on our part. It doesn't matter how difficult the crises, but how disciplined is our response. Will we demonstrate the faith and fruit of a godly life or will we display an attitude that portrays an immature life?

We must learn to live in the spirit of Christ. When we do, He will allow His Holy Spirit to flow through us in whatever response is necessary for the event. Let us be faithful and fruitful in our disposition and direction of life. It will provide a peace, a power and a proper response to every crisis we face.

As we stand, we will be equipped, enriched and enabled to stand unmovable and abounding in the work of the Lord.

Although I dwell in the fearful, frail, feeble tabernacle of the flesh; I will not succumb to the enemy. I will be an overcomer, operating on divine principles and using every opportunity to grow in the Lord and gain the victory

Talk With God:

".I am glad and grateful O Lord, that you have given humanity the essential armor, attitude and aspiration to stand firmly, faithfully and fervently in a relationship with you. It is a privilege to surrender my life to you and stand for your righteousness. Undergird me, uphold me and utilize me. Amen!"

October – Day 20

Text: I Peter 5:8-9 KJV

"Be sober, be vigilant; because your adversary the devil, as a roaring lion, walketh about, seeking whom he may devour; whom rest steadfast in the faith"

Thought: "Good News & Bad News!"

The pastor of a local church stood before his congregation and announced, "I have bad news, I have good news, and I have bad news."

"The bad news is, the church needs a new roof!" The congregation groaned.

"The good news is, we have enough money for the new rook." A cheer went up from the congregation.

"The bad news is, it's still in your pockets."

Friend, I have some bad news, good news and a simple truth.

The bad news is that you have an enemy in the world that is out to deceive you, destroy you and deny you access to heaven.

The good news is that Jesus Christ died for our sins and is daily available to assist you in being faithful and fruitful.

The simple truth is that it is up to you to tune him in and trust Him.

As you walk and work during the course of this life, you will face disappointments, decisions, delays and detours. Yet in each occasion you can find the strength and stability to weather the situation and stay on course. However, you must rely on the wisdom, the word and the work of Jesus Christ to remain faithful and fruitful.

Talk With God

"Because it is up to me to choose to participate, I renew my commitment today. I will get involved in building the Kingdom of God. I will do my part. I will resist the enemy and resign my total being in service to you O Lord. Take my life and let it be totally consecrated to you. Amen!"

October – Day 21

Text: Psalm 51:12-13 KJV

"Restore unto me the joy of thy salvation; and uphold me with thy free spirit. Then will I teach transgressors thy ways; and sinners shall be converted unto thee."

Thought: "Let Me See & Share!"

Sam Jones once stated, "The mountains are God's thoughts piled up. The ocean is God's thoughts spread out. The flowers are God's thoughts in bloom. The dew drops in the morning are God's thoughts in pearls."

How true it is! As we view the things of life we see the thoughts of goodness that only God can portray.

Daily we see the thoughts of God displayed around us and directed to us. Yet do we express the thoughts we have of God? How often have we spread good cheer and spoke words of commendations to others in our daily living? Christ sees His thoughts materialized and you can be assured He sees out thoughts. Therefore let the beauty and the blessings of God be expressed through your life -- Share a smile, sing a song or say a kind word.

Talk With God:

"How true it is O Lord, I do behold thy beauty each and every of my life. I do see the magnificent and majestic glory of your creation. Therefore, let me share the reality and the revelation of your splendor and your saving grace. Amen!"

October – Day 22

Text: Acts 2:38 Amplified Bible

"And Peter answered them, Repent – change your views, and purpose to accept the will of God in your inner selves instead of rejecting."

Thought: "Caught In The Act!"

I like this little story I heard several years ago. It told of a woman who had just returned home from Sunday evening service when she was startled by a burglar. With great biblical authority she yelled, "Stop! Acts 2:38!" which implies "turn from your sin."

The thief stopped dead in his tracks. Then the woman calmly called the police and explained what she had done.

As the officer cuffed the man, he asked the burglar, "Why did you stop? All the old lady did was yell a Bible verse at you."

"Bible verse?" replied the crook, "She said she had an axe and two .38s!"

I believe there are two great lessons we can draw from this strange, simple and to some degree silly little story: First, the power of God's Word to intercede for us and secondly, the challenge of the truth of God's Word.

You see, God's Word is powerful. When we study the Word of God, the Holy Spirit will inspire us in times of crises (however, don't tempt God by placing yourself in dangerous situation).

God's Word does reveal truths that need to be shared -- Shared in a way to uplift and give understanding or to uncover the sins and challenge our unbelief.

We have been caught in the act of sin; therefore, let us surrender and switch our devotion in life from self-centered to savior-directed.

Talk With God:

"Lord, search me and if I possess any intent of evil; freeze me in my tracks, forgive me and free me of the bondage. I desire to be caught in the act of serving you and my fellow man. In Your Name I pray!

October – Day 23

Text: Daniel 6:26 KJV

"Men fear and tremble before the God of Daniel: for He is the living God, and steadfast for ever, and his Kingdom that which shall not be destroyed, and His dominion shall be even unto the end."

Thought: "God Is Real!"

The most revealed fact in the universe is "God is real."

The whole universe bears witness to His presence. The sunlight that floods the earth; the seasons that change and clothe the landscape; the showers that nourish both creatures and cultivation; and the spacious universe in all its beauty declare that the Creator is everywhere in His world.

The laughter of little children, the love of friends, the living beauty and fragrance of flowers and the luscious tasting produce of the fruit trees establishes the reality of a precious and providing God.

The cry of a newborn, the conversion of a soul, the comfort of the Bible and the challenge of the Spirit declare the reality of a supreme, super-natural and sovereign God.

Yet it is up to you and I to notice the revelation of God rather than just taking all the grandeur and glory for granted. It is up to you and I to consider His presence and accept His perception in focusing on the things of wonder in this world.

There is a song that echoes the reality of this thought. It says, "My God is real for I can feel Him deep in my soul." God is real because of the conviction we feel, the creation we behold and constant intervention in everyday life.

Talk With God:

"Thank you Lord, for making yourself real: righteous in character, redeeming in purpose and revealing in nature. Help us never to be so foolish that we fail to accept and acknowledge your revelation. Amen!

October – Day 24

Text: Isaiah 55:1 NIV

"Come, all you who are thirsty, come to the waters...come...without cost."

Thought: "Fountain Of Life!"

The hart or deer is fond of feeding near the waters. When hunted the deer will take to the river and stay submerged as long as his breath permits. They will then swim downstream to escape from their pursuers. The water sustains his daily life and also provides protection in time of danger.

What an illustration of the individual who has an appetite for spiritual things. The deer senses it will expire if it does not find water.

A man can go without food for weeks, perhaps even months; but he can go only a few days without water. The unbeliever tries to satisfy his spiritual thirst in many ways. The awakened soul of the believer knows there is only true satisfaction, God himself.

Have you tried quenching your thirst in the river of God –the fountain of life?

God doesn't promise a fountain of youth, but a fountain of renewal. Jesus has made the provisions for any and all to drink freely of the living waters of salvation and find satisfaction.

Talk With God:

"Lord, I am aware of what a cool refreshing drink of water will do for someone who is hard at labor. It will refresh them. And I am glad that I have experienced the refreshing drink of living water found flowing from the Rock of Ages, Jesus Christ. I am also glad that I have the privilege to drink from that fountain each and every day of my life. Thank you for the living waters, Amen!"

October – Day 25

Text: 2 Corinthians 4:16 Amplified Bible

"Therefore we do not become discouraged – utterly spiritless, exhausted, and wearied out through fear. Though our outer man is (progressively) decaying and wasting away, yet our inner self is being (progressively) renewed day after day."

Thought: "He's Getting Better At It!"

I like the story of a little girl comparing her skin with grandfathers. Consider the beauty and blessings of it as I share with you.

A little girl sat on her grandfather's lap one day as he read her a bedtime story. From time to time, she'd reach up and touch his wrinkled cheek. Then she'd touch her own cheek thoughtfully.

Finally she spoke, "Grandpa, did God make you?"

"Yes, sweetheart," he answered, "God made me along time ago."

"Did God make me, too?" she asked.

"Yes, indeed, honey," he answered. "God made you just a little while ago."

She touched his face again, and then her own. "He's getting better at it, isn't He?" she stated.

God doesn't need any improvement for He is perfect and never changes. Yet, we change each day. We grow older and our external structure begins to fade and fail. However, our spirit is the Spirit of Godliness – it is constantly and progressively being renewed and restored. And as we are renewed day by day, step by step; we find our relationship with God grows stronger and sweeter.

No matter what our physical condition, let us have a great day because of our spiritual condition.

Talk With God:

"Thank you Lord for being our daily provider of strength. Thank you making it possible for us to have a song of praise. Let us rejoice and be glad in this the day you have made. Amen!"

October – Day 26

Text: 2 Timothy 2:15-16 The Message

"Concentrate on doing your best for God, work you won't be ashamed of, laying out the truth plain and simple. Stay clear of pious talk that is only talk. Words are not mere words, you know. If they're not backed by a godly life, they accumulate as poison in the soul."

Thought: "Dear Old Book!"

A lonesome woman parishioner demanded a home visit from her pastor. So, as promised, the pastor showed up and sat by the woman's bed listening to her litany of woe. Finally he asked to read some passages from her Bible.

In a much-too-sweet voice she called to her little daughter playing in the near room, "Darling, please bring Mother that dear old book that she reads every night." Promptly the little girl brought in a copy of a popular TV-movie magazine.

If the truth were known (and it is by God), what type of literature do we enrich our minds with each day – sports, science fiction, steamy love stories, solved mysteries, simple comics, seductive adult books, or the scriptures of God's Holy Word. Remember, it has been said, you are what you read. I wonder what type of book others are reading in our lifestyles.

It is only as we apply the words of Truth found in God's Word that we are able to verbally and visually demonstrate our commit to God. What we fill our minds with, sooner or later, will be portrayed as evidence of our real commitment. Therefore, let the dear old book be the book of life – God's holy Word!

Talk With God:

"Without the conveyed and conviction of your Word we would not enjoy a warm and wonderful relationship with you. However, I'm glad that I know you and you know me – we are connected. Therefore, reveal to me your Truth as I study your Word and search the Scripture to learn how to live a life that will honor you. Amen!"

October – Day 27

Text: Song of Solomon 2:4-5 NIV

"He has taken me to the banquet hall, and his banner over me is love. Strengthen me. . .refresh me. . .with love. His left arm is under my head, and his right arm embraces me."

Thought: "Something For God to Do!"

Today is a day that God is willing to handle all your problems.

If life happens to deliver a situation to you that you cannot handle, do not attempt to resolve it yourself! Kindly put it in the SFGTD (Something for God to do) box. Don't fret but allow God to do it in His time.

Once the matter is placed into the box, do not hold onto it by worrying about it. Instead, focus on all the wonderful things that are present in your life now.

Solomon in the second chapter is allowing the bride to remember her satisfaction in her beloved. Likewise with God, he loves and literally embraces His bride, the believer, and desires that she willingly be reinforced in His strength, rested in His strong arms and reassured of victory in His sincere love.

Therefore, even if you find yourself the victim of other people's bitterness, ignorance, smallness or insecurities; remember things could be worse. You could be one of them! Rejoice in having given your thoughts, your time, your talents, your trials and your temptations to the one who loves you more than anyone – God.

Talk With God:

Lord, thank you for allowing me to give you my praise and my problems. I know you will be a victorious banner of love as I walk in obedience to your commandments and under your command. I accept your leadership and your love. Please accept my sincere and surrendered love in return. In you name I pray. Amen!"

October – Day 28

Text: Psalm 4: 14, 16 KJV

"Let them be ashamed and confounded together that seek after my soul to destroy it; let them be driven backward and put to shame that wish me evil. . .Let all those that seek thee rejoice and be glad in thee: let such as love thy salvation say continually, The Lord be magnified."

Thought: "Blessings At The Devil's Expense!"

I read a cute story about witnessing of which I thought would be a blessing to pass on to you this morning.

On a particular Sunday morning, a pastor challenged his congregation to be aware of opportunities to testify for Jesus. One little elderly lady named Annie was known for her faith and her boldness in talking about the Lord. She was known to stand on her front porch and for the benefit of her atheist neighbor, shout, "Praise the Lord!" resulting in her godless neighbor's response, "There ain't no God!"

When hard times set in, Annie stood on her porch and prayed, "Praise the Lord! Please God; send me some groceries for things are tight this month." The next morning she found a large bag of groceries on her porch, which caused her to shout loudly, "Praise the Lord! Thank you, Jesus!"

On cue, her neighbor jumped out from behind a bush and cried, "Hey, don't give God the credit – I bought those groceries, He didn't!"

Annie laughed, jumped up and down, clapped her hands, and shouted, "Praise the Lord! He not only sent me groceries, but he made the devil pay for them!"

Friends, when we trust God; He will see us through and He will come through for us. The enemy will be put to shame.

Talk With God:

"O Lord, I trust you and truly depend on you to minister to my every need. I will rejoice because of your compassion and care and be not ashamed to let the enemy know that I am in love with you. Keep me from discouragement and cause me to delight in you each step of the way. Amen!"

October – Day 29

Text: Joshua 24:14 KJV

"Now therefore fear the Lord, and serve him in sincerity and in truth."

Thought: "Whole Hearted!"

Following the Sunday morning service, families headed for home to prepare their noon meal then relax for the afternoon. One particular family had a little girl named Anna. After washing their hands, Anna and her family sat at the table. Anna's mother brought heaping plates of dinner and set them in front of the family members. As he always did, Anna's father grumbled about the meal then asked the blessing.

Looking confused, little Anna asked, "Daddy, does God hear us when we pray?"

"Why, of course, Anna," he replied. "He hears us every time we pray."

"And does he hear everything we say the rest of the time?"

"Yes, every word," he answered, encouraged that he had inspired his daughter to be curious about spiritual matters.

Innocently she burst his bubble with her next question. "Then which does God believe?'

We must serve God whole hearted in sincerity and in single-focus. We must attempt to be devoted in our conversation, conduct and conscience all the time and in every situation. We will fail to please Him and promote Him if we are double-minded.

Talk With God:

"O Lord, how foolish man is sometimes. He speaks out of both sides of his mouth – words of encouragements and words of cursing. Help me O Lord, to be straight-forward, sincere and singular in my speech and my steps. Help me, O Lord, to honor you with my words and my works. And in doing so, I am a testimony of praise to your Name. Amen!"

October – Day 30

Text: Titus 1:9 KJV

"Holding fast the faithful word as he had been taught, that he may be able by sound doctrine both to exhort and to convince the gainsayers."

Thought: "Being Ecumenical!"

A story is told of the church secretary's confrontation with the postal clerk regarding a stamp purchase. The secretary stopped by the post office to pick up stamps for the church's Christmas mailing.

"What denomination?" asked the clerk.

"Oh, good heavens, have we come to this?" asked the secretary. "Well, let's be ecumenical; give me one hundred Baptist, seventy-five Catholic, fifty Presbyterian, and fifty undecided ones."

Now, we know the clerk did not mean church affiliation; but he was referring to the choice or price of stamps: post card stamps, first-class stamps, etc.

We know that this world thinks in terms of organizations, classifications, groups, species or divisions. God, however, thinks in terms of "whosoever believes." It is not the church philosophy or the community status or the constitutional right; but sound Biblical doctrine that makes the differences. When we believe in an unbiased God, we receive the ability to be converted and to convince others of the way of righteousness.

Talk With God:

"Lord, thank you for your word: pure, powerful and personal. Thank you for including me in your plans of abundant life. As I learn your Word and lean on its promises, lead me in the way that I may rejoice and reach others. Amen!

October – Day 31

Text: 1 Corinthians 3:11 KJV

"According to the grace of God, which is given unto me, as a wise master builder, I have laid the foundation, and another buildeth thereon. But let every man take heed how he buildeth thereupon."

Thought: "Be A Wise Builder!"

The other day, I watched my youngest grandson construct a four-car train out of Lego blocks. There were different sizes, shapes and colors. He carefully read each step of the instruction sheet and builds according to that particular step; then he proceeded to the next step. Several hours later he had a complete four-car train assembled. He had no spare parts. He proudly announced his accomplishments and of course, congratulated for a job well done.

Friends, God has laid the foundation for us in the work of His Son on Calvary and printed the instructions to a solid beginning of an abundant life in His Holy Word. It is up to us to follow the divinely inspired information for having a solid foundation and a sure fixture (life) constructed on the foundation.

When this physical race has been run and life on earth ends, we can receive our reward as a wise builder from the gracious and glorious Architect of life, Jesus Christ.

If I am looking forward to being congratulated on a job well done; I must take precaution and follow the plans for building my life on the perfect foundation, Christ's work on Calvary. It is a step by step process. Follow the divine directions and fulfill the daily task of living.

Talk With God:

"Thank you for laying the foundation for my spiritual building. Thank you for helping me follow the instructions found in your Word. Enrich me and encourage me to stay on track each step of the way. Amen!"

Thanksgiving Blessings To You And Yours

Step 11 – November

"Blessings & Gratitude "

As the year continues to fly by, we find our self in the month of November. A month of expressing gratitude for the many blessings we have as Christians and as Americans. November is a month in which we observe Election Day, recognize Veteran's Day and enjoy Thanksgiving Day Celebration. All of these events express blessings received of which we should be thankful.

Thankful that we can enjoy a democracy that allows us to voice our opinions and support the candidates and policy that we feel is most beneficial to our welfare. Thankful that we can recognize our soldiers that fought and continue to fight for our liberties. Thankful that our forefathers expressed years ago a grateful heart for the grace of God that enabled us to established rightful relationships in the new land and that we continue to celebrate that heritage with family and friends with food and fellowship.

I am thankful that I can see, hear and feel; that the love of God is genuine and real. I am thankful that I can enjoy my family, my friends; and when I fail, make amends. I am thankful when I am misunderstood; I am still considered a part of the brotherhood. I am thankful that I can experience God's peace; which offers to me sweet release. I am thankful that I can know God's power; that will sustain me in my troubled hour. I am thankful I can share some cheer; and to my neighbor cause courage to appear. Therefore, let your hearts not be troubled, neither let it be afraid. God loves us and desires to live in you.

Let the words of the Apostle Paul echo in your mind throughout this month: "rejoice evermore. Pray without ceasing. In everything give thanks for this is the will of God in Christ Jesus concerning you. Quench not the Spirit" (1 Thessalonians 5:16-19 KJV).

November – Day 1

Text: Romans 8:31 KJV
"If God be for us, who can be against us?"

Thought: "Mix-up!"

It was the grand opening for a business that had moved to a larger space. When one of the clients sent flowers for the occasion, the business owner was surprised by the message on the accompanying card—Rest in Peace.

When the owner contacted the client to thank him, he mentioned the obvious mix-up on the card. As soon as they hug up, the client called the florist and vented his displeasure.

After a moment's silence, the florist said, "You think you're angry. Imagine this. Somewhere there is a funeral today and they have a flower arrangement with a note saying, "Congratulations on your new location."

It seems this is a fulfilling of my mother's words. On occasion, she would tell me, "Son, you going to have days when it seems every effort you make will fail – things will go wrong. And I have had several of those days already in my life and I am sure now that I will encounter many more. (However, I hope they will not be to the degree of the opening story of our devotion today.)

We do experience mix-ups, misunderstandings and miss-directions every now and then. No matter how confident we are, we will encounter difficulties. We will also experience calm and cheerful days too (hopefully more than the cluttered and confusing ones).

Just keep in mind, as a believer, God is own side. We must trust Him to guide us and make the necessary adjustments to correct our mistakes and misalignments.

Talk With God:

"Lord, I love you. I love you because I know you care about me. You care when things go hay-wire and I am having a bad hair day. You care about me when I am happy and having a great time. Thank you for your constant abiding presence. Thank you for your comfort and courage when I stumble and slide. Amen!"

November – Day 2

Text: Matthew 14:28 NIV
"Lord, if it's you, Peter replied, tell me to come to you on the water."
Thought: "Don't Make Me Do it!"

A story is told of a woman who bought a bottle of cod liver oil (ugh!) to give to her dog so he could have a healthier and shinier coat of hair. Every morning, she pried the dog's jaws open and forced the liquid down his throat. He struggled, but she persisted. He doesn't know what's good for him! She thought. Faithfully, each day she repeated the process.

One day, however, the bottle tipped over and she released her grip on the dog for just a moment to wipe up the mess. The dog sniffed at the fishy liquid and began lapping up what she had spilled. He actually loved the stuff. He had simply objected to being coerced!

Sometimes our lives are like that when it comes to taking God's instruction and being an inspiration to others. We may desire to be obedient in following His leadership and use every opportunity for witnessing the message of Jesus; however, we find our self resisting and others repelling from our testimony.

We are called to be enriched by God's salvation and to encourage others to know Him. However, we must realize that the Holy Spirit is a gentleman and will not force himself on us nor will He force conviction on someone through us. He will not coerce us but will loving convince us to accept Christ and loving conceive the seed of the Gospel in others through our testimony. We must allow Him to give us His instruction and His inspiration. He will not treat us like a dog for we are His crowning creation.

In our text, Christ pronounced peace to the disciples; yet never demanded them to settle down and step out of the boat and come to Him. He offered peace in the storm and gave opportunity for Peter (who asked) to come to Him on the water.

As you commune with Him today, ask Him to give you what is essential for a good day and a giving (sharing) day.

Talk With God:
"Lord, today, help me to be sensitive to Your Word and Your Wisdom as I receive Your instruction and inspiration for a good day. Enable me to be led of You as I share Your good news with others by my walk, my words, my works, and my manners. This I ask in your Name. Amen!"

November – Day 3

Text: 2 Timothy 3:16 KJV

"All Scripture is given by inspiration of God, and is profitable for doctrine, for reproof, for correction, for instruction in righteousness."

Thought: "Thankful For The Word!"

When a traffic cop pulled over a local pastor one day for speeding, the minister reminded the officer, "Blessed are the merciful, for they shall obtain mercy." The policeman handed the minister the ticket and quoted, "Go thou and sin no more."

The Word of God is powerful, however, let us beware that we do not justify our wrong doing by using the goodness and graciousness of God's loving Word. For you see the Word is like a rubber ball, it will come bouncing back to you – it will bring revelation and realization of doing what is right or wrong.

We must heed the words of walking in righteousness and the words of warning against self-righteousness.

The Word will make us strong and stable if we will hear and hearken to its truths.

Thank God each day for His wonderful Word that will guide us and grant us wisdom as we apply it to our hearts.

Talk With God:

"Lord, your Word is life to me. It is a light to my path. It is a liberty for my spirit. It is a story of love to my heart. Teach me to honor it and hold its principles and promises high. I want it and need it. Amen!"

November – Day 4

Text: Matthew 6:24 KJV

"No man can serve two masters: for either he will hate the one, and love the other; or else he will hold to the one, and despise the other."

Thought: "The Opposites In Life Repel One Another!"

A lecturer from a denominational seminary was conducting an adult education class. In his attempt to illustrate some point or other, he asked, "What is the opposite of joy?" "Sadness," answered a student.

The academic instructor nodded approvingly and continued, "And the opposite of depression?" "Elation," another student volunteered.

Undeterred the lecturer persisted with her questioning, "And what about the opposite of woe?' Quick as a flash, an old-timer in the class fired back, "I reckon that would be giddy up."

Funny response, yet a factual realization. Opposites repel one another. They are different in purpose.

Allow me to give you a quick quiz: What is the opposite of saved? (Lost) -- What is the opposite of satisfaction? (Discontentment) – What is the opposite of Truth? (False) – What is the opposite of faith? (Fear)

God designed us to be able to perceive the good and the bad, the pure and the unclean. He has given us His Spirit and His Scriptures in order for us to know the opposites in life; then choose that which is best.

We can be funny and make rash justifications or we can be knowledgeable and make rational choices. Receive Christ and rejoice in life! Reject Christ and be a rebel of life.

We can be funny in life; but I am also glad we can face reality. We can't laugh our way out of facing the fact that we have to receive or reject, accept or alienate, adhere to or alter.

Talk With God:

"Lord, I am glad that you have given us the ability to enjoy life and be enriched in life by accepting the foundation of truth. I ask your guidance in living a pure, positive and progressive life for you, my Lord. Amen!

November – Day 5

Text: Job 1:10 KJV

"Hat not thou (God) made an hedge about him, and about his house, and about all tht he hath on every side?"

Thought: "Hedge of Praise!"

I remember two wonderful thoughts that has kept me focused when things go wrong or bent out of shape – "Hem in your blessings with praise if you don't want your joy to unravel" and "a Bible that is falling apart at the seam usually belongs to a person whose life is not." People who become discouraged and despondent usually overlook the bountiful gifts that God is constantly showering upon them. But when they begin counting their blessings rather than nursing their troubles or airing their complaints, life takes on a different hue. The comforting promises of the Word of God and the strengthening of our lives through the Spirit of God are benefits that should not be forgotten.

Therefore, let us delight in the Lord and dwell in the seemingly "taken for granted items of daily living." Let us turn our thoughts heavenward and allow the raindrops and showers of blessings to soak our lives.

Job loved God! Job lived for God! Because of this, God built a hedge of provision and protection around Job. He honored Him and considered him righteous. In the midst of trials, temptations and tribulations: Job did not waver in his love for God.

Praise will always produce a perpetual hedge in our life. We will have to suffer in the flesh, but God's hedge will provide personal communication with the source of power and peace we will need.

Sin is a constant thorn in the flesh. It creates suffering, sorrow and separation. However, God has promised peace, power and personal confidence if we will walk in praise of Him.

Talk With God:

"Thank you for your promises of peace, power and personal communion each step of the way. Thank you for your gracious consideration of our encounters, experiences and eruptions of the flesh. Forgive us, fortify us and fence us in as we praise you each day. Amen!

November – Day 6

Text: Matthew 10:29-31 KJV

"Are not two sparrows sold for a farthing? And one of them shall not fall on the ground without your Father. But the very hairs of your head are all numbered. Fear ye not therefore, ye are of more value than many sparrows."

Thought: "You Are the Crowning Creation of God!"

Listen to the conversation of the robin and the sparrow: "Said the robin to the sparrow: I should really like to know Why these anxious human beings rush about and worry so." "Said the sparrow to the robin; friend, I think that it must be That they have no Heavenly Father such as cares for you and me."

God made provision for everything He created. Even before a need arises, usually access to provisions is available. Before we ever felt cold, God began storing up oil, coal, and gas to keep us warm. He knew we would be hungry so even before He put man on the earth, God put fertilize into the soil and life into the seeds and made provisions for rain and sunshine. Even as we sin and forsake His will, He has a ready extended hand of forgiveness and fortitude for our lives.

He cares, do you?

God desires us to worship Him and witness of His goodness and grace to all mankind.

Talk With God:

"Heavenly Father, thank you for caring about your creation. Thank you for considering man at the top of the list. I appreciate you and desire to prove my love to you. Help me to praise you and present you to others. Amen!"

November – Day 7

Text: Genesis 6:8 KJV

"But Noah found grace (favor) in the eyes of the Lord."

Thought: 'Favored!"

All of us favor things. We see things and set higher priority on substances and subjects. We show and shower special graces on individuals of whom may gain our favor.

Gaining the favor of others may give us concessions on certain privileges, cut-rate deals on items or considerations toward awards and prizes.

However, what an honor it is to have found favor in the sight of God like Noah. God was about to destroy the world because of the rampant influence and influx of sin in the mind and manner of mankind. Yet, Noah honored God with his words, his walk and his worship. And because God is aware of our intents of life, He considered Noah worthy of honor. He requested Noah build an Ark. God was about to sent a mighty flood to clean up the corruption of the world and compassionately grant man another opportunity to enjoy a renewed life with Him.

Now, let keep this in mind. God would have saved every individual who came to grips with the revelation that judgment day had come. Instead, mankind mocked Noah and the plan God gave him. Humanity rejected the grace of God. Noah found the grace.

We have the same opportunity today. God examines every life during their time on earth and offers His grace (favor). Yet, self-centered man rebels and rejects God. Those who accept His grace, uses the favor to grow in the knowledge of the Lord.

You are favored, yet it is up to you to acknowledge it, accept it and apply it to your life.

Talk With God:

"What a delight it is to be favored by you O Lord. I acknowledge my sin, accept your saving grace and adhere to your way of life. I look forward each step of every day. I desire to be content, committed and constantly aware of your amazing grace. Amen!"

November – Day 8

Text: Acts 4:13 KJV

"Now when they saw the boldness of Peter and John, and perceived that they were unlearned and ignorant men, they marveled; and they took knowledge of them, that they had been with Jesus."

Thought: "Does God Recognize Us?"

I read an account of a person who had a near death experience. Her name was Bertha Jones, a middle-aged woman who had a heart attack and was taken to the hospital. While on the operating table the event occurred.

During the experience she saw God and asked if this was the end of the road for her. God said no and explained that she had another thirty years to live.

Upon her recovery she figured if she had thirty to forty more years, she might as well stay in the hospital and have a face-lift, liposuction, tummy tuck, hair transplant and coloring, and a nose job.

After her hospital stay, she walked out of the front door and was killed by a delivery truck. When she arrived in front of God, she asked, "I thought you said I had another thirty to forty years left?"

God replied, "Sorry, Bertha, I didn't recognize you."

Although God is very much aware of who we are and what we look like; I wonder if He is pleased with our character and our countenance. Do we possess an attitude and action that will honor Him? You see, He is not overly concerned if we change our appearance by diets, dress, dazzling jewelry or cosmetics; He's concern is with our heart and how it affects our external responses and reflection.

Talk With God:

"Thank you for Lord for granting us life and giving us blessings within life. Please enable me to maintain the disposition and the demonstration of a relationship with you. I desire to please you and promote your Kingdom. Amen!"

November – Day 9

Text: Ephesians 2:5 KJV

"By grace are you saved!"

Thought: "Points For Heaven!"

I have this story repeated over the years and it holds a great truth in it.

When Ted Martin died and went to heaven, he was met at the front gate by St. Peter, who let him know that he needed one hundred points to make it in the pearly gates. "You tell me all the good things you've done, and I'll award you points according to your deeds. When you reach one hundred, I'll swing open the gates."

"Okay," Ted reported, "I was head usher at the church I faithfully attended."

"That's wonderful," says St. Peter, "that's worth three points."

"I was faithfully married to the same woman for almost sixty-five years," Ted said.

"Remarkable," Peter declared, "let's add four more points."

"Only four?" Ted frowned. "How about this? I started a soup kitchen in the inner city and worked in a homeless shelter."

"Terrific, and here are five more points."

Ted's eyes opened wide, and he yelled, "Five points! At this rate the only way I'll get into heaven is by the grace of God!"

"One hundred points! come on in!"

We can not earn our way to heaven. We can not buy our way into heaven. We can not barter our way into heaven. We can not beg our way into heaven. But we can have access to heaven by the grace of God.

Yes, we must walk according to the way of God. Yes, we must adhere to the will of God. Yes, we must study the Word of God. Yes, we must commune daily with the Creator of our new life. But it is His grace that redeems us and it is up to us to accept it.

As the song says, "Amazing grace how sweet the sound, that saved a wretch like me; I once was lost but now I'm found, was blind but now I see."

Talk With God:

"Thank you Lord for your amazing grace. I love you and desire to live for you. Amen!"

November – Day 10

Text: Psalms 100:5 KJV

"For the Lord is good; his mercy is everlasting; and his truth endureth to all generations."

Thought: "The Lord Is Good!"

Sometimes, when people ask how I am doing, I respond with this little story. It is not a true story but a comical response to the question asked.

I am doing good. In fact, my mother never had to pay me to be good. I was good for nothing.

However, according to God's Word I am good and He is excellent. I am good for He loves me and literally died for me.

He is good because He included you and me in His plan of salvation.

He is merciful in that He is willing to forgive you and me of our sins and set us free. Not just the day we accepted Him as our Savior but on every occasion when we fail and falter, then seek His forgiveness.

His truth will never waver. It will remain steadfast, sincere and satisfying. It will always be dependable.

Yes, the Lord is good! He is merciful! He is the Truth! We must learn to listen to Him, lean on Him and allow Him to lead us.

Talk With God:

"It's me again Lord. I come before you to tell you that I appreciate you. I desire to always acknowledge your goodness, your gentle mercy and your glorious truth. I will praise you and perform my duty of service for you. Amen!"

November – Day 11

Text: Numbers 6:24-26 KJV

"The Lord bless thee, and keep thee; The Lord make his face shine upon thee, and be gracious unto thee; The Lord lift up his countenance upon thee, and give thee peace."

Thought: "The Beauty Of The Lord!"

The great commentator, Matthew Henry, once stated, "the flower of life never appears more beautiful than when it bends toward the son of righteousness."

How true! Each of us wishes to blossom into a beautiful being in life. However, we feel at times the crises of life has scorched our petals and wilted our leaves and dried our roots out. But friend, despite the fact crises are inevitable in life, we have a source of provision, protection and power to enable us to appear always beautiful, bold and blessed.

That source is the son of righteousness, Jesus Christ. He is the element of real nourishment.

Let Him shine upon your life. And as you do, He will enhance your countenance and enrich your character. He will cause you to be purified and prosperous. He will keep you and make you keenly aware of His abiding presence.

As you walk and work this day, remember, God desires for you to sparkle like freshly polished gold. He wants you to shine knowing He cares for you and is constantly aware of your every step.

Talk With God:

"Lord, I know I will be happy and hopeful when I humble my being to you at the start of each day. Therefore, I surrender my will afresh to you. I submit to your plan for me this day. I will make every effort to laugh, labor and listen to your voice of leadership. In your Name I pray, Amen!

November – Day 12

Text: Proverbs 18:24 KJV

"A man that hath friends must shew himself friendly and there is a friend that sticketh closer than a brother."

Thought: "Friendship!"

Mrs. Browning, the poet in conversation with the novelist, Charles Kingsley, spoke these words, "What is the secret of your life? Tell me, that I may make mine beautiful also."

Thinking for a moment, the beloved old author replied, "I had a friend."

Individuals have many an associates during their life span; however, to have a friend who is truly a friend is not often the case.

For you see, the friend Mr. Kingsley spoke of was the truest friend of man, Jesus Christ.

He is always near and always really to offer comfort, provide cover, promote courage, and abide continually along side.

A blessed thing is for any man or woman to have a friend – one whom we can trust utterly, who knows our worth and the worst of us, and who loves us in spite of all our faults, and who will speak the honest truth to us.

Jesus is such a friend. He is always straight-forward, sincere and attempts to strengthen us on every occasion.

The world flatters us to our face, and laughs at us behind our back; then we are left alone to fight our own battles.

To have a friend is to be friendly. In other words, to experience friendship, we must desire friendship by expressing friendship. This is true in our social relationships and our spiritual relationship.

Christ desires to be a friend like a family member. Accept Him!

Talk With God:

"Lord, thank you for being a friend in times of celebration and in confrontation of crises. I am grateful and I gladly return the friendship by accepting your invitation to be a part of your family – a child of God. Uphold me with your goodness and grace. Amen!"

November – Day 13

Text: 1 Corinthians 9:22 Amplified Bible

"I have [in short] become all things to all men, that I might by all means – at all costs and in any and every way – save some [by winning them to faith in Jesus Christ]."

Thought: "Jack-Of-All-Trades!"

I'm sure you have heard the remark, "I am a jack-of-all-trades but a master-of-none."

This statement is true when applied to humanity. However, the Son of God is master of every situation. He has displayed his power over sickness and the storms of life. He has demonstrated His authority over every work of evil.

Jesus has shown His willingness to help the sinful individual, the social outcast and those who are eager to submit to His will.

When you are faced with problems, perplexing situation and personal inadequate; you can go to the Giver and Girder of life. For His Word declares that His anointed touch cooled the fever brow, the authority commanded by His words calmed the raging sea, the absolute power of His voice expelled the demon and melted the possessed individual into a peaceful, pure and positive state of being.

Jesus not only can help, he will help! His instruction and inspiration still stands ready to minister to each of us. Call on Him today and feel his touch.

Let Him direct you in ways that will touch and transform a life. God will undergird us an help us become a helping hand, a happy person, a hurting friend (filled with apathy), a hearing (listening) individual, a healing (comforting) source and a honorable example of Godliness.

Let us refrain from being haughty, hateful, hurtful, heartless, or hypocritical.

Talk With God:

"Yes, Lord, I will be what I need to be to touch and transform a life. Give me the will power, the Word power and Your personal anointing power. Lord guide me steps, guard my mind, and govern my words. Amen!"

November – Day 14

Text: Matthew 11:28 NIV

"Come unto me, all you who are weary and burdened, and I will give you rest!"

Thought: "In Need Of Rest!"

I awoke the other morning, feeling very weary – tired and troubled. Yet, I knew I had much to do that day. I made my way to the shower and with the clean, clear and cascading flow of water pelting my face, I seem to become revived. As I added the suds of soap and fresh scent of Coast soap, I soon became refreshed and renewed. Thus, I proceeded to fulfill my duties of the day.

How often have we been down, feeling rough when we needed to be up, revved up for the day? Many times for we all grow tired and troubled.

The Bible tells us that the outward man will perish – grow weary, worn and wasted. Man is limited to his days of strength and accomplishments. However, the inward man may be renewed day by day and instead of growing powerless, it grows more powerful.

Does your inner man need an eye opener? Remember the Coast Soap commercial: when you are tired and weary from a day's work, you shower with Coast soap. It is the eye opener. It will revitalize your being.

Sometimes, we need something to refresh and renew the control center of our life? If so, turn to God's Son and God's Word for strength. I have found a moment with God during the night or during the day; in the morning or at the close of day, will renew your mind with peace, your body with restfulness and your spirit with strength.

Check it out! It works!

Talk With God:

"I am glad that the times of refreshing comes from the presence of you O Lord. I am grateful that you have extended an invitation to us to come and find the renewal we need. Help me to always be reminded of this realization. Amen!"

November – Day 15

Text: Proverbs 28:20 KJV

"A faithful man shall abound with blessings."

Thought: "Count Your Blessings!"

Have you ever stop to count your blessings?

Oh, yes, we each have many benefits. God has blessed us and continue to bless every individual. We enjoy and are enriched with shelter, substance of nourishment, sources of transportation, and sufficient clothing.

Many would state that God does not provide such; it is obtained by toil and tears. While it is true that we must apply ourselves to labor and earn the essentials of life; we must never forget that it is God that provides the body and brain in order that we may engage in activities that produce the benefits we need. It is God that produces the raw materials that are used in supplying the goods for use. God gives the strength, the stamina and support for our interest and involvement.

But did you know that God has given us more – yes, an opportunity of a new creation brought about by His Son, Jesus Christ. This is one blessing of life that we must not avoid but accept with all our heart. It is a blessing and benefit that will make a difference in every thing you do in life.

If you have not counted your blessings, pause and personally add them up. As a wonderful old hymn states, "Count your blessings, name them one by one; count your blessings, see what God has done."

Talk With God:

"We are blessed O Lord, there is no doubting the reality of that. Therefore, I wish to express thanks for each and every blessing and benefit you have bestowed upon my life. I want to demonstrate my appreciation by loving and laboring for you. Amen!"

November – Day 16

Text: Psalm 107:8 KJV

"Oh that men would praise the lord for his goodness, and for his wonderful works to the children of men."

Thought: "More Blessings Than You Can Shake A Stick AT!"

A man kept bragging to his neighbor about how smart his bird dog was. Growing weary of the boasting, the neighbor finally said, "Let's see what that dog can really do!"

Early the next morning, the trio tromped through a cotton field stopping at a small clump of bushes. The dog's owner sent his dog into the bushes. When the dog emerged, he patted his foot one time. "There's 1 bird in the bush," said the owner. He gave the command and the dog flushed out one bird.

Walking on, they came to a second clump of bushes and repeated the exercise. This time the dog patted his foot twice. "There are two birds in the bush," said the owner. Sure enough, the dog flushed two birds.

The two men and the bird dog approached a corner full of bushes. Once again, the dog disappeared. After a minute, he ran out of the bushes and went berserk. He yanked cotton off the stalks with his teeth, and then he grabbed a stick and started shaking it vigorously.

"What is wrong with that crazy dog?" asked the neighbor.

"He's saying that there are more cotton-picking birds in that bush than you can shake a stick at."

Humanity is blessed! We are undeserving and at times unthankful; yet God, who is rich in love, sprinkles our life with His benefits. It should amaze us and cause us to arise in honor and hallelujahs of worship.

In the devotion yesterday, I encouraged you to count your blessings; yet in all reality, it would be impossible to do so. He has blessed us in so many ways, they are too numerous to count. Just acknowledge them and accept the given of them.

Talk With God:

"Thank you Lord for every blessing each day of our life. Cause us to be grateful and to give ourself to you on a daily basis. Use us for your glory. Amen!"

November – Day 17

Text: Psalm 103:2 KJV
"Bless the Lord, O my soul, and forget not all his benefits."

Thought: "A Failure of Expression!"

I came across an article while reading one day that issued a challenge worth repeating. A noted editor once noticed a particularly fine achievement by a friend, also an editor. He thought he would write immediately a letter of congratulations to his friend. But he didn't. There was a day or two of delay, and then he said to himself, "Oh, pshaw! He will get hundreds of other notes about it, so I shall not bother him with mine." Then he met his friend and told him how it happened he had failed to send his letter of commendation. "How many do you think I did receive?" asked the friend. The editor guessed that many were received. But the real answer was, "Not one."

Friend, did you not know you were created by a wonderful Lord for a wonderful purpose. But how long has it been since you expressed thanks for your daily benefits – family and fitness; food and friends (always goes together); job and joy (yes, these two go together); transportation and temptation (these go together because most temptations come when driving – aggression, attitude, etc); power and promises (to live in hope and look for that blessed hope).

When was the last time we celebrated our relationship with Him (by reading His Word) or was challenged to share His message of life?

Today is a wonderful opportunity to be filled with a dose of thanksgiving and display an expression of gratitude.

Talk With God:

"O Lord, I do thank you for each blessing. I refuse to be robbed of the memory of those blessings or the moment to thank you for them. Let my expressed gratitude privately and publicly be received by you and reach out to others. Amen!

November – Day 18

Text: 2 Corinthians 12:9 NKJV

"And He said unto me, My grace is sufficient for you, for My strength is made perfect in weakness."

Thought: "God's Grace Is Sufficient!"

It has been said that the first sacred concert ever held in Europe was performed by just two artists, without piano or any other musical instrument to accompany, and that it was held in a dungeon; yet it literally brought the house down.

Of course, I am referring to the singing of praises by missionaries Paul and Silas in the midnight hour while being residents in the grand prison of Philippi.

Every person alive is in a prison. He is in the prison of the flesh which places him in the midnight hour of hardships, heartaches and headaches. However, with the joy of knowing Christ we can sing the song of freedom.

God's grace is sufficient for your trials. Yes, his marvelous light hath shone in the darkness – therefore, praise Him.

In His unmerited favor (which is what grace is), we are made strong, stable and sufficient for the task. Nothing came overcome the amazing grace of God.

Talk With God:

"Lord, I am glad to know that you give us a joy that will bring contentment and celebration regardless of the circumstances. Enable us to experience this delight daily in order that we may express it throughout the day. Let us lift up the downhearted and brighten the darkness of any situation with your gracious justification and joy. Amen!"

November – Day 19

Text: Deuteronomy 6:6-7 NIV

"These commandments that I give you today are to be upon your hearts. Impress them on your children. Talk about them when you sit at home."

Thought: "Focus On The Family!"

I remember when I was at home during my school days that my mother would always have time for family devotion with her four children. She would prepare our hearts with the Word of God and then pray for each of us. I am grateful today for her focus on the family.

Not many families gather for family devotions any more, but I read about a family that gathered each evening for a Bible story and prayer. One evening, the story was about Lot and his wife escaping from Sodom and Gomorrah. As we know, the great climax of the narrative is when Lot's wife looked back and turned into a pillar of salt.

The story sat well with one of the children, Tommy. He raised his hand the second the story was over and told his father, "That's like when mom was driving home in the car; she looked back at Rachel and me and turned into a telephone pole."

I had to insert a bit of humor, but back to the serious side. The purpose of family devotions is the focus on the family and the opportunity to fan the flame of God's love and law. The family is our nation's one hope of reestablishing our trust in the Lord! Therefore, let us accept the challenge to "bring our children up in the admonition of the Lord."

Talk With God:

"Thank you Lord for giving to me the opportunity to share your Word with my family. Help me to study and share the simple, stable and scriptural truths available in your Word. Give me the willingness to take the time and the wisdom to "rightly divide the truth." Amen!"

November – Day 20

Text: Acts 11:26 KJV

"And the disciples were called Christians!"

Thought: "Portrait Of Christ!"

A children's Sunday school teacher encouraged her five year olds to create an art masterpiece that related to the Bible. A she wandered around the room looking at the pictures, she came to little Alice. "Alice, what are you drawing?"

"I'm drawing God."

"But no one knows what God looks like, Alice."

Without missing a beat, Alice replied, "They will when I'm finished."

While it is true, no man has seen God. We do not know what God looks like, because He is Spirit. However, man has seen God in the person of Jesus Christ and in the character of Christ-likeness in man.

Think about it for a moment. You and I have the opportunity to paint a portrait of God by the works, the words and the walk of our life. As we learn and live the ways of God, we exemplify the character of godliness – Chris-likeness. As the name of every believer states, we are Christians, reflections and representatives of God.

We, as the children of God, can paint a picture of God that the world may see. This is the whole message of the Beatitudes Jesus shared in Matthew chapters 5 and 6. And once He ascended to the heavens following His resurrection, His followers took on His characteristics (not His physical features).

Therefore, let us paint a portrait of Christ by our life style.

Talk With God:

"Lord, I am feeble and frail in my attempt to portray you to the world. However, I am willing to make an effort each day to let your life shine through me. I live by the faith you have given me and caused to grow in me. I am what I am by your grace. Give me the confidence, courage and companionship that I may communicate a true image of you through my life. Amen!"

November – Day 21

Text: I Corinthians 2:2 KJV

"For I determined not to know anything among you, save Jesus Christ and Him crucified."

Thought:

The story is told of a mail-boat returning from the West Indies. On board were a man and his dog. One day a child was playing with the dog by allowing the dog to fetch a stick he was throwing. On one occasion the child threw the stick overboard. The dog jumped into the waters. The owner quickly ran to the captain and asked him to stop the boat. The captain refused. The owner replied, "If you will not stop for a dog then you will for a man, and into the water he dove. Both were rescued.

Attachment is very important. The man was attached to his dog. The child was attached to the dog. The captain was attached to the safety of his crew and passengers. Attachment will produce intervention when dangers exist.

Jesus Christ became attached to humanity when he came into the flesh and dwell among man. That attachment grew out of a love to lift man from the dangers of sin. In our danger, He came to rescue. We all have jumped into the sea of self and sin, yet Jesus followed suit and bailed us out.

Do you give thanks each day for His spiritual and secular blessings? Are you eager to be identified and become attached to His love and life?

The Apostle Paul was a learned man yet he claimed to know nothing except Jesus Christ as the Redeemer of life. He only wanted to be known as one who was attached to the will and way of Christianity. He only wanted to be identified as a follower of one who gave His all for him.

Is that our desire? Is that our determination? Is that our devotion? Do we want to live this life in the flesh attached to Christ and acknowledging His Name in all we become?

Talk With God:

"Lord, I know I must perform task that will meet my everyday need of life and enable me to enjoy this life; however, I want to please you in all that I do and in all that I am. Give me your grace and the gifts of your spirit to accomplish this task. Amen!"

November – Day 22

Text: 2 Thessalonians 1:11 KJV

"Wherefore also we pray always for you, that our God would count your worthy of this calling, and fulfill all the good pleasure of his goodness, and the work of faith with power: that the Name of the Lord Jesus Christ may be glorified in you, and ye in him."

Thought: "Approved and Appreciated!"

Did you know that one of the strongest cravings of our lives is the hunger to be appreciated? Humanity desires and delights in being loved.

In fact, I am reminded of the old commercial about an after shave lotion, where the man would rub the lotion in his hands then slap his face with it and say, "thanks I needed that." For it seems at times life is a drag and if we do something that produces a response of gratitude; it will boost us and build us up.

As we praise those about us it seems they blossoms into a better person. They become more positive and progressive. Maybe we need to do it more often.

God has shown praise for us in providing creation, in continual daily blessings and in the care of our eternal destination. From this praise by the Creator of life, we should desire and devote our selves to becoming a better person each day. In our responsibilities and in our relationships of life, we must demonstrate gratitude and graciousness of being appreciated.

We must also praise God. We can do this by reading His Word, reflecting a smile to those we come in contact with and rendering a prayer for guidance and grace for daily living.

Praise in performing a task or enjoying personal fellowship is a shower of approval and appreciation. Do it more often. You will be glad you did.

Talk With God:

"Lord, thank you for counting me worthy in saving me and enabling me to serve you. You saw in me what I did not. Your approval and appreciation of me gives me the challenge and courage to move forward faithfully and fervently. Amen1"

November – Day 23

Text: Acts 17:28 NIV

"For in Him we live and move and have our being. As some of your own poets have said, We are his offspring."

Thought: "Only by the enablement of God!"

Have you ever stopped to count you blessings?

Oh, yes, we have bountiful bundles of blessings and benefits that fill our life each day. Abundant food, adequate transportation, available shelter, affordable clothes, abiding friends, accessible churches and adaptable jobs fill our life each day with enjoyment and enrichment.

And these are possible by our own desire and delight to have; as well, as our determination to pursue and perform the work that provides them.

But when you get right down to the bare facts, where does our muscle, motive and mental capabilities originate? God is our source. He instilled within us the abilities to develop, devise and direct our lives to achieve and accomplish.

We sometimes do not like to admit it. But God created us with all we needed to get started in achieving the impossible.

However, the most important aspect of our creation is that ability to know Him and walk in a renewed relationship day by day.

This is a blessing that we cannot afford to develop and delight in. Is it a blessing of which you can count in your life?

Talk With God:

"Lord, thank you for every blessing you have made possible for me to experience and enjoy. May I always look to you with gratitude and share with others the precious promise of my relationship with you. Amen!"

November – Day 24

Text: Galatians 6:7 NIV

"A man reaps what he sows."

Thought: 'A Day Is What You Make It!"

J. H. Newman once said, "Life is a web, time is a shuttle, and man is the weaver. The principle of action is a thread in the web of life. Of that web, two things are true, that which enters therein will reappear, and nothing will reappear which was not put therein."

Therefore, if man is to bring forth honor, harmony, holiness and honesty; he must first put into his life that which would produce such character. He must become renewed.

It is up to each of us each day to portray a character that would be edifying: to God, to self and to others. If we fail to express a pure and positive note; why should we expect a return or response any different in our walk of life?

I am glad that God's truth will enable us to live a triumphant life. As we begin this day asking of Him, we shall surely receive. As we receive, let us apply the truths that will enable us to walk the liberty of an abundant life.

Therefore, before leaving home each day, look into the mirror and ask yourself "what type of person and what kind of day are you going to experience?" Then walk away with an air of courage, confidence and contentment. You and God are partners and nothing or any one will spoil the relationship

Talk With God:

"Our most gracious and glorious God, we are thankful for the blessings made available to us this day. It is our desire to live in them and become a blessing to others. Forgive us, fortify us and frame us in your Spirit. For this is our sincere prayer. Amen!"

November – Day 25

Text: Matthew 14:27 KJV

"Be of good cheer; it is I; be not afraid!"

Thought: "Tap On The Shoulder!"

I just have to share this cute, comical story with you.

"A passenger in a taxi leaned over to ask the drive a question and gently tapped him on the shoulder to get his attention. The driver screamed, lost control of the cab, and nearly hit a bus, drove up over the curb and stopped just inches from a large plate window.

For a few moments everything was silent in the cab. Then, the shaking driver said, "are you OK?" I'm so sorry, but you scared the daylights out of me."

The badly shaken passenger apologized to the driver and said "I didn't realize that a mere tap on the shoulder would startle someone so badly."

The driver replied, "No, I'm the one who is sorry, it's entirely my fault. Today is the very first day driving a cab; I've been driving a hearse for 25 years."

I really believe many born-again believers get scared when the enemy Satan taps them on the shoulder with a temptation, troubling thought or outright terrible confrontation. However, let us be still and silently commune with the Heavenly Father. He will grant us peace and give us power to resist the enemy.

The cab passenger did not know the past of the cab driver. Yet, Satan knows our past waywardness and he knows our present weakness. Yes, he even knows our commitment to God. However, God encourages us to "be still and know that He is God – a very present help in time of need and a God who is all-powerful.

So, remember: when life startles us or Satan strikes a blow at us; stop, still your heart and let God speak to you.

Talk With God:

"Lord, I am thankful that when life's situation seems to tap us on the shoulder, we do not have to lost control. We can simply become still and sense your holy presence. Our confidence in you will give us the comfort and courage to counter any moves by the enemy of the soul. Teach me how to be sensitive to your word and your will as I travel the road of life. Amen!"

November – Day 26

Text: Proverbs 17:22 KJV

"A merry heart doeth good like a medicine."

Thought:

Dr. James Walsh of Fordham University says, "Few people realize that their health actually varies due to the factor of joyous expression – laughter. When you laugh, your diaphragm goes down, your lungs expand, and you take in two or three times more oxygen than usual. As a result, a surge of energy runs through your body."

And the real source of good laughter (joy) comes from the Lord. The bible says, "Happy are His people." He gives a joy that is unspeakable and full of glory."

A ransomed soul and a reverence for God radiate genuine joy that adds value to life. Therefore, let the joy of Christ be a stimulus for real living.

The joy of the Lord will become our strength. It will enrich our life and bring rest and restoration to a weary, worn, worried and even a wicked soul. Therefore, allow God to enter your life and enhance your outlook.

Talk With God:

"Lord, I know that in this life, we face many situations that cause sadness and sorrow; yet I also know that in you we are able to find a peace and a perpetual joy that will flow like a river washing away our distress and filling our life with your presence. That you for that awareness. Amen!"

November – Day 27

Text: I Corinthians 13:1-3 NCV

"I may speak in different languages of people or even angels. But if I do not have love, I am only a noisy bell or a crashing cymbal. I may have the gift of prophecy. I may understand all the secret things of God and have all knowledge, and I may have faith so great I can move mountains. But even with all these things, if I do not have love, then I am nothing. I may give away everything I have, and I may even give my body as an offering to be burned. But I gain nothing if I do not have love."

Thought: "Love Is The Key!"

Scientists have declared that "genuine love when properly applied could virtually empty our asylum, our prisons and our hospitals."

Love is the touchstone of psychiatric treatment. Love can eradicate deep internal hate and hurt. Love can build positive and pure thoughts preventing disappointments, distrust, and downcast attitudes that produce many illnesses.

More and more clearly every day; out of the research of biologist, anthropologist, historians, economist, psychologist, and plain everyday common practices; the necessary mandate of survival is being confirmed and reaffirmed. That is why Christ gave us one great commandment – Love.

Now let us go to the laboratory of life – every day living – with a love for our Heavenly Father and for all humanity. Yes, those we work with, those we worship with, and those we walk with.

Loving God and loving each other is the key element missing in so many lives today; however, it is available to all who desire it.

It is the key to unlock the hearts of man, understand the will of God and undergird us with strength and stability.

Talk With God:

"Lord, thank you for loving me! Thank your for giving me your love in order that I may be able to return love to you and share love with one another. I find in doing this I will be satisfied and will prove to be successful in life. Amen!"

November – Day 28

Text: Matthew 5:16 The Message

"Here's another way to put it: You're here to be light, bringing out the God-colors in the world. God is not a secret to be kept. We're going public with this, as public as a city on a hill. If I make you light-bearers, you don't think I'm going to hide you under a bucket, do you? I'm putting you on a light stand. Now that I've put you there on a hilltop, on a light stand—shine! Keep open house; be generous with your lives. By opening up to others, you'll prompt people to open up with God."

Thought: "Gratitude Is Contagious!"

Returning from a trip to visit her grandmother, a woman was pulled over by a state trooper for speeding. When the trooper gave her a verbal warning rather than writing a ticket, the grateful driver gave him a small bag of her grandmother's homemade chocolate chip cookies to thank him.

Ten miles than the road, another trooper stopped the same care. "But officer, I wasn't speeding, was I?" the woman asked.

"No, "the trooper said with a smile. "But I heard you were passing out great chocolate chip cookies."

Once we have received the awareness, the anointing and the attitude of gratitude from our Heavenly Father, we will because a contagious individual. The words, the work and the walk of our life will radiate thanksgiving to the Lord for his many blessings and benefits – physically and spiritually. When we do, others will take note and inquire regarding the blessings we enjoy.

Let us shine for Jesus! It is better than passing out cookies.

Talk With God:

"Today, Lord, I am grateful for the relationship that I enjoy with you. I pray that I will be able to challenge someone to see You in me and desire to enter into and enjoy a relationship with you. Amen!"

November – Day 29

Text: Isaiah 65:4 NKJV

"Behold, My servants shall sing for joy of heart."

Thought: "Joy Is The Fire Of Life!"

Helen Keller once said, "Joy is the holy fire that keeps our purpose warm and our intellect aglow."

Another writer stated "if I were to evaluate the condition of the joy of our world today, I would probably find that our purpose is cold and our sound intelligence burns low."

How true! Many individuals exist without an ounce of happiness, hope and harmony. They simply go with the flow – up and down, around and around. No contentment and no commitment! For such individuals, life has no perpetual flow of joy.

However, let me share with you a source of real joy. Jesus Christ offers a joy that is unexplainable concerning its fullness. It is free for the asking. He waits to give you his peace which in turn will produce a joy that is full of His glory.

Regardless of what one may encounter or experience in the journey of life – the coldness of rejection, the chilling winds of adversity or the cowering fear of temptations and tribulations; we can find welcome warmth in the joy of the Lord. His Word will build a holy fire within our spirit and bring courage to our life.

Tune in to Him in the morning, trust Him at noon, and thanks Him in the evening for His abiding presence that warms our soul and wraps us in His love.

Talk With God:

"Lord, thank you for the promises, provisions and privileges we can enjoy as a believer. Thank you for the warmth of your love and your Word in times of pleasure and problems. I lift my voice in praise and desire for you to light my life with perfect peace and perpetual joy. Amen!"

November – Day 30

Text: John 21:6 KJV
"And he said unto them, Cast the net on the right side of the ship, and ye shall find. They cast therefore, and now they were not able to draw it for the multitude of fishes"

Thought: "Thank God, You're on the Right Side!"

Four old men were out golfing.

"These hills are getting steeper as the years go by," one complained.

"These fairways seem to be getting longer, too," said another.

"The sand traps seem to be bigger than I remember them," said the 3rd senior.

"Hearing enough complaints from his senior buddies, the oldest and the wisest of the foursome piped up: "Just be thankful we're still on the right side of the grass!"

In all things, we can be assured that there is a positive view of which we can take. In Christ we can enjoy a positive and a pure concept of life.

If we are obedient to the voice of God's Word and God's will, we will find ourself viewing life from the right perspective and valuing our life through participation in the right things. Grumbling and gripping will distort our thinking and detour our enjoyment of life.

So, whether we are fishing or growing older or whatever; we can view life in the proper perspective.

Talk With God:

"It is so human for us to always look on the dark side of circumstances rather than the delightful side. However, Lord, it is my desire to be positive and progressive by listening to your Word and allowing you to lead my thoughts in expressing the right and righteous words that will uplift and undergird my life and those around me. Give me strength this day to be on the right side. Amen!"

Step 12 – December
"Bountiful Gifts of Life "

December is a month noted for its exchange of gifts, particularly on Christmas Day morning. However, December holds the day of celebration for the greatest gift ever given unto humanity – the birth of the Son of God, Jesus Christ.

Because of the purpose of His coming, we have every good gift available unto us – love, life, light (revelations), laughter (happiness), liberty (mind and spirit), and leadership. And if we leave Christ out of the celebration of this season, we rob our being of these and many other bountiful gifts. James declares in his New Testament book that "every good and perfect gift is from above, and cometh down from the Father" (James 1:17).

Therefore, let us enjoy the gifts of the Lord during each day of this wonderful month of celebration. Let each step be filled with praise, peace and precious memories of His wonderful gift given unto mankind over two thousand years ago. Let our words and our works be times of worship to our Heavenly Father for being so gracious and good to humanity that He allowed His Son to be identified with our confrontations, circumstances and conditions of daily living. Let us be excited and extremely grateful that He allowed not only His Son to identify with us but to grant us the pleasure and privilege of being identified with Him.

For it is in our relationship with Him that we are able to enjoy life, endure the hardships and heartaches, and enter into the everlasting abode with our Savior Jesus Christ, the gift of God.

Therefore, let us agree and aggressively express that the reason of this season is the celebration of the birth of the Savior of the world, Jesus Christ!

December – Day 1

Text: I Corinthians 13:12 The Message

"We don't yet see things clearly. We're squinting in a fog, peering through a mist. But it won't be long before the weather clears and the sun shines bright! We'll see it all then, see it all as clearly as God sees us, knowing him directly just as he knows us!"

Thought: "We Don't Understand!"

In the middle of a snowstorm on a very dark night, a man was trying to hitch a ride with no luck. The snow was so blinding, he could barely see his hand in from of him. Suddenly, car light appeared behind him. It stopped!

The guy immediately got into the backseat of the car before realizing that nobody was behind the wheel.

The car started slowly. The guy looked at the road and saw a treacherous curve ahead. He started praying loudly. Just in time, a hand appeared through the driver's window and turned the steering wheel. This happened over and over again.

Finally, he had seen enough. The guy jumped from the car, and ran to the nearest town. Cold, covered with snow and in shock; he ran into a café and downed two cups of hot coffee before recounting his horrible ordeal.

About half an hour later, two other guys walked into the same café, cold and covered with snow. Pointing to the man at the counter, one said to other, "look! That's the crazy guy who climbed into the car while we were pushing it into town!"

Just as the guy who was hitching a ride and didn't understand what was going on became filled with fear; we too, so often, are faced with needs and thinking we have found the solution are fooled and filled with fear.

We must learn to lean on God Who knows the coldness of life and can see clearly what will supply our need.

Talk With God:

"How true it is God, we don't understand all things that happen. We are faced with circumstances that chill us to the bone. We are filled with fear. Yet, it is an honor to know that you care for us and will direct us through our situation and reassure us that we will understand it by and by. Amen!"

December - Day 2

Text: John 19:5 The Message
"Here He is: the man!"

Thought: "Behold the Man!"

I read a wonderful comparison that proved Jesus is better than Santa Claus. Read the following words with praise.

Santa is said to live at the North Pole; Jesus is everywhere.

Santa is said to ride in a sleigh; Jesus rides on the wind and walks on the waves.

Santa comes but once a year; Jesus is an ever present help.

Santa is reported to come down your chimney uninvited; Jesus stands at the door of your heart and knocks.

Santa makes you stand in line to see him; Jesus is as close as the mention of His Name.

Santa lets you sit on his lap; Jesus lets you rest in His arms.

Santa asks, "little boy, little girl, what is your name?" Jesus knew our names before we did.

Santa has a belly like a bowl full of jelly; Jesus has a heart full of love.

Santa offers "Ho, ho, ho"; Jesus offers hope, help and happiness.

Santa says, "You better not cry"; Jesus says, "Cast all your cares on me for I care for you."

Santa's little helpers make toys; Jesus makes new lives, mends hearts, and repairs broken homes.

Santa may make you chuckle; Jesus gives you perpetual joy.

Santa is said to put gifts under tree; Jesus became our gift and died on the tree.

Just as Pilate rendered the words, "Behold, the man." There is no comparison that can be made with Jesus Christ. He is the One and Only! Therefore in this Christmas Season let us come to realize that Jesus is the reason for the season.

Talk With God:

"I am glad to know that you are real and you are the reason for the season. Therefore, I will accept and acknowledge this great truth. Amen!"

December – Day 3

Text: Ephesians 4:14-15 NCV

"We will not be influenced by every new teaching we hear from people who are trying to fool us. They make plans and try any kind of trick to fool people into following the wrong path. No! Speaking the truth with love, we will grow up in every way into Christ, who is the head."

Thought: "A Portrait Of Truth!"

A woman decided to have her portrait painted. She told the artist, "paint me with diamond rings, a diamond necklace, diamond bracelets, a diamond brooch, and a diamond-encrusted gold Rolex watch."

'But you're not wearing any of those things," he replied."

"I know, "she said, "It's in case I should die before my husband. I'm sure he'll remarry right away, and I want his new wife to go crazy looking for the jewelry."

This story may appear funny, factious and maybe a fantasia; yet a fantastic lesson to learn.

One may get by with pulling a practical joke, but let us be careful as to the image of character that we live today and leave behind.

However, God will never present a false image of Himself just to see our reaction. His love for humanity is real. His liberty for mankind is genuine. Therefore, let us consider His portrait of Truth found in the Bible and apply it to our smile, our service and our steps. And as we do, we will present a portrait of character that will not drive one crazy looking for it; but will cause a devotion to search and find the treasure of truth found in a relationship with Jesus Christ.

It has been said, "you may fool some people some of the time, but you cannot fool all the people all the time." Portraying a false image will catch us to us sooner or later. It is important that we present our true image and if it is not an image of Truth, ask God to change you and give you the image of Truth.

Talk With God:

"I am glad to know that you, O Lord, never change. Your character and commitment will remain unmoved. Therefore, as I learn from You, enrich and enable me to walk in truth portraying an image of You. Amen!"

December - Day 4

Text: Psalm 89:28 NIV

"I will maintain my love to him forever, and my covenant with him will never fail."

Thought: "Nothing Can Go Wrong!"

The world's first fully computerized airliner was ready for its maiden flight without pilots or crew. The plane taxied to the loading area automatically, its doors opened automatically, the steps came out automatically. The passengers boarded the plane and took their seats.

The steps retracted automatically, the doors closed automatically, and the airplane taxied toward the runway. Everything happened without a hitch.

As the passengers leaned back in their comfortable seats, a voice came over the intercom. "Good afternoon, ladies and gentlemen. Welcome to the debut of the world's first fully computerized airliner. Everything on this aircraft is run electronically. We're cruising at 35,000 feet. Just sit back and relax. Nothing can go wrong. . .nothing can go wrong. . .nothing can go wrong. . .."

As Murphy's law states, "if it can go wrong, it will."

And as a simple proverb declared, "To err is human."

Hardly a day passes that we do not perceive a thought, perform an act, or proclaim a word that after the fact, we wish we could take it back or do it a different way. The flesh is fragile and subject to failure; however, God's grace is sufficient. Just as the inventors of the computerized craft did not think it would fail in any phrase of operation; we do not plan on failure in living for God during the day. Yet, it may happen.

However, God never fails in His plan and purpose nor his protection and provision for His chosen people. He will be faithful and fervent in maintaining His love for His people.

When we fail, we must pay the price; yet God perfect love will rescue us and restore us.

Talk With God:

"O Lord, I am sorry when I fail to maintain the love and commitment that is essential to a godly life. However, I am glad that your faithfulness will never cease but understand me and uphold me. Love me and lead in the way everlasting for your glory and honor. Amen!"

December - Day 5

Text: Ephesians 3:17 KJV

"That Christ may dwell in your hearts by faith; that ye, being rooted and grounded in love."

Thought: "Who's In Your Heart?"

Recently I read a great story about sharing Jesus. It was not intended to be a witness opportunity but it worked out that way.

Four-year-old Brianna was at the pediatrician for a check-up. When the doctor looked in her ears, he asked, "Do you think I'll find Big Bird in here?" Brianna only giggled.

Next, the doctor took a tongue depressor and looked down her throat, this time he asked, "Do you think I'll find the Cookie Monster down there?" Brianna giggled again.

Then the doctor put a stethoscope to her chest. As he listened to her heartbeat, he asked, "Do you thin I'll hear Barney in there?"

"Oh, no!" Brianna replied. "Jesus is in my heat, Barney's on my underpants."

What a wonderful message the children's chorus says, "Into my heart, come into my heart Lord Jesus; Come in today, come in to stay; Come into my heart Lord Jesus!"

What a time to allow Jesus to come into your heart (your life). Our thought, our talk, our thrust in life is motivated by the love of God when Jesus abides within our heart.

Knowing that Christ abides within enables us to live externally in courage, confidence and comfort.

Keep this little thought in mind: when temptations come knocking at your heart's door; since Jesus lives within our heart, let Him answer the door.

Talk With God:

"Today Lord, I will allow you to dwell in my heart that I might not sin against thee. I will meditate on your Word that I may progress and prosper in my relationship with you and with my fellow man. I will allow your Word to guide my steps and govern my speech. I will proclaim your truth in the way I live. Amen!"

December – Day 6

Text: 1 Chronicles 28:9 KJV

"And thou, Solomon my son, know thou the God of thy father, and serve him with a perfect heart and with a willing mind: for the LORD searcheth all hearts, and understandeth all the imaginations of the thoughts: if thou seek him, he will be found of thee; but if thou forsake him, he will cast thee off for ever.".

Thought: "Imagination!"

A Sunday school teacher was telling a group of 4-year-olds about Jesus, Joseph and Mary. After the lesson the kids were asked to draw a picture depicting their favorite part of the story. The teacher received pictures of the baby Jesus in the manger surrounded by animals, pictures of the three wise men and the like.

One drawing puzzled her. It was a picture of an airplane with four people in it. She called the young artist up to explain his picture. Little Johnny pointed out Mary, Joseph, and the baby Jesus, and said this was their "flight" to Egypt. The teacher then asked about the other man in the plane. "Oh, that's Pontius, the pilot."

It is great to have an imagination. And I love to watch in wonderment as I observe children and see their imaginations materialize into moods and motion. However, we must also accept reality.

Within the Bible, we find many references to vain, vulgar and void imaginations; but we also find sincere and sober imaginations. It is of the latter that we must develop and demonstrate in true expressions of glory and honor to our Heavenly Father who has blessed us with the good news of our Christmas Season. It is of this truth and testimony of reality that we build our assurance in God.

Talk With God:

"Lord, thank you for the gift of imagination and thank you for the manifestation of good imagination in the lives of your creation. Enrich me and enable me to give evidence of the truth that you have helped me to express. I pray it helps establish me and encourages others. Amen!"

December – Day 7

Text: Ephesians 5:15-17 KJV

"See then that ye walk circumspectly, not as fools, but as wise, Redeeming the time, because the days are evil. Wherefore be ye not unwise, but understanding what the will of the Lord is."

Thought: "Time Flies!"

When I was a youngster, we use to tell little moron jokes. One was "why did little moron throw the clock out the window?" The answer was "to see time fly."

And how time does seem to fly. My, it is as if school was just beginning, then the Fall Season with its cooler weather was approaching. And now it is almost Thanksgiving Day and soon the Christmas season will be here.

It is true that time goes by quickly, how then should we make use of it?

Each day is a gift – a trust – from God. We need to be good stewards of that time. Let us use each day wisely.

The Bible says for us to devote ourselves to a relationship with God, being watchful and thankful. Be wise in the way you act toward others, make the most of every opportunity. Let your conversation be always full of grace, seasoned with reason.

We can't recall time, yet we can redeem it. That is, we can use it beneficially in accordance to the Word of God.

In fact, when you think about it; time is the only real thing that we have. Money and material matter can disappear in a moment. A person can lose their mental capabilities and mobility of their physical being in a brief encounter. However, time continues. Therefore, while it is present let us participate in those activities and relationships that will prepare for hereafter.

Talk With God:

"Oh how foolish we humans are sometimes O Lord. We waste our most precious commodity – time. Therefore, help us to redeem the time by relying on your omniscience, omnipotence and omnipresence. In you we may achieve the essential goals in the time allotted us. Amen!"

December – Day 8

Text: Philippians 2:15 The Message

"Do everything readily and cheerfully—no bickering, no second-guessing allowed! Go out into the world uncorrupted, a breath of fresh air in this squalid and polluted society. Provide people with a glimpse of good living and of the living God. Carry the light-giving Message into the night so I'll have good cause to be proud of you on the day that Christ returns. You'll be living proof that I didn't go to all this work for nothing."

Thought: "The Only Entrance!"

A shopkeeper was nervous when a brand-new business just like his own opened up next door. The new owners hung a huge sign: Best Deals.

His anxiety grew when another competitor opened up on the other side and announced its arrival with an even larger sign: Lowest Prices.

Then the shopkeeper got an idea. He put the biggest sign of all over his own shop. It read: Main Entrance.

The world offers all kinds of deals and deflated standards to attract us. Yet God has always been the only entrance to the best deals and highest quality of life.

And He has made us His shopkeeper. It is up to us to out deal and out wheel all other seekers of the soul. And the best way we can do this is simply and sincerely declaring that Jesus is the only entrance to the real deal.

People are looking for a guarantee for life, a genuine product and a good price. Friends, the only genuine product is the salvation offered by Jesus Christ. It is free to all who come into and request it. It is guaranteed for life if the word of God (warranty) is kept.

Therefore, let us put up the biggest and best advertisement available – our life as a proven entrance to the item that man is looking for. Let us shine like stars in the heavens, like spotlights reflecting the product, like spiritual lighthouses scanning the dark, deep seas of life.

Talk With God:

"Yes, I know there are choices available to mankind, yet only one offers genuine life. Thank you for that gift. And O Lord, remember, I am not a salesman; but I will be a living sanctuary for you. I will present you in who I am, what I am and where I am. Amen!"

December – Day 9

Text: I Peter 1:4 KJV

"To an inheritance incorruptible, and undefiled, and that fadeth not away, reserved in heaven for you."

Thought: "What Do You Expect?"

A wealthy man died and his family anxiously gathered together for reading of his will.

"To my precious wife, whom I loved dearly, I leave the house, fifty acres of land, and ten million dollars. To my wonderful son, who loves automobiles, I leave my Lexus, Jaguar, Ferrari and $500,000. To my darling daughter, who loves the ocean, I leave my yacht and $500,000. To my one and only sister, I leave $250,000. And to my brother-in-law, who always insisted that health is better than wealth, I leave my sunlamp and barbells.

We should be very careful with our declaration in life. For what we speak may become a reality to us.

What is our focus? What do we figure will be our inheritance? Will our life be enhanced by the dedication and declares we make during our life time?

If our focus is on Christ and we are pursuing eternal life, then my friend, your life will be enhanced by what you dedicate your time to, devote your talent and treasures for and declare in conversation, conduct and countenance during this life time.

Talk With God:

"Lord, I may not receive much in worldly goods and my family may not get much in worldly goods when I depart. However, I pray that I have already planted the seeds of the greatest inheritance that I or my family can inherit and enjoy – a relationship with you and a godly inheritance in heaven. For this I am thankful. Amen!"

December – Day 10

Text: Hebrews 10:23 KJV

"For He is faithful that promised!"

Thought: "Promise Keeping!"

I read a beautiful and uplifting story of little Johnny and his Christmas promise. It went like this. It was the day after Christmas at a downtown church in San Francisco. The pastor was out in front looking over the manger scene set up on the front lawn when he noticed the Christ Child figure was missing.

Right on cue, he turned to see a little boy with a red wagon coming down the street and in the wagon was the figure of the infant Jesus. So the pastor walked up to the boy and asked, "Well young man, where did you pick up your passenger?"

Little Johnny replied, "I got Him here, from the church."

"And why did you take Him" the pastor asked?

Little Johnny replied, "Well, about a week before Christmas I prayed to the little Lord Jesus, and I told Him if He would bring me a red wagon for Christmas, I would give Him a ride around the block in it."

The Word of God declares that God will "grant the desires of our heart" if we live in obedience to Him and His Word. Even in the small things of life, when we really believe, God will supply and satisfy. God always keeps His promise.

Now, the question we must answer is, are we faithful to keep our promise to God? Are we willing to be content with the blessings and benefits that God honors us with? Are willing to fulfill our commitment to Him?

Let us promise and proceed to walk in the reverence, responsibility and relationship that God requires of us. Let us live in the contentment, commitment and compassion that God desires to see in us.

Talk With God:

"God, we could never repay you for the blessings you have given us; but we can live for you. Therefore, it is my desire and my delight to daily surrender my will to you and sincerely serve you. Amen!"

December – Day 11

Text: Romans 12:2 KJV

"Be not conformed to this world: but be ye transformed by the renewing of your mind, that ye may prove what is that good, and acceptable, and perfect, will of God."

Thought: "It Is Like A Battle!"

Our youngest grandson is hooked on Transformers. You know those toys that can change from one thing to another. He talks of the good guys, the Autobots, and bad guys, the Decepticons, doing battle.

Well, the other day, when he came in to the house from the school bus, he told me that he and one of his friends was talking about whether God was real or not. He explained it in terms of "it being a battle between the idea that God was real and the idea that God was not real." His friend told him that God was just an opinion people take. He shared that he told his friend that God was real and that he could find the story about God in the Bible. In fact, he preached a little sermon about God being the creator of all things. He also told him that God lives in a person's heart.

Now folks this was amazing even to me. For you see, our youngest grandson is only seven years old. However, the youngest mind, inspired by God, can perceive that there is a battle between the good and the bad.

We are in a battle of the good and the bad, the righteous and the rebellious,

Therefore, it is important that we choose the side that is right, the side that relies on facts and faith, and the side that will reign one day. The side that proves best is the side of the Lord.

Talk With God:

"Lord, it is very obvious that we are engaged in a real battle. But it is so wonderful that we can be transformed by your amazing love and grace; and live in the truth which will prevail in any warfare. Keep us as we keep on battling against the enemy of life. For we shall win in You. Amen!"

December – Day 12

Text: Galatians 5:25 KJV

"If we live in the Spirit, let us also walk in the Spirit."

Thought: "Living In the Spirit!"

Men everywhere are living in the ideas and character of others. He who lives in the spirit of Raphael, becomes a painter; He who lives in the spirit of Milton, becomes a poet; he who lives in the spirit of Bacon, becomes a philosopher; he who lives in the spirit of Caesar, becomes a warrior; he who lives in the spirit of Christ, becomes a man.

For to be in Christ, is to live in His ideas (purpose), His image (character) and in His spirit (attitude).

For you see no man has made the impression as Christ has. He has changed the course of history itself. His appearance on earth redirected humanity to a new and living way.

We must accept His teachings, His training, His tenderness and His triumph; we are declaring that we will walk in the Spirit of all that represents Him. Our thoughts, our talk, our travels down life's road becomes influenced and inspired by our Lord and Savior, Jesus Christ.

As the Apostle Paul said, "I live, yet not I; but Christ lived in me and the life that I now live in the flesh I live by the faith of the Son of God" (Galatians 5:24).

Talk With God:

"Lord, I have a single goal in life and that is to praise you and present you to others. If I do this, I will be blessed in everything else. I am convinced that I can be a worthy ambassador for you. Grant me your anointing. Amen!"

December – Day 13

Text:	Proverbs 4:23 NCV
"Be careful what you think, because your thoughts run your life."

Thought:	"Too Big For Our Britches!"

A college freshman was 5 feet, 9 inches tall when he left for school in the fall. He worked through the Christmas holidays and didn't return again until the February break.

When he got off the plane, his mother was startled at how much taller he looked. Getting the tape measure out at home, they discovered he had grown three inches! The student was as surprised as his mother. "Couldn't you tell by your clothes that you'd grown?" she asked him.

"Well, since I've been doing my own laundry," he replied, "I just figured everything had shrunk."

Sometimes, we get to big for our well-being. We allow our achievements, acquisitions or accolades to give us the big head. Although we should be grateful for all that we acquire or accomplish, we should hope that it would give us a big heart.

We must always keep in mind the words of the Lord to Pilate at Judgment Hall, "Thou couldest have no power at all against me, except it were given thee from above" (John 19:11). It is the pleasure of God to bless us and grant us the ability to achieve the task before us.

Let us thank God for honoring us with the ability to achieve but let us humble ourselves before Him in appreciation.

Talk With God:

"Thank you for enriching me and enabling me to advance and achieve; however, never let me accomplish anything without honoring you and expressing my appreciation. I can do all things through your strength and your scriptures. Amen!"

December – Day 14

Text: 2 Timothy 4:7-8 NCV

"I have fought the good fight, I have finished the race, I have kept the faith. Now, a crown is being held for me—a crown for being right with God. The Lord, the judge who judges rightly, will give the crown to me on that day —not only to me but to all those who have waited with love for him to come again."

Thought: "Consistent Efforts Will Be Crowned!"

After spending a fortune hunting for King Tut's tomb, Lord Carnarvon stood with archaeologist Howard Carter before a door more than 3,000 years old. Tension gripped the pair as they pried open the seal. Would their many years of effort and expense be rewarded? On that November day in 1922, they would open the door to find the long lost tomb crammed full of treasures they had not even imagined. It took nearly ten years for all the treasure to be transferred to museums. Their patience had paid off.

Billy Sunday, a fiery preacher at the turn of the 20th century, echoed the words, "payday someday," over and over when he challenged people to surrender their life to Christ and serve Him wholehearted. He emphasized that a dedicated life to Christ made life worthwhile and the afterlife worth the wait.

Each morning should be a precious moment of anticipation as to the treasures God has in store for us. As we take each step, it should be like opening the door to the enjoyment and enrichment of a treasured tomb. We should awake each morning with anticipation of enjoying the genuine treasure – family, friends and food; health, home and happiness; shelter, secular employment and a satisfied mind - available to us.

And of course, we should always look forward to the opening of the door of heaven that is accessible to all who accept Jesus Christ as Savior and remain faithful to His will.

Talk With God:

"Lord, how foolish we are at times, complaining about having to seek and slave to experience the genuine treasures of this life. Let us be willing to work at enjoying God's goodness and your graciousness. Knowing that if we experience you, we will enjoy life and expect a greater pleasure in the future. Amen!"

December – Day 15

Text: Luke 2:10-11 NCV

"I am bringing you good news that will be a great joy to all the people.[11] Today your Savior was born in the town of David. He is Christ, the Lord."

Thought: "Happy Holy-day!"

It seems today that society desires to delete the real reason for the Christmas season. Retailers promote popular items and updated versions of 'whatever.' They substitute "Happy Holidays" for "Merry Christmas." Schools allow students to enjoy "Winter Breaks" instead of "Christmas Celebration!" And I will agree that it is a break from school in the winter months and it is a time to be happy and it is a holiday from work.

However, it is more. It is the celebration of the birth of the Son of God, Jesus Christ. No other celebrated holiday other than Easter should be declared holy and keep its reason of being in tack.

Therefore, let us enjoy the festivities, the fancy wrapped presents, the family get-togethers; but let us keep our focus on the reason why we are happy. It is a Holy-day! It is a Happy Holy-day!

A day of reverence in which the human race began to rejoice over the fact that the Person Who would forgive us our sins, free us from its bondage and fill our life with the promises and privileges of genuine life had come into our midst.

Have a happy holy-day!

Talk With God:

"O Lord, let us not disrespect your birth and the purpose of your coming in the flesh. Open our eyes and ears that we may experience the true joy of such a holy day. Amen!"

December – Day 16

Text: Revelation 22:12 KJV

"And, behold, I come quickly; and my reward is with me, to give every man according as his work shall be."

Thought: "He is Coming!"

Someone shared a hilarious story of a preacher who was humiliated and humbled at the same time. The new pastor of the community church was so nervous about delivering his first sermon that he'd not gotten much sleep for several nights. Matter of fact, he was so tired he could barely make it up the steps to his pulpit. Fortunately, he found his text and began preaching. But nervousness soon overtook him, and the outline flew right out of his mind.

Now, in the Bible school he'd been taught that if a lapse of memory occurs, it is wise to repeat your last point. And so he did. "Behold," he quoted, "I come quickly," but his mind was still a blank. He tried one more time, still no memory of what was to come next. Another attempt, but no results.

Finally, he stepped way back, made a lunge toward the pulpit, shouted out, "Behold, I come quickly," tripped, and fell into the lap of a little old lady in the front row. Flustered and embarrassed, he picked himself up, apologized profusely, and started to explain what had happened. "That's all right, young man," said the kindly old lady. "It was really my fault. You warned me three times that you were on your way down here. I should have just gotten out of your way."

At this time of the year, we heard the echo of the chorus, the commercials, the comments all challenging us to get ready for Santa Claus is coming to town. Well, let me echo another great challenge: Jesus Christ is coming to your heart's door and to open heaven's door to those prepared.

Yes, the prophets announced His birth (Isaiah 9) and the Holy Spirit announced that He would deal with man (Revelation 3) and the Holy Son of God gave anticipation to all that He would come again to gather His family together (I Thessalonians 5). The Scriptures said it once, they said it twice and they repeated it again and again – He is coming! Watch out and be ready to welcome Him.

Talk With God:

"Lord, thank you for your prophecy and your promise. Search my heart and secure my spirit in the safety of your will. I am listening and looking for your appearing. Amen!"

December – Day 17

Text: Isaiah 1:18 NIV

"Come now, let us settle the matter," says the LORD. "Though your sins are like scarlet, they shall be as white as snow."

Thought: "A Christian Is Like A Snowman!"

Recently, we had an unusually amount of snow for our area. School was out for the Christmas break. Therefore, grandmother and our youngest grandson build a snowman. Then, he and I built a snowman. Later, on the local television weather report, a picture of a very large snowman build by our son's children was shown on the screen. We all had a blast building snowmen and throwing snowballs during this Christmas season snowfall.

But did you know that believers can compare their life to the created snowmen. As believers we are created in image of our Heavenly Father. The snowman is created by snow gently given from the heavens.

The snowman is packed and patterned with pure white substance. Our renewed life in Christ is filled with the purity of His holiness and affects every area of our life.

The snowman will not melt from the cold chill of winter but will gently humble to the warmth of the sunlight. Likewise, with our life; if we abide in the purity of God's Word and God's love, we will not melt away in fear and failure in the chilly winds of adversity or the coldness of this world's society. However, we will gently humble to the warmth of the amazing love and grace of God's SON.

Therefore, when the snow falls, we are viewing a perfect picture of the purity of God freely given, falling fresh for us to gather in, to form an image of our Heavenly Father and firmly standing for all to see.

Talk With God:

"Thank you Lord for your purifying power that can be applied to our lives. I am glad to know if I confess my sins, you are faithful and just to cleanse me from all unrighteousness. Search my heart each day and create within a clean and pure heart. Amen!"

December – Day 18

Text: John 1:14 Amplified Bible

"And the Word (Christ) became flesh (human, incarnate) and tabernacled (fixed His tent of flesh, lived awhile) among us; and we [actually] saw His glory (His honor, His majesty), such glory as an only begotten son receives from his father, full of grace (favor, loving-kindness) and truth."

Thought: "Christmas!"

I enjoy using acronyms to help me remember things. Therefore, allow me to share a personal acronym of Christmas that will help us remember what and why we celebrate the event.

Of course, "C" is for the Christ Child who came fulfilling prophecy and laying a foundation to eternal life.

The "H" stands for Humanity, the object of the Heavenly Father's love.

The "R" represents the Relationship that the Son wishes to have with all humanity.

The "I" is for the each Individual who must recognize for themselves the importance of Christmas.

The "S" stands for the Sacrifice that the Son of God would become for mankind.

The "T" represents the Truth. Christ is the answer to all man's problems.

The "M" is for Music. Christ produces a melody and provides a song in our heart.

The "A" stands for Ally. It means that we shall never stand alone. He is with us always.

The "S" stands for the Satisfaction that we experience in our daily life as we walk with the Son of God.

I know you may have special words or different thoughts you could share as to the why you celebrate Christmas. And this season should have personal meaning to us.

Enjoy the celebration of the season and experience a wonderful time with family and friends.

Talk With God:

"Thank you Lord for your birth and your willingness to build a relationship with us. I am grateful for your inception into humanity, your identity with our conditions and circumstances and giving us inspiration. I realize it all began in this celebrated season. I rejoice and radiate my appreciation. Amen!"

December – Day 19

Text: John 3:16 NIV

"This is how much God loved the world: He gave his Son, his one and only Son. And this is why: so that no one need be destroyed; by believing in him, anyone can have a whole and lasting life."

Thought: "Christmas Is A Significant Day!"

Christmas is a time of remembering, a time of rejoicing and a time of readiness.

It is a time of remembering that God provided a great plan of salvation for all mankind and brought it into existence through His Son, Jesus Christ (John 3:16). No other event in history produced the love and liberty that the coming of Christ brought. Had the Son of God not came into the flesh, there would not have been a physical identity with man; a path of righteousness to walk; a pardon for sin obtained; a power demonstrated over death, hell and the grave; nor an interceding High Priest. Don't forget why He came!

It is a time of rejoicing. The reason is that you and I are included in the benefits of His coming. He came to rescue us from sin, restore us to right relationships with Him, and reinforce us against the enemy of our soul.

It is a time of readiness. Jesus is coming again; therefore, we must prepare our lives by surrendering our will to Him (Romans 6:12-13), submitting to His will (Hebrews 12:1-2) and sincerely look for His appearing (Titus 2:13).

"Every day is a special day; but Christmas Day is a significant day. It is a day that is marked in the hearts and minds of many who believe that Jesus came to redeem mankind and help make the readjustment to the life of everyone who trust in the Lord.

It is our sincere desire that you have a Merry Christmas!

Talk With God:

"Thank you Lord for making a very special and significant day for every person who believes in you. What a delight to know that you will cause a new birth in the life of each one who puts their trust in you. Amen!"

December – Day 20

Text: Luke 1:31 KJV

"Shalt call His Name Jesus!"

Thought: "The Christmas Candy Cane!"

Allow me to share with you the legend of the making of the Christmas candy cane. I believe you will find it self-explanatory and simple satisfying.

There once was a candy maker who wanted to make a candy that would be very special for Christmas. He decided to make a candy cane because he knew he could include a lot of signs and symbols to celebrate the true meaning of Christmas.

He began with a stick of pure white hard candy. He used white as a symbol that Jesus was born of the Virgin Mary who was always so pure and holy. He made it hard and crunchy to symbolize the solid rock on which the church is founded.

He bent over the top of the candy cane to make a hook like a shepherd's staff. He remembered that Jesus called himself "The Good Shepherd" The candy maker remembered too that the first people who come to worship Jesus at the manger after he was born were shepherds. Then the candy maker looked at his candy cane and thought it looked a little plain. "It needs some color," he said. Something red," he thought. "That will give it Christmas look!" So, he began to stain the white candy cane with red stripes. First, he put on three thin red stripes. You see, he remembered that Jesus went through terrible torture before he died and was whipped across his back. The candy maker decided that the red stripes on the candy cane would remind everybody that Jesus shed his blood for us when he died on the cross on Good Friday.

The candy maker was doing well with his candy cane. He had a lot of signs of Jesus in there but he wasn't satisfied. Then he began to pray, "Dear Jesus, help me to make my candy cane show the true meaning of Christmas." Then suddenly the candy cane slipped from his hands. It fell upside down on the floor. When he looked, he noticed that the candy cane was no longer a candy cane, but it was the letter "J". It stands for "Jesus." Jesus is really what Christmas is all about.

Talk With God:

"Lord, thank you for giving humanity the desire to praise you and present you in many special forms. Please take this feeble bit of flesh that I am and use me to exemplify your special birth, your sinless life, your sacrificial death, your supernatural resurrection and your spiritual presence today and your second coming promise. Amen!"

December – Day 21

Text: Luke 2:14 NCV

"Then a very large group of angels from heaven joined the first angel, praising God and saying: Give glory to God in heaven, and on earth let there be peace among the people who please God."

Thought: "A Personal Christmas Carol!"

At Christmas time, you usually hear the sound of music and song everywhere you go – the mall and the market, the church and at concerts, on television programming and theaters, on the radio and in reading material. Christmas music fills the air.

Well, on that very first Christmas Day celebration, singing was a vital part. On the hillside of Judea, the heavenly host lifted harmony of praise to God.

Just as Christmas can not be Christmas without a song, neither can believers be true worshippers without a song. A song of praise for what God has done for each of us. A song of peace for the blessed quality of life that we experience. And a song of proof that our relationship with Christ is a living reality (Psalm 40:1-2)

Therefore, in the season of celebration, let us sing a personal Christmas carol of thanksgiving and testimony.

Talk With God:

"Thank you Lord, for your personal gift – Your Son – and for your personal carol of praise – honor and humility before your Son. O Lord, you have blessed me with spiritual life, therefore I will sing praises to your Name. Amen!"

December – Day 22

Text: John 6:63 NCV

"It is the Spirit that gives life. The flesh doesn't give life. The words I told you are spirit, and they give life."

Thought: "Reason For The Season!"

I read a beautiful comparison between Santa Claus and Jesus Christ. It is like comparing a fairy tale with reality. Read it slow and let it saturate your heart and mind.

"Santa Claus is said to live in the North Pole; Jesus is everywhere.

Santa is thought to ride in a sleigh; Jesus rides on the wind and walks on the water.

Santa comes but once a year bringing gifts to all; Jesus is an ever present help 24/7.

Santa has been said to come down your chimney uninvited; Jesus stands at your heart's door and knocks waiting for an invitation..

Santa makes you stand in line to see him; Jesus is as close as the mention of His Name.

Santa lets you sit on his lap; Jesus lets you rest in His arms.

Santa asks, "Little boy, little girl what is your name?" Jesus was aware of our names before we were.

Santa has a belly like a bowl full of jelly; Jesus has a heart full of love.

Santa offers, "Ho, ho, ho"; Jesus offers help, happiness and hope.

Santa says, "You better not cry"; Jesus says, "Cast your cares on me for I care for you."

Santa's little helpers make toys; Jesus makes new lives, mends hearts, and repairs broken homes.

Santa may make you chuckle; Jesus give you perpetual joy.

Santa puts gifts under your tree; Jesus became the gift and died on the tree."

There's really no comparison. Jesus is the reason for the season. He is the Giver of life!

Talk With God:

"Although things of this earthly life fails to give satisfaction and secure for us life; the Words of the Lord is truth and provides for us true contentment and commitment for living. Thank you for your Word that reveals you and reinforces us in living successfully. Amen!"

December – Day 23

Text: Psalms 111:10 Amplified Bible
"The reverent fear and worship of the Lord is the beginning of wisdom."

Thought: "Wisdom to Walk"

Burt Jr., was one of the Three Wise Men in the Sunday school pageant, and so was his father, one Christmas long ago. "Well, Dad," he said, "wisdom must run in the family."

What a cute story but what a greater challenge it issues.

While it is true, man is superior to the beast of the field, the birds of the sky, and fish of the sea; he still seems to lack common sense and competent wisdom to live a life beneficial to himself and all inhabitants of this great planet.

Man seems to stumble at decision making, sputter at direction in life and split hairs over doctrine and devotion to God. Heaven help us.

We must develop and become determined to wake each day with a reverence for the most powerful and precious Person ever—God Himself! We must accept the fact that without such an acknowledgement and acceptance of God, we will never acquire "the know how" (wisdom) to live this life successfully.

Let us approach God each day with a desire and a decision to hear His voice and determine to obey His voice. When this is done, we will be able to walk life's roadway and anticipate the wonderful victory that awaits us.

Talk With God:

Today is the day, O lord that I lean on you. I acknowledge who you are and what you have to offer that will assist me in living a valid and victorious life. I will make every effort to walk in reverence and responsibility. I desire to live a full life and a fruitful life that is found in you.. In your Name I pray. Amen.

December – Day 24

Text: John 1:11 KJV

"He came unto his own, and his own received him not

Thought: "The Night Before Christmas!"

I love the poem, "Twas the Night before Jesus Came," by Dianne Donenfeld. She wrote the poem in 1988, as a spiritual rendition of "The Night before Christmas." She wrote the poem to emphasize the reality of the coming of Jesus as the Savior of the world and the unprepared state of the world for His appearance.

The secular poem, "The Night before Christmas!" leaves the implication that all was ready for Saint Nick to appear. They had been forewarned he was coming to bring gifts to all. And were there not prophecy regarding the coming of Christ, both as the child in the manger and the Crowned Lord of Lords in the rapture of the church. The Holy Spirit and the Holy Scriptures bear record that this is true

I do not have the space to put the complete poem in this devotional but I do wish to refer to an important truth conveyed by the poem. That truth is that many were not prepared for His coming. Society was to busy to pray, pursue His truth found in the Word, or properly develop their character.

So often, people refuse to accept the forewarning regarding events that are predicted. However, it is better to be prepared than to perish!

Let this Christmas season be a time of devoting our life to Jesus. Let us learn to praise Him. Let us seek His face in prayer. Let us search His Word for guidance. Let us share His love with others. Let us live a life in anticipation of celebration tomorrow of His birth and a greater anticipation of His coming again in the Rapture.

Talk With God:

"Lord, I need your comfort and your courage to face the challenges of being prepared. I want to awake each day ready to listen to you, lean on you and learn from you that I may lead others to you. Grant me your perfect love, perpetual joy and patience to endure. Amen!"

December – Day 25

Text: Isaiah 9:6 KJV

"For unto us a child is born, unto us a son is given"

Thought: "The Gift!"

We read a lot of Christmas stories during this season but it is important that we keep our focus on the real account of the story of the birth of Christ. Therefore, I wish for us to simple share the Christmas announcement of the birth of Christ by the angels to the shepherds. It is an announcement of the gift of God given to humanity.

"There were sheepherders camping in the neighborhood. They had set night watches over their sheep. Suddenly, God's angel stood among them and God's glory blazed around them. They were terrified. The angel said, "Don't be afraid. I'm here to announce a great and joyful event that is meant for everybody, worldwide. A Savior has just been born in David's town, a Savior who is Messiah and Master. This is what you're to look for: a baby wrapped in a blanket and lying in a manger."

At once the angel was joined by a huge angelic choir singing God's praises: "Glory to God in the heavenly heights, Peace to all men and women on earth who please Him."

What a gift! It was a delightful expression of God's love. It was a divine intervention in the affairs of mankind. It was a direct offer and opportunity for mankind to have a relationship with the Creator and Caretaker of the Universe. However, like man does with many of the gifts he receives, he crams it in a storage box or cast it aside. Let us receive the satisfaction that it brings and share it with others.

Talk With God:

"Lord, there is no greater gift than the gift of life found in the coming of you as the Babe of Bethlehem. The marvel of the event and the masterful effects it can have on our life, if we simply believe. Help us to believe! Amen!"

December – Day 26

Text: Luke 2:20 The Message

"Mary kept all these things to herself, holding them dear, deep within herself. The sheepherders returned and let loose, glorifying and praising God for everything they had heard and seen."

Thought: "The Day After Christmas!"

I read a story one day of a merchant who related to a minister who was in his store the day after Christmas. The merchant was busy removing Christmas decorations and reducing Christmas items in price. As he worked feverishly, he began sharing, "I got to get rid of Christmas today. It is over and I must begin making room for the next holiday promotions.

The minister responded to the merchant's statement with a statement of his own. "You know while you are discarding the image of Christmas in one day; I find that I am responsible to maintain the image of Christmas each day throughout the year."

Folks, is it our desire to continue our celebration of the birth of Christ throughout the following year? I hope so.

Think about it. If someone has given you a gift for Christmas, do you put the gift up or do you use the gift and allow its blessings to fill your life throughout the days ahead. If it is a tool or an appliance, we will use it. If it is a cosmetic item, we will allow it to enhance our beauty and give us a fresh air of fragrance on our person. Do we enjoy the treats or allow them to get old and stale. See what I mean.

Should we not enjoy the gift of God – the Son of God – in our every day experiences following our acknowledgement and acceptance of Him? Should we not allow the beauty and the blessed fragrance of the fruit of the Spirit to radiate from our lives? Should we not indulge in partaking of the promises and privileges that the gift of God provides for us?

Don't let the day after Christmas be a putting away (other than the trash of wrapping paper – or maybe the debris of a wasted life). Let is be a dawning of a new day, utilizing the gift of Christmas.

Talk With God:

"Lord, let me not hasten to rid myself of the blessings of Christmas, but enable me to make haste in sharing a continual and compassionate message regarding the events of the first Christmas. Amen!"

December – Day 27

Text: Titus 2:13-14 NIV

"while we wait for the blessed hope—the appearing of the glory of our great God and Savior, Jesus Christ, [14] who gave himself for us to redeem us from all wickedness and to purify for himself a people that are his very own, eager to do what is good."

Thought: "The Messiah Has Come – It's Payday!"

Everyone looks forward to payday, some more than others. The elderly or those on fixed incomes may live from week to week or month to month, therefore, the anticipation of payday is a high priority – paying bills, purchasing food, prescriptions filled and personal items bought. Many self-sufficient individuals could care less – they do their own thing.

However, I wonder if we are anticipating the dawning of a new year. This year could be different. A reverse of things could occur.

I believe that is why Christmas is celebrated prior to the New Year. For the coming of the Son of God as the Messiah – Savor of the world—prepares hearts for the dawning of a new day. If we could only anticipate the differences Jesus would make in our daily lives, we would look for Him, love Him and live for Him.

The Messiah has come. He brings the comfort, courage, and confidence we need to live our daily lives. He provides reassurances, rest and restoration to our lives whether we have great resources or simply live from day to day on merger assets.

However, to experience His blessings and benefits, we must anticipate His presence, acknowledge His person, accept His promises, awake to His power, and advance on His path.

Talk With God:

"I believe your Word regarding your promise to return. Therefore, I desire for you to enrich my life with your Word and equip me to do your will. I want to be ready for your coming. I miss the privilege of seeing your birth but I shall not miss out on the Blessed Hope

December – Day 28

Text: Hosea 7:9 Amplified Bible

"Strangers have devoured his strength, and he knows it not; yes, gray hairs are sprinkled here and there upon him, and he does not know it."

Thought: "As We Grow Older!"

Yes, we are all growing older. As one writer put it, "the foot of time falls as softly as ever, and the current of life flows on as smoothly as ever. Months and years pass away without special observation and we begin to get old before we think of it. And when we sit down to a simple sum in arithmetic – the subtraction of the year of our birth from the current year – we are astonished at the answer, and are so doubtful of its correctness that we go over it a second time, but always with the same results."

Time stands still for no one. Age is a progressive act for all mankind. And if we do not take a day at a time, we will wake up one morning and where in the world has time gone. Our hearing is dull. Our sight is dim. Our teeth are decreased in number (or been replaced). Our hair has turned dingy gray or gone completely, our walk is with dips, and our strength has diminished.

Having experienced the above let me ask this important question. What plans have you made for the future?

Oh, I am sure that you have insurance policies and an individual will; but do you have blessed assurance. Do you have the assurance that heaven is yours to gain? Have you committed your life to Christ, thus being a joint heir with Him of eternal life?

The year is almost gone. Our time on earth could expire any moment. We have no guarantee of tomorrow. Therefore, let us do one of two things: Commit our life to Christ or renew our commitment to Christ. Either way we are prepared for what the day may hold.

Talk With God:

"I am glad that I have an opportunity at this moment to consider my relationship with you O Lord. Confirm my relationship with you by giving me a fresh touch of your spirit, and guiding me throughout this day. Amen!"

December – Day 29

Text: Isaiah 42:16 KJV

"And I will bring the blind by a way that they knew not; I will lead them in paths that they have not known: I will make darkness light before them, and crooked things straight. These things will I do unto them, and not forsake them."

Thought: "Hitch Your Wagon to a Star!"

Ralph Waldo Emerson once stated, "Hitch your wagon to a star." One can see in these six words the summary of human achievement and an everlasting inspiration to the future. It has been said that every forward step taken by mankind throughout the centuries and each advancement by humanity toward the ultimate goal has been led by some valiant dreamer whose eyes were fixed upon the dawn.

Moses saw a star that blazed in the Promised Land. The radiance of an eternal star led three-wise men to the manger in Bethlehem where the Christ-child lay. Christopher Columbus pinned his faith in the dawn of a new day when he set sail across the Atlantic Ocean. Each of these looked beyond and into the future.

Have you given consideration to the future? Do your daily steps today mark a path that will lead to a brighter and better future? Set your sights on possessing eternal life by inviting Christ into your life today and determine to live each day walking the path of righteousness.

Hitch your life to the Maker of the stars and He will pull you through every situation you encounter on your journey through life. Trust Him!

God will make a way. The Word tells us that He will make a way even when our vision is darkened. He is the light, the life and the liberty that we seek.

Talk With God:

"Lord, I don't want to be a star-gazer but I want to go beyond the stars. I want to reach out and touch the Creator of the Universe. And I can by believing in you and building my life on the foundation of Your Son and Your Scriptures. Thank you for that privilege, Amen!"

December – Day 30

Text: 1 Thessalonians 5:6 KJV

"Therefore let us not sleep, as do others; but let us watch and be sober."

Thought: "Stay Focused!"

The Sunday school teacher was describing how Lot's wife looked back and turned into a pillar of salt (Genesis 19:26).

"Oh thats nothing, my mommy looked back once while she was driving," a little boy interrupted excitedly. "She turned into a telephone pole."

It is very important that we stay focused.

The year is almost gone, but allow me to ask. "Are you still focused on the things of God?" Is our resolve (New Year Resolution) still just as meaningful as it was when we made it?

December is a wonderful month of celebration and challenge. It gives us reason to celebration in the acknowledgement of the birth of Christ. It gives us challenge in helping us realize that God created us to know Him.

It is not good for us to slumber and stumble in our self efforts to be the person we need to be. We need to focus our attention on the Word of God and forwardly progress as we adhere to the principles and promises we find in that Word.

Talk With God:

"Lord, you have been good to each of us during this year. Even in moments of distress, disease and disaster; you have proven your readiness to reassure and reinforce us to endure. I truly thank you for walking with us each step of the way. I am grateful for your forgiveness when we failed to be on guard against the enemy of the soul, to be glad for life and to give you the glory due your Name. Amen!"

December – Day 31

Text: Romans 6:1 Amplified Bible

"What shall we say [to all this]? Are we to remain in sin in order that God's grace (favor and mercy) may multiply and overflow?

Thought: "What If!"

As we look back over the past year, I am sure we ponder the consequences and ask our self what if? What if we had taken a different direction than we took? What if we spoke with a different tone or used different words to express our self? I really believe we would reconsider some of our words, our ways and our works. However, we can not relive any of our days. They are history.

Yet think with me for a moment.

What if God didn't take the time to bless us today because we didn't take the time to thank Him yesterday?

What if God decided to stop leading us tomorrow because we didn't follow Him today?

What if the day of beauty, blessings and benefits ceased because we ceased to reach out a helping hand to others?

What if God answered our prayers the way we offer praise?

God would not rob His creation of the blessings He designed for them (Matthew 5:45). Yet, so often we are guilty of robbing God of praise due His Name. We fail to praise Him, seek His purity and maintain a positive outlook on life.

What if God had not sent His Son to be born in the framework of the flesh – to identify with man and intercede for man's sin nature? There would be no Christmas Season.

Yet, we know man look forward from January 1 to the celebration of the Christmas Season. And if that is true and it is – then we should celebrate not with a "What If" attitude but with "I know."

Let us not let a slothful or sinful state exist in our life if we have been exposed to the grace of God. Let us accept His grace and alienate our life from sin and self-centeredness.

Talk With God:

"Lord, so often we take our blessings for granted. I am guilty and ask your forgiveness. You are worthy to receive glory, honor and praise. You are faithful and true in caring for your creation. Thank you. Amen!

Step 13 – The Future

"Building a Future"

An unknown author penned the words of the poem entitled, "An Uncertain Future!"

"We know not what the future holds in times like these today;

The castles that we start to build may crumble and decay.

With all earth's vast uncertainty – some poverty, some wealth,

For some the best that heart could wish; for others failing health.

Hold on to God's unchanging hand no matter where you go;

Relinquish not your trust in Him though weakened by the foe.

May God's eternal leadership our stronghold ever be,

Oh, strengthen, Lord, our faith and hope for what we cannot see!"

I do not know what the future holds in this life, but I do know who holds the future. George Truett stated, "Because of the character and the invincible purpose of God, there can be no doubt of the ultimate triumph of righteousness."

Patrick Henry on March 23, 1775, said, "I know of no way of judging the future, but by the past." Therefore, if we commit our lives to Jesus Christ, commune with Him on a daily basis, and conduct our lives appropriately and in accordance to the principles of God's Word; we shall have the promise of a glorious future. So, put it simply – the only preparation for tomorrow is the right use of today.

Let me share with you a story I read once. The story is told of a man who dreamed one night that he was carried to a conference of evil spirits. They were discussing the best means of destroying men. One rose and said, "I will go to earth and tell them the Bible is a fable, and not God's Word." Said another, "Persuade them that Christ was only a man." Still another said, "Let me go; I will tell them there is no God, no Savior, no heaven, no hell." "No, that will not do," they said. "We could never make men believe that."

Finally one old devil, wise as a serpent but not as harmless as a dove, rose and said: "Let me go, I will tell them that there is a God, there is a Saviour, there is a heaven and a hell, too. But I will tell them there is no hurry; tomorrow will do; tomorrow will be even as today!" And he was the devil they sent!

We know the story is fiction, but its message is a fact. The devil is among us today. He is alive and is actively engaged in deceiving humanity. Yet, let us be wise, and be not deceived by his trickery and traps.

Time passes so quickly. In fact, do you realize that as soon as today is complete, it becomes yesterday and what was tomorrow becomes today. The future has a way of slipping quickly into the past. What a person plans to achieve, accomplish and accept must do it NOW.

Did you know that you were building the future throughout the past year as you paused and enjoyed each daily devotional? If your attention was captivated for just a moment; the devotional thought, the divine presence of the Holy Spirit and the dedication to the will of God laid a stepping stone toward a good, godly and glorious future.

As the old year passed and the New Year begins, I recall an article I once read in House & Garden magazine. It was about the Italians, who have a custom on New Year's Eve. As midnight on New Year's Eve approaches, the streets are clear. There is no passing traffic; there are no pedestrians; even the policemen take cover. Then at the stroke of twelve midnight, the windows of the houses fly open. To the sound of laughter, loud music and lit fireworks, each member of the family pitches out old crockery; ornaments detested; odd, old and hated furniture plus a whole catalogue of personal possessions which remind them of something in the past year they are determined to wipe out of their minds."

Such an experience reminds me of the words of the writer of the book of Hebrews where he exhorts followers of Christ to "let us strip off and throw aside every encumbrance (unnecessary weight) and that sin which so readily (deftly and cleverly) clings to and entangles us" (Hebrews 12:1).

Friends, I do not know what the coming year may hold for me or you; but I do know who holds the future in the palm of His hands and I do know if I have placed my faith in the past work of Calvary and walk faithfully each day; I shall have a promising year. For I believe that if I have placed my life in His hands and I walk the path of life fervently and faithfully, I will be happy, hopeful and live in harmony with my Heavenly Father and humanity. I am willing for Christ to allow me to enjoy and experience His compassion and care as I yield my will to Him and become yoked together with Him. The Word of God clearly states, "The steps of a good man are ordered [established] by the Lord: and He delighted in his way. Though he falls, he shall not be utterly cast down: for the Lord uphold him with hid hand" (Psalm 37:23-24 KJV).

God may know (and he does) what lies in the future, whether tomorrow, two weeks from now, ten months from now, or a thousand years from now. He will renew me and route me in the direction that I need to go day by day. He unfolds my future step by step.

Yes, He may give me a glimpse of my future by enabling me to consider His promises and precepts. However, I must learn to listen and lean on Him in the morning, then at noon and in the evening. Consider the words of the Psalmist: "Evening, and **morning**, and at noon, will I pray, and cry aloud: and he shall hear my voice" (Psalms 55:17 KJV). Check out the advice of Solomon, "Trust in the LORD with all thine heart; and lean not unto thine own understanding. In all thy ways acknowledge him, and he shall direct thy paths (Proverbs 3:5-6). We must neither fear tomorrow nor the troubles it may bring, but have faith that leads to a triumphant day. We must not worry about what tomorrow may bring; but willingly give Him our hand to guide us, guard us and grace us with His power, peace and presence.

As the words of the song, "One Day at a Time"; so beautifully and boldly declares: "I'm only human, I'm just a man (or woman). Help me believe in what I could be and all that I am. Show me the stairway, I have to climb. Lord for my sake, teach me to take one day at a time."

The Bible declares that "man born of woman is of few days and full of trouble" (Job 22:21 KJV). Therefore, you may be assured the fierce winds of adversity will blow into our minds, the frigid waters of affliction will billow against our bodies, and the fiery attacks of the spiritual enemy will beat against our spirit; HOWEVER, the future is in the hands of He Who stills the wind, settles the waves and stops the fiery darts of Satan. We must remind ourselves of His faithfulness and remain faithful to Him, Who is our foundation, our focus and our future.

Consider the Parable of the Builders in Matthew chapter 7. One builder was foolish and laid a foundation on sand. The other builder was wise and laid a foundation on solid rock. When the storms of wind and rising water hit the structures, different consequences occurred – the fixtures were sound but the foundation of sand began to shift and slide until the structure fell. The foundation of solid rock stood firm and enabled the frame of the structure to hold and withstand the onslaught of the storm.

Once we lay the foundation of a life surrendered, sanctified and satisfied with a relationship with the grand and glorious architect of lives, Jesus Christ; we can proceed to build our future a step at a time and one day at a time, maturing and manufacturing a structure able to withstand the storms of life.

The love of God, the leadership of the Holy Spirit and the Lordship of Jesus Christ are the essential ingredients for building the future. And the instructions and inspiration of each of these are found in God's Holy Word. As we spend time in worship of the Lord, walking in God's presence each day, waiting before Him in prayer, wrapping ourselves in the knowledge of God's Word through daily study of the Bible, and witnessing a godly lifestyle before the world; we will build our future on solid ground.

Now, as we face the new year, the future; let us face it with purity of life, a positive outlook, and a progressive determination. If we do not, we are defeated already. This thought reminds me of the words of the Psalmist. He said, "Teach us how short our lives really are so that we may be wise" (Psalms 90:12 NCV).

In fact, let me share a story about a college student who had a wonderful view of the future – the New Year. She was tacking the new calendar on the wall of her dorm room. As she finished, she turned to her roommate and said, "It is going to be a beautiful year."

Her roommate was taken back with such a positive statement and asked, "How do you know?"

At this, the young lady replied, "if I take a day at a time and make sure something beautiful happens through my efforts each day; then I will have a beautiful year."

How wise and what a wonderful plan! Now, if each of us would allow God to work through us by creating something beautiful, something good; what a difference it would make during the year in building our future. It would make for a better self, a better society, a better sign for eternal preparation.

Therefore, let us hear and heed the words of Peter in his second epistle (2 Peter 1:1-4). God has invested His life, His Son's life, and His nature in us. He provides whatever we need to succeed in our lives (in the church and in the community). He wants us to develop His character and nature in our lives. Our efforts benefit us and bless God. Jesus teaches us that God expects a return on that investment. What kind of return are you giving Him on His investment in you?

Made in the USA
San Bernardino, CA
08 November 2015